Praise for *The Commander-in-Chief Test*—

"The best book yet written on the relationship between public opinion and foreign policy. With a rare combination of truly superb quantitative and qualitative analysis, Jeffrey A. Friedman shows us not just that the public matters but how it matters."
—**Brian Rathbun, University of Southern California, author of**
  Reasoning of State

"A must-read for anyone interested in American presidential leadership. Using a sweeping range of survey data, experiments, and case studies, Friedman persuasively shows that democratic political leadership has much less to do with responsiveness to the public's policy preferences than with the positive images citizens look for in leaders."
—**Robert Y. Shapiro, Columbia University, coauthor of**
  The Rational Public

"Provocative and persuasive. In this elegantly written book, Friedman overturns conventional wisdom about the relationship between public opinion and foreign policy, showing how voters reward politicians who appear competent even as they pursue policies voters disagree with. Image-making, as Friedman compellingly argues, is central to the domestic politics of international affairs."
—**Joshua Kertzer, Harvard University, author of**
  Resolve in International Politics

"In this pathbreaking book, Friedman masterfully combines quantitative and archival data to show that presidents' hawkish foreign policy actions reflect the public's preference for strong leaders. This book will surely be seen as the authoritative treatment of how American foreign policy works and what can be done to improve its democratic basis."
—**James N. Druckman, Northwestern University, coauthor of**
  Who Governs?

The Commander-in-Chief Test

A VOLUME IN THE SERIES

Cornell Studies in Security Affairs

Edited by Austin Carson, Alexander B. Downes, Kelly M. Greenhill, and Caitlin Talmadge

Founding Series Editors: Robert J. Art, Robert Jervis, and Stephen M. Walt

A list of titles in this series is available at cornellpress.cornell.edu.

The Commander-in-Chief Test

Public Opinion and the Politics of Image-Making in US Foreign Policy

JEFFREY A. FRIEDMAN

Cornell University Press

Ithaca and London

First published 2023 by Cornell University Press

Publication of this book was made possible by a generous grant from Dartmouth College.

Library of Congress Cataloging-in-Publication Data

Names: Friedman, Jeffrey A. (Jeffrey Allan), author.
Title: The commander-in-chief test : public opinion and the politics
   of image-making in US foreign policy / Jeffrey A. Friedman.
Description: Ithaca : Cornell University Press, 2023. | Series: Cornell
   studies in security affairs | Includes bibliographical references
   and index.
Identifiers: LCCN 2023006822 (print) | LCCN 2023006823 (ebook) |
   ISBN 9781501772924 (hardcover) | ISBN 9781501772948 (pdf) |
   ISBN 9781501772955 (epub)
Subjects: LCSH: Presidents—United States—Public opinion. |
   Political culture—United States. | United States—Foreign
   relations—Public opinion. | United States—Politics and
   government—Public opinion.
Classification: LCC JZ1480 .F75 2023 (print) | LCC JZ1480 (ebook) |
   DDC 327.73—dc23/eng/20230302
LC record available at https://lccn.loc.gov/2023006822
LC ebook record available at https://lccn.loc.gov/2023006823

For Kathryn

Contents

CONTENTS

Acknowledgments

It is a pleasure to have so many people to thank for their help with writing this book. Top billing goes to Mike Poznansky and Megan Stewart. For more than two years, the three of us met twice a month to discuss each other's book projects. Those conversations shaped every part of *The Commander-in-Chief Test*. Mike and Megan's collegiality was particularly welcome during the COVID-19 pandemic, which would otherwise have been a much more isolating environment in which to produce a manuscript.

I held three workshops to critique draft versions of the book, with Peter Feaver, Josh Kertzer, Peter Liberman, Andrew Payne, Phil Potter, Brian Rathbun, Dustin Tingley, Elizabeth Saunders, and Melissa Willard-Foster. I think that these kinds of workshops represent the apex of the academic profession, as they involve colleagues devoting substantial amounts of time for little reason beyond improving their colleagues' research. These workshops were extremely useful in helping me to hone the book's argument and to shore up weak spots in my analysis. It was also simply a lot of fun to spend time discussing the politics of US foreign policy with a group of people who have so much expertise on that subject.

Dartmouth College is one of the best places there is to study international security and US foreign policy. Steve Brooks, Jennifer Lind, Ed Miller, Nick Miller, Katy Powers, Ben Valentino, and Bill Wohlforth provided especially helpful feedback on early versions of the book's arguments. I regret that I may have worn out some of my Americanist colleagues, especially Mia Costa, Brendan Nyhan, and Sean Westwood, with what must have seemed like a very large number of very odd questions about public opinion and presidential politics. Their knowledge and patience were greatly appreciated.

Another privilege of working at Dartmouth is the opportunity to collaborate with excellent undergraduate researchers. Marco Allen, Claire Betzer, Naina Bhalla, Neil Choudhary, Charles Chen, Maggie Doyle, Luca Fagotti, Alex Fredman, Gabe Gever, Naomi Gonzalez, Natalia Henry, Emilia Hoppe, Zac Jaynes, Jolie Kemp, James Lawrence, Lila McKenna, Annie Michalski, Alexa Paladino, Noa Phillips, Owen Ritz, and Anna Wilinsky contributed to nearly every part of the book's analysis, helping me to get up to speed on presidential elections, to design survey experiments, and to code open-ended data.

The ideas presented in this book were sharpened by presentations at the University of California, Berkeley, Boston University, the Dickey Center for International Understanding, the Five College International Relations Workshop, the American Political Science Association, and the Institute for Advanced Study in Toulouse. IAST was a particularly stimulating home for conducting my research: I began the book during a fellowship at the institute during the 2017–2018 academic year and completed it on a return visit for 2021–2022. Shana Gadarian, Michael Joseph, Jonathan Markowitz, Eleonora Mattiacci, Rachel Myrick, Robert Ralston, Alexander Stephenson, and Jordan Tama also provided helpful input at various stages of the book's development.

The book required substantial funding in order to support nationally representative surveys and research at seven archives. For that purpose, I am grateful to the Charles Koch Foundation, the Marion and Jasper Whiting Foundation, and the Susan and Gib Myers Fellowship. Special thanks go to Andrew Byers for his enthusiastic support of the project along with Charlotte Bacon and Cate Homicki for helping me to navigate the grants process. Funding from the French Agence Nationale de la Recherche (under the Investissement d'Avenir programme, ANR-17-EURE-0010) is gratefully acknowledged. Michael McGandy and Jacqulyn Teoh guided the project through Cornell's review and publications process, during which Caitlin Talmadge provided exceptionally constructive editorial feedback.

Conducting archival research for this book was a terrific experience, especially since every one of the archives I visited was such an interesting and well-managed institution. The project benefited, in particular, from the support of Stacey Chandler at the JFK Presidential Library, Allen Fisher at the LBJ Presidential Library, Aimee Muller at the Reagan Presidential Library, Brittany Paris at the Carter Presidential Library, Mackenzie Ryan and Drew Hogan at the Minnesota Historical Society, Adele Leigh Stock at Stanford's Hoover Library, and Julie Tanaka at Arizona State University's Hayden Library.

I'm lucky and proud to be part of the Friedman, Odel, and Vuarchex families, which are filled with role models who have given me invaluable support, especially over the last year.

My late wife, Kathryn Schwartz, provided encouragement and advice throughout this project. A self-described "miracle genius," Kathryn was an inexhaustible source of interesting conversation, irreverent wit, loving companionship, and intelligent (if frequently unsolicited) criticism. Every day was better because of her presence. I remain filled with admiration and gratitude for all the wonderful things she brought to my life, especially our daughter, Violet, who smiles just as brightly as her mother.

The Commander-in-Chief Test

Introduction

How Does Public Opinion Shape Foreign Policy?

In his 1961 inaugural address, President John F. Kennedy called on his fellow citizens to "pay any price, bear any burden, meet any hardship, support any friend, oppose any foe to assure the survival and success of liberty." These words capture the vigor and confidence of Kennedy's leadership. They are a classic piece of political rhetoric, taught in countless public speaking classes, and carved in stone at Kennedy's gravesite in Arlington National Cemetery. Perhaps you, too, find something inspirational in Kennedy's call to arms.

But do you agree with what Kennedy said? Should the United States pay *any* price to promote its foreign policy objectives? Do you think the United States should raise its spending on national defense at all? Today, most Americans say their government already spends enough, or too much, on its foreign policy agenda. And, when Kennedy ran for president in 1960, less than a quarter of Americans thought the defense budget was too small. Kennedy nevertheless believed that promising to raise military expenditures would help convince voters that he was a strong leader who would energetically promote US interests around the world. This strategy was very successful, helping Kennedy to build an inspiring personal image that continues to resonate with the American public today.

Kennedy's appeal to "pay any price, bear any burden" is an example of what this book calls an issue-image trade-off: a policy position that is not popular on its merits but that leaders nonetheless use to craft favorable impressions of their personal qualities. This book will offer many more examples of how issue-image trade-offs steer US foreign policy in a direction that is more costly and less cooperative than what voters want. For instance, Lyndon Johnson asked Congress to provide open-ended authorization for the use of force in Vietnam as a way to rebut charges that he was soft on communism, even though voters did not support escalating the war. Bill

Clinton's presidential campaign manager advised him to "bomb Serbia to look strong," even though a minority of voters supported military intervention in the Balkans. George W. Bush turned substantive criticisms of the Iraq War into a narrative that he was willing to "stick to his guns" in the face of political pressure, thereby translating public opposition to his policies into an indication of leadership strength. Donald Trump publicly criticized allies to show that he was a hard-nosed bargainer who would prevent other countries from taking advantage of the United States, even though most voters disliked Trump's abrasive posturing in its own right.

These examples involve Democrats and Republicans, incumbent presidents and presidential challengers, decisions made in and out of wartime, and policies developed in election and in nonelection years. Despite all the analysis that scholars, journalists, and pundits devote to understanding what voters think about foreign policy issues on their merits, we will see that leaders often pay more attention to determining how those issues shape perceptions of their fitness to serve as the country's commander in chief.

Public Opinion and the Politics of Image-Making in US Foreign Policy

How does public opinion shape foreign policy? The standard answer to this question is that leaders build public support by making popular policy choices.[1] This is a simple and intuitive idea of how democracy works. And, by this logic, US foreign policy does not seem to be particularly democratic. Some of the most significant features of US foreign policy—rising defense budgets, open-ended military interventions, and a tendency toward unilateralism—frequently conflict with voters' policy preferences. A large volume of scholarship thus portrays US foreign policy as being "disconnected" from public opinion, reflecting the attitudes of elites and special interests rather than the input of ordinary citizens.[2]

I argue that this conventional wisdom underestimates the role that public opinion plays in shaping foreign policy. Though voters certainly prefer presidents who share their views on foreign policy issues, I show that they place greater emphasis on selecting a commander in chief who seems competent at foreign policy decision making writ large. This means that leaders can sometimes cultivate public support by pursuing foreign policies that violate voters' preferences, so long as those choices help to build or maintain impressions of competence.

What should those impressions of competence entail? Voters generally want presidents to possess two attributes. They should be strong leaders who will vigorously promote US interests. And they should possess the good judgment to avoid taking unnecessary risks. To the extent that presidents and presidential candidates need to show voters that they are fit to be commander in chief, this challenge largely revolves around conveying impressions of strength and judgment.

In principle, voters value the attributes of strength and judgment in roughly equal measure. Yet, in practice, good judgment is hard to evaluate. Good judgment is context dependent: a foreign policy decision that is reasonable in one situation might be too risky or too cautious in another. International relations scholars frequently struggle, even with the benefit of hindsight, to distinguish skill from luck in foreign policy decision making.[3] It is genuinely challenging to know what good judgment entails when it comes to managing geopolitics.[4]

By contrast, it is fairly easy for presidents and presidential candidates to use hawkish foreign policies to indicate that they are standing up to adversaries in a manner that voters intuitively associate with leadership strength. I argue that this unusually clear connection between hawkish behavior and perceptions of leadership strength encourages leaders to expand the scope of US foreign policy, to be more aggressive on the international stage, and to avoid making compromises that could be portrayed as backing down under pressure, even when voters do not agree with the substance of those choices. In doing so, I demonstrate that the relationship between public opinion and US foreign policy is both more extensive, and more problematic, than the conventional wisdom allows.

Rethinking the Politics of US Foreign Policy

This book explains how the role foreign policy positions play in US politics resembles a "MacGuffin": a literary object whose primary function is to advance a broader narrative. A classic example of a MacGuffin is how the title character in the 1941 film *Citizen Kane* utters the word "Rosebud" while dying. The rest of the film revolves around searching for what the word "Rosebud" means. Viewers eventually learn that Rosebud is the name of a sled, which itself represents the loss of childhood innocence. In some sense, *Citizen Kane* is thus a movie about a sled. But no one would gauge an audience's response to *Citizen Kane* by asking viewers what they think about the sled. The sled is simply a device for conveying other elements of the story. I similarly show that, when leaders debate foreign policy issues, their stances serve as devices for conveying other messages about their personal qualities. It is thus a mistake to gauge the public's reaction to foreign policy debates by asking voters what they think about the issues—even though that is the focus of the vast majority of existing research on public opinion and foreign policy.

This argument helps explain why Americans are consistently frustrated with the cost and scope of their country's foreign policy. The frustration comes from the fact that leaders consistently reject public demands to restrain the growth of military expenditures, to curtail open-ended military interventions, or to share more of the burden of global leadership with allies. And this behavior remains consistent because leaders are not simply ignoring public opinion. Instead, leaders frequently face trade-offs between satisfying voters' policy preferences and cultivating impressions of foreign policy competence. Aligning US foreign policy with voters' preferences is thus easier said than done, and it is not always the best way for leaders to maximize their public standing. We should not expect this tension to disappear any time soon.

Issue-image trade-offs have significant implications for the conduct of international affairs. In particular, the book's case studies reveal a consistent pattern of presidents and presidential candidates trying to prove their fitness to be commander in chief by taking foreign policy positions that are more militaristic and less cooperative than those of their rivals or predecessors. Even if these choices have a marginal impact on individual foreign policy decisions, their effects can accumulate in important ways over time. For example, American voters have opposed raising military expenditures in nearly every year since World War II. Leaders have nevertheless continually increased the defense budget over time, such that the United States now accounts for roughly 40 percent of global military spending, an amount that is equivalent to the defense outlays of the next nine countries combined.[5]

Today, this tendency to push foreign policy in hawkish directions is particularly worrisome with respect to US-China relations. The book's theory explains how presidents and presidential candidates have incentives to use their China policies as proving grounds for demonstrating their vigilance against great-power competition, for showing that they will not back down in the face of aggression, and for portraying their rivals as complacent about threats to US national security. Candidates in any given election cycle have incentives to avoid taking their hawkishness too far, lest they be accused of possessing poor judgment. But if every new set of leaders pushes that envelope, then US-China relations could end up in a place that is substantially more conflictual than what anyone would deliberately choose in advance.

Finally, the book reveals important flaws with the United States' foreign policy discourse. Though it seems entirely reasonable for voters to subject potential presidents to a "commander-in-chief test," I explain that these efforts end up distorting US foreign policy. These distortions stem from the fact that it is relatively simple for presidents and presidential candidates to use hawkish foreign policies as tools for crafting impressions of leadership strength. That logic is similar to how car commercials often focus on sleek visuals rather than providing information about how well cars run. Even if customers do not place a particularly high value on a car's aesthetics, it is easier for television ads to make cars look visually appealing, and so that is where advertisers focus. I similarly show that conversations about foreign policy competence naturally gravitate toward considerations of leadership strength, because that attribute is relatively straightforward for voters to evaluate.

This argument does not imply that voters should delegate the commander-in-chief test to experts, because I doubt that most experts can do a particularly good job of assessing foreign policy competence, either. A large volume of research demonstrates that it is inherently difficult to assess the personal attributes of people we do not know well. This is true even when experts have substantial incentives to make accurate judgments, as with employers conducting job interviews or judges making bail decisions.[6] In many cases, attempting to judge other people's personal traits can be actively counterproductive, because these judgments end up serving as vehicles for biases and stereotypes. Such difficulties are likely to be especially severe when attempting to assess the competence of political leaders who specialize at image-crafting, who employ large teams of public relations specialists to enhance their personal appeal, and who—as we will see—can be remarkably cynical in seeking to manipulate public perceptions of their fitness to be commander in chief. If anything, the following chapters suggest that it is harder for voters to form accurate beliefs about presidential candidates' foreign policy competence than to develop reasonable preferences on major foreign policy issues. If citizens stuck to the issues when deciding who would do a better job of serving as commander in chief, they might end up being better off.

Isn't It Just "The Economy, Stupid!"?

This book does not argue that foreign policy plays a dominant role in US politics. Decades of scholarship on political behavior in the United States have demonstrated that the vast majority of vote choices can be predicted on the basis of factors such as partisanship, voters' socioeconomic status, and recent economic conditions.[7] For the most part, I agree with the famous mantra of Bill Clinton's 1992 campaign manager, James Carville, who said that the key to winning presidential elections is "the economy, stupid!" Indeed, the quantitative evidence that I present throughout this book suggests that presidential candidates' foreign policy positions might explain just one or two percentage points of presidential voting, at the margin.

Shifting a candidate's vote share by one or two percentage points might not make much difference to a statistical model that aims to explain political behavior writ large. But that kind of swing can very well change an election's outcome. And, in the context of a competitive presidential campaign, we should expect candidates to scrape and claw for every slice of the vote they can get. The book's theory and evidence explain how those efforts have significant consequences for US foreign policy—including the way that Bill Clinton chose to take a hawkish stance on intervening in Bosnia when he ran for president in 1992.

Evidence and Case Selection

The book contains three kinds of evidence. First, I present preregistered survey experiments that examine how voters assess presidential candidates' fitness to be commander in chief. Next, I analyze survey data to demonstrate that the book's experimental findings are consistent with voters' attitudes across more than half a century of presidential politics. Finally, I present case studies that show how the politics of image-making shape presidential candidates' foreign policy platforms. Where possible, I base these case studies on archival records, including strategic memoranda and private polls commissioned by presidential campaigns. These documents provide unique insight into how leaders perceive issue-image trade-offs and how they use foreign policy debates as vehicles for crafting personal images, even if that requires taking foreign policy positions that voters oppose on the merits.

The book's empirical analyses focus on presidential elections for methodological reasons, and not because my argument applies solely to that context. Vote choice provides a clear measure of the extent to which citizens support some leaders over others. Elections also encourage leaders to maximize public approval in the short term. This short-term focus minimizes concerns about how leaders pursue unpopular foreign policies that they expect to gain popularity over time. The idea that leaders seek to maximize anticipated public opinion poses notorious methodological challenges, because there is no reliable way to know what voters will think in the future. Surveys can only measure current public opinion; current public opinion matters most during elections; elections thus provide the best opportunities to test my theory against other ideas for how public opinion shapes foreign policy.

The book's case studies examine the seven presidential elections since 1960 in which foreign policy issues played the most salient role.[8] These should be relatively hard cases for my argument to explain. When foreign policy issues are unusually salient, then we would expect voters' policy preferences to have their largest impact on electoral outcomes, and leaders should have their strongest incentives to take foreign policy positions that align with public opinion. If I instead focused on cases in which foreign policy issues had low salience, then it would be less surprising to find that presidential candidates are willing to take unpopular foreign policy positions in order to bolster impressions of their foreign policy competence.

I determined the salience of foreign policy issues in each presidential election by examining two sources. The first of these sources is a database of public opinion surveys that ask voters to identify the "most important problem" facing the country.[9] I used this database to identify the proportion of voters in each presidential election who claimed that some foreign policy issue (such as counterterrorism or the Vietnam War) was the problem that concerned them most. I also examined open-ended survey questions from the American National Election Studies (ANES) that asked voters to explain

Table I.1 Salience of foreign policy issues across presidential elections

Presidential election	Pct. voters listing foreign policy issues as the country's "most important problem" (rank)	Pct. ANES candidate evaluations involving foreign policy issues (rank)
1960 (Kennedy, Nixon)	61% (1)	8% (7)
1968 (Nixon, Humphrey)	49% (2)	8% (6)
2004 (GW Bush, Kerry)	36% (3)	21% (2)
1972 (Nixon, McGovern)	35% (4)	21% (1)
1984 (Reagan, Mondale)	30% (5)	12% (4)
1964 (Johnson, Goldwater)	29% (6)	7% (9)
1980 (Reagan, Carter)	20% (7)	18% (3)
2008 (Obama, McCain)	17% (8)	–
2016 (Trump, H Clinton)	15% (9)	–
1988 (GHW Bush, Dukakis)	14% (10)	7% (8)
2000 (GW Bush, Gore)	7% (11)	2% (12)
1976 (Carter, Ford)	6% (12)	4% (10)
1996 (B Clinton, Dole)	5% (13)	3% (11)
2012 (Obama, Romney)	4% (14)	–
1992 (B Clinton, GHW Bush)	3% (15)	9% (5)
2020 (Biden, Trump)	1% (16)	–

The book provides case studies of the highlighted rows and discusses most of the others elsewhere in the text.

why they support or oppose presidential candidates. I used these data to identify the proportion of voters in each presidential election who invoked some element of foreign policy to justify their candidate preference.

I started my case selection process by identifying elections that fell into the top six rankings for either measure of foreign policy salience. Table I.1 shows how this approach captured seven cases: 1960–1972, 1980–1984, and 2004. The 1992 election also fits my case selection criterion because it placed fifth on the ANES measure of foreign policy salience, but the data show that this case rates quite low—fifteenth place—on the "most important problem" measure. These divergent scores make it hard to claim that foreign policy played a significant role in the 1992 election. And, as noted earlier, conventional narratives broadly agree that this contest largely revolved around economic issues. I therefore excluded the 1992 election from my primary set of qualitative analyses in chapters 4 through 6.

Chapter 7 then shows how my argument applies to US military interventions in the post–Cold War era. This chapter confirms that the politics of image-making shape foreign policy in cases where international affairs have relatively low salience (such as President Obama's 2009 decision to approve the Afghan Surge), shows that my argument applies to foreign policy decisions that occur outside of presidential campaigns (such as Bill Clinton's 1995 decision to send US forces to Bosnia), and describes how issue-image trade-offs can shape congressional behavior (as with debates over authorizing the

Iraq War in 2002). Altogether, the book's qualitative research thus shows that my theory sheds light on a wide range of historical material and contemporary policy debates.

Key Terms and Scope Conditions

This book examines mass public opinion, which reflects voters' collective preferences and beliefs. For the rest of the book, all references to "public opinion" refer specifically to mass public opinion. This does not mean that I ignore variations in voter demographics. For instance, I will show that my analyses of survey data generally hold when examining the opinions of partisans as well as political independents, men and women, white voters and nonwhite voters, highly educated voters and less educated voters, voters with high and low levels of foreign policy knowledge, and so on. This is important for demonstrating that my theory does not simply apply to peculiar segments of the electorate whose views skew aggregate survey results.

I use the term "leaders" as a shorthand for describing presidents and presidential candidates. I focus on presidents and presidential candidates because they face the strongest pressure to demonstrate their fitness to serve as the country's commander in chief. The book's theory also presumably applies to people who plan to run for president in the future. This scope condition includes some cabinet officials (such as Hillary Clinton during her tenure as Barack Obama's secretary of state), some military officials (such as General Douglas MacArthur during his service in the Korean War), some private citizens (such as Donald Trump before declaring his presidential candidacy), and many US senators. Yet, since it is difficult to estimate the strength of any individual's presidential ambitions—and, since presidents play the greatest role in shaping US foreign policy anyhow—the book's empirical analysis focuses on presidential politics.

The book's case studies focus on national security policy, and specifically the areas of defense spending, military interventions, and unilateralism. I focus on these issues because they play central roles in debates about democratic responsiveness in US foreign policy. As noted above, scholars frequently argue that elites and special interests have hijacked US national security policy in order to pursue objectives that are more militaristic and more cooperative than what voters want. One of the book's primary contributions is to show that the story is not that simple, and that US foreign policy has more to do with public opinion than the conventional wisdom allows. Yet, there is no reason to think that my argument applies solely to national security policy. The book's conclusion describes how my argument plausibly extends to debates about issues such as trade and immigration.

Finally, it is worth noting that the book examines foreign policy promises made by presidential candidates as well as actual foreign policies implemented by incumbent presidents. Throughout the book, I will treat both behaviors—position taking and the execution of actual foreign policies—within the same theoretical framework. This move raises two questions: Why should voters believe the promises presidential candidates make on the campaign trail? Do campaign promises matter for the conduct of US foreign policy?

If presidential candidates' statements were mere rhetoric, then voters would have little reason to pay attention to candidates' policy positions, those positions would not help candidates to cultivate impressions of competence, and this process would have little practical significance for the actual conduct of foreign policy. However, a significant body of research demonstrates that leaders suffer "audience costs" for breaking their commitments, that presidents believe they will be held accountable for implementing the policies they proposed, and that presidents implement most of their campaign pledges.[10] These findings show that the proposals presidential candidates make on the campaign trail are not just cheap talk: they are indications of what leaders would do if elected, if only to avoid being accused of breaking their promises.

Of course, presidents do not fulfill all of their commitments, and so campaign statements provide weaker indications of competence than actual foreign policy decisions. This means that nonincumbents likely have more reason to behave in the manner that my theory suggests, because they need to go to more extreme lengths in order to convey their competence to skeptical observers. But I expect that this difference is largely a matter of degree, and I will show that my argument explains behavior by presidential candidates and incumbent presidents alike. For the rest of the book, I will thus use the term "foreign policy positions" to reflect either campaign statements or actual foreign policy decisions, in order to avoid clogging the text.

Plan of the Book

Chapter 1 presents my theory of how public opinion shapes US foreign policy. Chapter 2 then tests the book's claim that voters generally place a higher priority on supporting leaders who seem competent at foreign policy decision making than on supporting leaders who take appealing foreign policy positions. I back this claim by analyzing seventy years of open-ended and closed-ended ANES data, by conducting an original survey of voters' attitudes during the 2020 presidential election, and by administering two preregistered survey experiments to nationally representative samples of voters. Chapter 3 combines similar evidence gathered from surveys and experiments to test my argument about how leaders' foreign policy positions shape their personal images, and to demonstrate that this relationship systematically favors foreign policy hawks.

Chapter 4 shows how my theory sheds light on the politics of defense spending, based on case studies of the 1960, 1980, and 1984 presidential elections.

The chapter's evidence revolves around archival records that I gathered from the JFK Presidential Library, the Carter Presidential Library, the Reagan Presidential Library, and the Minnesota Historical Society's Mondale Papers. These documents reveal how John F. Kennedy and Ronald Reagan used hawkish positions on defense spending to craft impressions of leadership strength, even when voters disagreed with those positions on their merits.

Chapter 5 explains how the politics of image-making shaped the life cycle of the Vietnam War through case studies of the 1964, 1968, and 1972 presidential campaigns. I show that none of the six presidential nominees during this period attempted to win public support by making proposals for handling the war that voters supported on their merits. Instead, debates about Vietnam largely served as vehicles for debating which candidates would provide stronger leadership, in a manner that escalated and prolonged US military intervention. These case studies revolve around archival records that I gathered at the LBJ Presidential Library, Arizona State University's Goldwater Papers, and the Minnesota Historical Society's Humphrey Papers, along with a substantial volume of digitized primary source material from the Nixon presidency.

Chapter 6 examines the politics of the Iraq War during the 2004 presidential election. Even though voters generally thought that President George W. Bush had mishandled the invasion of Iraq, I show that Bush nevertheless portrayed his wartime leadership as evidence that he was willing to "stick to his guns" in the face of public criticism. This case provides a vivid example of an issue-image trade-off: Bush explicitly leveraged public disapproval of his policies to craft an appealing personal image. I support this argument by relaying firsthand accounts from Bush's and Kerry's campaign advisers, and by analyzing a database of more than eighty thousand telephone interviews conducted by the National Annenberg Election Survey.

As noted earlier, chapter 7 shows how the politics of image-making shaped US military interventions in the post–Cold War era. In addition to demonstrating how my argument generalizes beyond the context of presidential campaigns, this chapter shows how the book's theoretical framework sheds new light on debates about why the United States has recently engaged in a series of "endless wars" that were not vital to US national security. The book concludes by drawing several implications from the book's analysis: it explains how the book's theory provides a novel lens for interpreting the politics of US foreign policy under Donald Trump; it develops practical implications of the book's argument; it suggests directions for future research; and it offers an overall assessment of how the commander-in-chief test ultimately distorts the politics of US foreign policy.

What Is the Commander-in-Chief Test and Why Does It Matter?

How the Politics of Image-Making Shape US Foreign Policy

In every presidential election, candidates, journalists, and pundits engage in extensive discussions about which leaders are "fit to be commander in chief." This is certainly a reasonable topic of concern. Who would not want to elect a president who can competently manage international affairs? Yet, that impulse can end up distorting the politics of foreign policy, by encouraging leaders to take foreign policy positions that are more militaristic and less cooperative than what voters actually want. I make this argument in five steps.

The chapter's first section explains why we should expect voters to place a higher priority on supporting leaders who seem competent at foreign policy decision making than on supporting leaders who take appealing foreign policy positions. I define foreign policy competence with respect to two attributes—strong leadership and good judgment—that ground the book's theoretical and empirical analysis.

The next section describes how leaders do not need to take popular foreign policy positions in order to craft favorable personal images. This claim is crucial to the book's overall argument, because it implies that we cannot say foreign policies are disconnected from public opinion just because they do not align with voters' policy preferences. Instead, I develop the concept of issue-image trade-offs: policies that are not popular on their merits but that leaders nonetheless use to convey favorable impressions of their personal qualities.

The chapter's third section explains why issue-image trade-offs tend to favor foreign policy hawks. Even if voters value strong leadership and good judgment in equal measure, I argue, they will generally find the first of those attributes easier to evaluate. This difference in evaluability gives presidents and presidential candidates special reasons to focus on cultivating perceptions of leadership strength. I describe how hawkish foreign policies are well suited for that purpose.

The chapter's last two sections identify some limits of my theory and then describe how my argument departs from prior research. Altogether, the chapter offers a new way to understand how public opinion shapes foreign policy, and a new explanation for why Americans are consistently frustrated by the cost and scope of their country's global role.

Foreign Policy Competence

The classic definition of political competence is "the ability to handle a job, an assessment of how effective a candidate will be in office."[1] Competence differs from likeability, because voters can find leaders to be likeable for reasons that have nothing to do with job performance. Competence also differs from the popularity of a leader's policy platform. Even if two leaders take identical policy stances, it is always possible that one leader would do a better job of implementing those policies.

There are several reasons to believe that voters will prioritize electing leaders who seem competent at foreign policy decision making. First, foreign policy decision making is frequently dominated by unexpected events. Many presidents' foreign policy legacies were defined by crises that they did not anticipate when they ran for office. Examples include Harry Truman's handling of the Korean War, John F. Kennedy's handling of the Cuban Missile Crisis, Jimmy Carter's response to the Iranian hostage crisis, George H. W. Bush's response to Iraq's invasion of Kuwait, Bill Clinton's handling of the Rwandan genocide, George W. Bush's response to the September 11 terrorist attacks, Barack Obama's response to the Arab Spring, and Donald Trump's handling of the COVID-19 pandemic. Voters thus have a legitimate interest in understanding how well leaders could handle unanticipated international problems that emerge on their watch. That is why presidential candidates are expected to demonstrate that they are ready to take the proverbial three-a.m. phone call.

Foreign policy also involves strategic interactions that make it difficult for leaders to say in advance exactly how they would respond to international crises. This is different from most areas of domestic policy, where governments provide goods and services directly to their citizens, and where leaders are therefore expected to say up front how they plan to design those programs. As Thomas Schelling famously explained, international conflict is essentially a form of bargaining, in which each side's best course of action depends on the choices of its counterparts.[2] Even the most sophisticated attempts to specify strategies for handling these situations require extensive simplifying assumptions.[3] Nor should voters want leaders to reveal their plans for crisis management, as adversaries could exploit that information.[4]

Voters must therefore trust that foreign policy decision makers possess the leadership qualities required to manage international crises effectively.

Finally, there is substantial evidence that leaders' personal attributes do, in fact, shape foreign policy decision making. Recent scholarship has documented that individual-level factors such as confidence, expertise, narcissism, rationality, and resolve affect foreign policy behavior.[5] This scholarship implies that voters have an interest in making sure that their presidents have the right personal qualities to be effective commanders in chief.

If anything, we should expect voters to place a higher priority on supporting leaders who seem competent at foreign policy decision making than on supporting leaders who take appealing foreign policy positions. Voters appear to possess limited knowledge of foreign affairs, and most foreign policy issues have relatively low salience in US politics.[6] By contrast, voters are naturally inclined to assess politicians on the basis of their personal attributes. Citizens make split-second judgments about political leaders' competence on the basis of cues such as gender, face shape, vocal pitch, and physical attractiveness.[7] One explanation for this behavior is that, while policy debates are complex things that rarely come up in voters' daily lives, most people have plenty of experience sizing up strangers.[8] Thus, whereas most voters pay limited attention to foreign policy issues, and thus end up holding policy preferences that are often weak and malleable, they intuitively form impressions of leaders' competence.

STRONG LEADERSHIP AND GOOD JUDGMENT

What, then, does it take to be a competent commander in chief? For one thing, a president should be able and willing to resist international aggression. This a basic requirement for protecting national security. Leaders who tend to back down when threatened will encourage predatory behavior by adversaries. Citizens also presumably want their leaders to be proactive when it comes to supporting allies, marginalizing adversaries, and negotiating international agreements that work to the United States' advantage. We can summarize these expectations by saying that voters should value having a commander in chief who is a strong leader, defined as someone who will vigorously promote US national interests and who will not back down when challenged by the nation's adversaries. A substantial volume of research indicates that voters do, in fact, value presidents who seem like strong leaders and that they associate leadership strength with making competent foreign policy decisions.[9]

Yet, leadership strength is only part of what it takes to be a competent commander in chief. Even if voters want a president who will not easily back down when challenged, they should also value having leaders who will avoid entangling the country in unnecessary wars. Similarly, even if voters value hard-nosed bargaining, this should not preclude a president from making pragmatic compromises when dealing with other countries. Thus, in addition to valuing strong leaders who vigorously promote America's national interests, we should also expect voters to prioritize selecting presidents who possess good judgment, which I define as the ability to avoid taking unnecessary risks and to avoid major mistakes in foreign policy decision making.

Identifying strength and judgment as the two crucial components for foreign policy competence resembles several prior studies of political leadership. For example, Margaret Hermann's research on leadership styles distinguishes "transformational" figures from leaders who provide a "safe pair of hands."[10] Donald Kinder's research on presidential personalities distinguishes leadership strength from more cerebral qualities such as knowledgeability and intelligence.[11] Brian Rathbun classifies the cognitive profiles of foreign policy decision makers with respect to "romantic" leaders who pursue ambitious visions and "realists" who carefully assess the costs, benefits, and uncertainties surrounding high-stakes choices.[12] Henry Kissinger characterizes foreign policy leaders as "prophets" who redefine conceptions of the possible versus "statesmen" who are adept at managing geopolitical constraints.[13] These authors all argue that effective leaders have assertive qualities that are associated with my definition of strong leadership along with rationalistic qualities that are associated with my definition of good judgment.

If strong leadership and good judgment always went together, then there would be no reason to treat these concepts separately. But it is easy to identify examples of leaders who excel on one of these dimensions and not the other. Ronald Reagan was straight out of central casting when it came to projecting an image of leadership strength in international affairs, but many voters also worried that he was a reckless warmonger who might entangle the United States in unnecessary conflicts. By contrast, George H. W. Bush possessed unusual foreign policy expertise and he styled himself as being a "prudent" decision maker, but he was saddled with accusations of being a "wimp."[14] The book's case studies will provide many other examples of how leaders struggle to craft images of strength and judgment simultaneously.

Even though my concepts of strength and judgment do not capture all of the characteristics that voters might associate with foreign policy competence, they cover most of what debates on this subject entail. To test this claim, I asked a research team to scour the LexisNexis news database, examining political commentary from the last twenty years of presidential campaigns that discussed the extent to which candidates seemed fit to be commander in chief. This exercise identified twenty-five attributes that journalists and pundits associated with foreign policy competence. The appendix for this chapter shows how twenty-two of those twenty-five attributes fit with my definitions of strong leadership and good judgment.[15]

How Foreign Policy Issues Shape Leaders' Personal Images

Leaders can take many steps to convince voters that they are competent at foreign policy decision making. These include highlighting prior military or diplomatic service, meeting with world leaders, and debating foreign policy issues on national television. Such actions can help leaders look presidential, and they may well play a crucial role in presidential politics, but they do not necessarily shape the content of US foreign policy.

By contrast, my theory explains why some foreign policy positions are more politically valuable than others. In particular, I argue that "hawkish" foreign policies generally bolster impressions of leadership strength while "dovish" foreign policies generally help to communicate good judgment. I also explain how these dynamics can distort the politics of foreign policy by encouraging leaders to take foreign policy positions that voters do not support on their merits.

USING FOREIGN POLICY ISSUES TO CRAFT IMPRESSIONS OF PERSONAL TRAITS

I use the term "hawkishness" to capture two dimensions of foreign policy. The first dimension is a leader's willingness to use military force instead of relying on nonmilitary elements of diplomacy. The second dimension is a leader's willingness to make compromises to work in concert with other countries. All things being equal, a foreign policy "hawk" is more likely to pursue militarized foreign policies and less likely to compromise with other countries. A foreign policy "dove" is more likely to pursue foreign policies that are less militarized and more cooperative.[16]

Militarized foreign policies are useful ways to convey leadership strength because they are easy to frame in terms of standing up to the United States' adversaries or remaining vigilant in the face of foreign threats. The main drawback to militarized foreign policies is that they can seem excessively risky, which raises questions about leaders' judgment. An example of this tension involves the 1964 Republican presidential nominee, Senator Barry Goldwater. Goldwater took several unusually hawkish stances with respect to the Vietnam War and the use of nuclear weapons. Chapter 5 will explain how Goldwater used those policies to portray himself as a strong leader, and to cast incumbent president Lyndon Johnson as being soft on communism. But Goldwater's hawkishness also caused many voters to question his judgment. Today, Goldwater is the archetypal case of a presidential candidate who could not be trusted with his thumb on the nuclear button, though almost no one ever questioned his commitment to national defense.[17] Goldwater thus exemplifies how hawkish foreign policy positions can bolster impressions of strength while undermining perceptions of judgment.

15

Likewise, leaders who are more aggressive when it comes to demanding diplomatic concessions from other countries can readily frame that behavior in terms of vigorously promoting US interests. The main drawback to this behavior is that it risks obstructing avenues for international cooperation—an outcome that voters might associate with poor judgment. Donald Trump's foreign policy provides clear examples of this tension. President Trump provoked tensions with US allies and terminated US participation in several multilateral agreements. The conclusion to this book will show how Trump used this behavior to portray himself as a hard-nosed bargainer who put America first, while claiming that other leaders let other countries walk all over the United States. At the same time, President Trump's critics warned that his confrontational behavior risked undermining US credibility and creating unnecessary conflicts. Trump's unilateralism thus helped him to convey leadership strength while exposing him to criticism for lacking good judgment.

ISSUE-IMAGE TRADE-OFFS

Viewing foreign policy positions as tools in the politics of image-making—not just as a means of appealing to voters' policy preferences—has two main practical consequences. First, leaders who are worried about looking weak should have incentives to pursue hawkish foreign policies, whereas leaders who fear criticism for lacking good judgment should have incentives to pursue dovish foreign policies. Second, there is no reason to believe that the most popular foreign policies will also be the ones that help leaders to establish the most appealing personal images. In other words, leaders who seek to cultivate mass public appeal do not necessarily have to adopt popular foreign policy positions. I use the term "issue-image trade-offs" to describe any situation in which the policy positions that maximize voters' collective policy preferences do not simultaneously maximize a leader's ability to craft impressions of foreign policy competence.

My theory even implies that leaders can sometimes convey competence by pursuing foreign policies on which voters have no coherent attitudes at all. Arguably the most important example of this phenomenon is how President Lyndon Johnson used the 1964 Gulf of Tonkin Crisis to gain open-ended congressional authorization for the use of military force in Vietnam. Chapter 5 will show that most voters were not paying much attention to political instability in South Vietnam, nor did they have firm preferences for handling that problem. Johnson nevertheless used the Gulf of Tonkin Crisis to demonstrate that he was tough enough to resist communist aggression.

It may not immediately seem troubling to find that leaders have incentives to take positions on issues where the public lacks coherent preferences. Yet, every public policy has opportunity costs. If the politics of image-making encourage leaders to devote time and resources to dealing with issues that voters do not care about, then that will drain attention from tackling other problems. So long as voters can imagine any other way that leaders could put their time and resources to better use, then these leaders would not be maximizing voters' policy preferences. Johnson's escalation of the Vietnam War provides a vivid example of how this behavior can impose substantial costs on US foreign policy.

Why the Politics of Image-Making Favor Foreign Policy Hawks

I have explained why we should generally expect hawkish foreign policies to bolster perceptions of leaders' strength while undermining perceptions of leaders' judgment. In principle, these countervailing effects could balance each other out. Yet, in practice, I expect that voters will find it easier to associate hawkishness with leadership strength than to associate dovishness with good judgment. This dynamic is important for understanding why the commander-in-chief test favors foreign policy hawks.

This argument builds on the phenomenon of evaluability bias, which is the well-documented tendency for individuals to weight the importance of an attribute in proportion to its ease of evaluation.[18] Evaluability bias is the reason why car commercials tend to focus on sleek visuals and gadgets. Even if customers primarily care about buying cars that run well, they may find it difficult to evaluate a car's performance. For example, one of the main criteria for judging the quality of a car's engine is its torque, but very few people have an intuitive understanding of what torque statistics mean. (If you learn that a car's engine has 180 pound-feet of torque, would you know how good that is? How much extra would you be willing to pay for an engine with 195 pound-feet of torque?) By contrast, most people can intuitively determine how much they like a car's exterior finish or whether they think the vehicle contains a suitable number of cupholders. Since these factors are easy to evaluate, they will likely play an outsized role in most customers' decisions.

Evaluability bias can be perfectly rational. If you lack the ability to evaluate an attribute, then it makes sense to assign that attribute less weight when making decisions. Yet, weighting attributes with respect to evaluability will generally lead people to make choices that do not reflect their true preferences. Advertising agencies exacerbate this problem by deliberately designing marketing strategies around easily evaluable details. Evaluability bias thus generates an equilibrium in which car manufacturers oversupply their customers with aesthetics and gadgets, and customers end up overpaying for features that they do not really want.

I argue that a similar phenomenon shapes the politics of image-making in foreign policy. Even if voters value strong leadership and good judgment in equal measure, we should expect leaders to focus their efforts on conveying whichever attribute is easier to evaluate. And, all things being equal, leadership strength is easier to evaluate than good judgment.

Good judgment is inherently difficult to evaluate because it depends on context. A foreign policy that is reasonable in one situation might be too reckless or too cautious in another. Since most foreign policy debates involve high degrees of uncertainty and subjectivity, it is usually hard to say, even with the benefit of hindsight, which foreign policy positions reflect better judgment than others.[19] To give one prominent example, it is essentially impossible to draw conclusive judgments about when the use of military force is more likely to escalate or to contain international crises. In some cases, military action is necessary to restrain aggressive opponents. In other cases, military force will only worsen spirals of hostility. International relations scholars have not yet developed clear rules of thumb for knowing which cases are which.[20] It is hard to expect that voters possess the time and expertise necessary to develop firm views on such subjects.

I am not claiming that voters will never form opinions about which leaders possess good judgment and which do not. Some voters may derive these opinions from partisan loyalties, assuming that copartisans have good judgment while leaders from the other party are all idiots. For other voters, perceptions of good judgment might be a straightforward function of preference alignment: leaders who share their policy views will seem to have good judgment while leaders who do not share their policy views will seem to have poor judgment. But if voters' assessments of good judgment simply reflect other attitudes, then we would not expect the politics of image-making to affect leaders' behavior. Returning to the car-buying analogy, car manufacturers would not put cupholders in vehicles unless they thought this would make customers spend more money on cars. Similarly, when I say that good judgment has low evaluability, I am claiming that foreign policy positions will have a relatively limited impact on voters' perceptions of leaders' judgment.

By comparison, it is straightforward to frame hawkish foreign policies as indications of leadership strength. Leaders who promise to spend more on national defense than their opponents can easily use that contrast to claim that they care more about national security. Leaders who propose to wind down military interventions can easily be criticized for backing down to America's enemies. Leaders who make diplomatic concessions to other countries can easily be criticized for not negotiating aggressively. It might be hard to say which of these policies are actually justified on their merits, but that is the point: leadership strength is more evaluable than good judgment.

A recent example of this contrast involves President Donald Trump's decision to assassinate Iranian general Qassem Suleimani in January 2020. After Trump ordered the strike, many observers accused him of recklessly risking war with Tehran.[21] Others said that the United States should have taken action against Suleimani long ago, and that the strike would help to deter Iran from challenging the United States in the future.[22] Even in hindsight, it is difficult to determine whether or not Trump's decision reflected good judgment. Since Iran's retaliation for the Suleimani strike was less severe than many people predicted, it is possible that Trump accurately understood that his decision was not as risky as his critics alleged. Or, maybe Trump just got lucky.

By contrast, the Suleimani assassination sent an unambiguous indication of how Trump was willing to punish Iranian aggression in a manner that other leaders would not. Trump's predecessor, Barack Obama, had declined to take direct action against Suleimani, and Trump's opponent in the 2020 presidential election, Joe Biden, explicitly said that he would not have approved the strike.[23] The Suleimani strike thus sent a message about Trump's leadership strength that was easier to evaluate than the indications the strike provided about Trump's judgment. Trump indeed appeared to view the Suleimani strike as a significant political asset, repeatedly highlighting this decision throughout his 2020 reelection campaign.[24]

What the Book Does—and Does Not—Argue

To summarize, I have made three main claims about how the politics of image-making shape US foreign policy. First, I argued that voters place a higher priority on supporting leaders who seem competent at foreign policy decision making than on leaders who take popular foreign policy positions. I defined foreign policy competence with respect to two attributes: strong leadership and good judgment.

Next, I argued that leaders do not need to take popular foreign policy positions in order to craft images of foreign policy competence. Instead, I explained how the politics of image-making can encourage leaders to take unpopular foreign policy positions, or to prioritize dealing with foreign policy issues on which voters have no coherent preferences at all. I coined the term "issue-image trade-offs" to describe this phenomenon.

Finally, I explained why issue-image trade-offs generally favor foreign policy hawks. This is because voters generally associate hawkish foreign policies with leadership strength. And, even though voters will also generally associate dovish foreign policies with good judgment, I argued that the first of these relationships is more evaluable than the second.

Altogether, my theory thus explains how voters evaluate leaders' fitness to be commander in chief and argues that these considerations steer US foreign policy in a direction that is more militaristic and less cooperative than what voters actually want. Now it is important to clarify what my theory does *not* argue.

My theory does not assume that leaders ignore voters' policy preferences. All else being equal, leaders should benefit from making popular foreign policy decisions. The problem is that popular foreign policy decisions are not all equal when it comes to crafting leaders' personal images. My argument explains how these trade-offs can shape the politics of foreign policy in significant ways.

My theory does not predict that leaders always benefit from making their policy positions more hawkish. So long as we assume that there are diminishing returns to conveying personal attributes such as leadership strength, then there will always be a point at which the marginal benefit of image-making falls below the marginal cost of reducing preference alignment. Barry Goldwater provides a good example of this risk, given how he adopted a foreign policy platform that was so extreme that he came across as a reckless warmonger. The book's case studies will show that presidents and presidential candidates generally work hard to avoid exposing themselves to such criticism.

My theory does not argue that hawkish foreign policies are the only way that presidents and presidential candidates can convey leadership strength. For instance, President Joe Biden claimed that withdrawing from Afghanistan demonstrated his willingness to make tough decisions.[25] Yet, that same rhetoric is usually available to hawkish leaders, too, as with George W. Bush "sticking to his guns" in Iraq. The difference between these cases is that Biden exposed himself to criticism for backing down in the face of enemy aggression, whereas Bush could more readily portray the invasion and occupation of Iraq as evidence that he was confronting his adversaries head on. This is the sense in which I expect that hawkish foreign policies will generally be more useful than dovish foreign policies when it comes to cultivating reputations for leadership strength.

My theory does not imply that leaders never benefit from pursuing dovish foreign policies. Harry Truman's Marshall Plan and Jimmy Carter's Camp David Accords are two prominent examples of dovish foreign policies that helped presidents to improve their public standing. Yet, both of those policies were popular on their merits.[26] There is no clear argument to be made about how the Marshall Plan or the Camp David Accords shifted US foreign policy in a direction that voters opposed. In other words, my theory does not depend on claiming that every foreign policy issue presents an issue-image trade-off. Instead, I claim that when issue-image trade-offs occur, they generally favor foreign policy hawks.[27]

Finally, my theory does not predict that foreign policy hawks will always win elections. For instance, Barack Obama won the 2008 presidential election despite being more dovish on foreign policy than his Republican opponent, Senator John McCain. Yet, once in office, Obama also proved to be less dovish than his supporters anticipated. Obama withdrew US troops from Iraq more slowly than he had promised, he escalated the war in Afghanistan, he toppled Muammar Qaddafi's regime in Libya, he authorized covert surveillance of US citizens, he ramped up the global use of drone strikes, and he broke his campaign promise to close the US prison camp at Guantánamo Bay. Chapter 7 will explain how at least some of these surprisingly hawkish elements of Obama's foreign policy reflected pressures that Obama faced to demonstrate that was not a weak commander in chief. Thus, while the book's theory does not claim that dovish politicians never win elections, it can explain why many of these leaders do not turn out to be as dovish as their followers might have hoped.

ALTERNATIVES AND QUESTIONS

It is worth addressing some alternative ideas for how the politics of image-making can shape foreign policy. First, voters might simply think that strength is more important than judgment when deciding which leaders are fit to be commander in chief. If that were the case, then we would still have reasons to believe that the politics of image-making pressure leaders to adopt hawkish foreign policies, but we would not have to invoke the concept of evaluability in order to explain that behavior. Yet, the book will deploy several forms of evidence to show that voters do, in fact, value good judgment as least as much as leadership strength when assessing foreign policy competence. We thus need to invoke some other phenomenon in order to explain why the commander-in-chief test has a hawkish bias. The book's quantitative and qualitative evidence will both show that this bias appears to result from the way that voters find leadership strength to be more evaluable than good judgment.

Another idea is that voters are naturally attracted to "change candidates" who promise to overturn the status quo. In this view, incumbent presidents face the disadvantage of having to defend their records, whereas challengers can criticize existing policies in a manner that makes them seem more competent at handling foreign policy issues. The book's case studies will indeed show that presidential challengers have more freedom to outflank their rivals in the politics of image-making. Yet, this does not explain why challengers consistently try to outflank incumbents by pushing foreign policies in hawkish directions. If voters were simply drawn to candidates who promised to revise the status quo, then dovish foreign policies should be just as valuable for that purpose. The book's quantitative and qualitative evidence will show that this is not the case.

A third question is whether the book's argument simply reflects the dynamics of partisan types. Since the start of the Cold War, Republicans have generally been seen as offering stronger leadership than Democrats on foreign affairs, but that often goes hand in hand with the perception that Republicans are more likely to start unnecessary wars.[28] In principle, this pattern is consistent with the book's argument: since Republicans tend to be more hawkish than Democrats on foreign policy issues, we would expect them to come across as stronger leaders with worse judgment. But if these reputations are simply a function of party brands, then the politics of image-making would not influence leaders' positions on foreign policy issues. To that end, the book's survey and experimental evidence will demonstrate that perceptions of strong leadership and good judgment are not simply the product of party brands. I will show that leaders' foreign policy positions do, in fact, shape the way that voters perceive their personal images. The book's case studies then show that leaders scrape and claw for those advantages, and that this competition pushes both Democrats and Republicans to support foreign policies that are more hawkish than what voters actually want.

A final question is whether the book's argument holds throughout the election cycle, or whether it only applies in the context of presidential campaigns, when leaders face the strongest pressure to win public approval. There are three reasons why I do not expect the book's argument to be limited to presidential campaigns. First, presidents have instrumental reasons to maintain high levels of public support, as this provides them with more political capital to use for implementing their policy agendas.[29] Second, presidents generally value their reputations and legacies as ends in themselves.[30] Third, and perhaps most importantly, chapter 7 will provide empirical examples of how the book's argument explains foreign policy behavior outside of presidential elections.

Comparisons to Existing Scholarship

My argument departs sharply from existing scholarship on "issue voting," which argues that leaders cultivate public support by taking policy positions that are more popular than their opponents'.[31] The issue-voting paradigm assumes that three conditions must hold in order for public opinion to shape foreign policy. First, voters must possess coherent foreign policy preferences. Second, voters must perceive clear distinctions between presidential candidates' positions on significant foreign policy issues. Third, voters must assign some weight to foreign policy issues when deciding which presidential candidate to support. When each of these conditions holds, presidential candidates should have incentives to take foreign policy positions that maximize voters' collective preferences.

My theory deviates from all three of the issue-voting paradigm's core assumptions. I explain why voters should value foreign policy competence even when they lack coherent preferences on any individual foreign policy issues. I describe how voters who perceive no significant differences among leaders' foreign policy platforms can still believe that one leader would do a better job of handling international affairs. And I argue that voters may support leaders who take unpopular foreign policy positions, so long as those positions appear to convey foreign policy competence.

It is worth noting that, even if the term "issue voting" comes from a specific body of scholarship, the basic idea is widespread in public discourse. Polls that elicit voters' policy preferences are the standard tool that journalists and pundits use to understand what citizens want. Vast reams of writing explore the nature, coherence, and sources of citizens' policy preferences. Researchers conduct these studies because they think voters' policy preferences play a significant role in the politics of foreign policy. In short, the issue-voting paradigm represents intuitive notions of how democracy works. This book explains how that idea provides an incomplete and often misleading lens for analyzing the relationship between public opinion and US foreign policy.

OTHER STUDIES OF HAWKISH BIASES IN US FOREIGN POLICY

Several other studies explore the factors that steer US foreign policy in hawkish directions. For example, several important works show that cognitive biases can lead people to develop hawkish foreign policy preferences.[32] My theory departs from this scholarship because it does not revolve around voters' policy preferences. Instead, I explain how the politics of image-making encourage leaders to pursue foreign policies that are more hawkish than what voters say they want.

Other research attributes the cost and scope of US foreign policy to the behavior of undemocratic elites. One example of this argument is the idea that a "military-industrial complex" agitates for hawkish foreign policies that benefit defense contractors, bureaucrats, and legislators even when voters do not support those policies on their merits.[33] Other scholars claim that the US "foreign policy establishment" is ideologically predisposed to pursue ambitious international goals that voters do not share.[34] Both of these arguments assume that leaders would behave differently if they followed mass public opinion.[35] Yet, this book explains how the politics of image-making naturally steer foreign policy in a direction that departs from voters' policy preferences. My argument thus suggests that the politics of US foreign policy are more democratic than they might otherwise appear.

OTHER STUDIES OF FOREIGN POLICY COMPETENCE

Several other studies claim that voters value foreign policy competence. However, this book offers new ideas about how perceptions of foreign policy competence shape international behavior. For example, a substantial literature on "retrospective voting" explains how citizens evaluate leaders' competence by judging the outcomes of their decisions.[36] In this view, voters do not really care what kinds of decisions leaders make so long as those decisions seem to work out in the end. My theory explains why we should also expect voters to evaluate leaders' competence based on the content of their foreign policy choices.

Scholarship on "audience costs" argues that foreign policy decision makers appear incompetent when they do not follow through on military threats or other international commitments.[37] Some leaders might take military actions to avoid the perception that they are breaking their promises, even if they think that backing down is the right decision. This scenario could force leaders to make a trade-off between preserving an image of competence and pursuing popular policies. My theory explains how similar trade-offs appear across a broad range of foreign policy issues, and why those trade-offs do not necessarily depend on leaders tying their hands with prior commitments.

Another relevant literature argues that voters assume competent leaders are more likely to undertake difficult tasks. This expectation can give leaders reasons to embark on activist foreign policies, simply as a way for these leaders to indicate that they can tackle tough challenges.[38] Yet, in principle, leaders could communicate competence by undertaking dovish policies, such as negotiating arms control treaties, brokering peace treaties, or building international institutions. My theory explains why leaders who seek to craft impressions of foreign policy competence do not just have incentives to be active in international affairs, but why the politics of image-making encourage hawkish actions, specifically.

OTHER THEORIES OF POLITICAL IMAGE-MAKING

Scholarship on "priming" explains how political leaders often seek to highlight their most popular policy positions in order to enhance their personal images.[39] This behavior does not necessarily promote democratic responsiveness, because leaders can exploit priming effects to make their policy agendas seem more popular than they really are.[40] That is different from how I argue that leaders can cultivate mass public opinion by taking unpopular policy positions, or by pursuing policies on which voters lack coherent preferences.

The literature on "issue ownership" argues that some candidates enter elections with preexisting advantages in their perceived ability to handle specific policy domains.[41] For instance, voters normally expect Democrats to do a better job of providing health care, and voters normally expect Republicans to do a better job of reducing crime. The literature on issue ownership describes how leaders can exploit those advantages by raising the salience of issue areas in which they are already perceived to be competent. By contrast, my theory explains how leaders attempt to change voters' perceptions of their competence in handling foreign policy issues.[42]

Finally, scholars have documented how elected officials frequently have incentives to conceal controversial policy views or to defer controversial policy decisions until elections have concluded.[43] Concealment and deferral can help leaders to avoid criticism that might undermine their reputations for competent leadership. By contrast, my theory explains how leaders make controversial choices as a way of building their reputations for foreign policy competence. This contrast offers another example of how the book's argument departs from prior scholarship on political image-making.

Personal Images, Policy Preferences, and Presidential Voting

Evidence from Surveys and Experiments

This chapter demonstrates that voters place a higher priority on selecting leaders who seem competent than on leaders who share their views on foreign policy issues. These findings ground the book's overall argument by showing that leaders have incentives to take unpopular foreign policy positions if that would help to bolster their personal images. I support this conclusion with four bodies of evidence.

First, I examine data from the American National Election Studies (ANES), a series of nationally representative surveys from every US presidential election since 1948. I use these data to show that citizens' foreign policy preferences explain less variation in presidential vote choice than their perceptions of presidential candidates' leadership strength. In fact, the ANES data suggest that there are effectively no areas of foreign policy in which presidential candidates would not benefit from taking unpopular policy positions if that helps them to seem like strong leaders.

The chapter's second section documents similar patterns using the ANES database of open-ended questions. Open-ended questions allow voters to describe, in their own words, how they view presidential candidates' strengths and weaknesses. I find that voters are roughly three times as likely to evaluate presidential candidates based on their competence as opposed to their foreign policy positions. I also find that perceptions of competence explain roughly twice as much variation in presidential voting relative to foreign policy issues.

It is always hard to draw causal inferences from political surveys, and so the chapter's third section presents two preregistered survey experiments that I designed to elicit voters' priorities when it comes to selecting a commander in chief. These experiments confirm that, when voters evaluate presidential candidates, they prioritize foreign policy competence over the substance of those leaders' foreign policy positions. Once again, these findings indicate that presidential candidates would benefit from taking unpopular positions on nearly any foreign policy issue if that helps to cultivate favorable perceptions of their leadership qualities.

Finally, I analyze original survey data that I gathered during the 2020 presidential campaign. This survey asked voters to assess Republican incumbent Donald Trump and his Democratic challenger, former vice president Joe Biden. Unlike ANES surveys, which ask voters to say what they like and dislike about presidential candidates in general, I asked voters to say which candidate they thought would make for a more effective commander in chief. Using both open- and closed-ended question formats, I found that voters were more than twice as likely to defend their judgments based on their perceptions of Trump and Biden's personal traits rather than invoking those candidates' stances on foreign policy issues.

The chapter's findings apply to Democrats, to Republicans, and to independents, to men and to women, to white and nonwhite voters, to voters with college educations and to those without college educations. When gathering my own survey data, I asked respondents to complete a battery of questions measuring foreign policy knowledge. My conclusions are robust to variations on that dimension, too. The results of my survey experiments hold regardless of whether respondents evaluated candidates from their own political party, as in presidential primaries, or whether respondents evaluated candidates from opposing political parties, as in general elections. Altogether, the evidence presented in this chapter supports the book's claim that the politics of foreign policy primarily revolve around leaders' personal images, rather than the content of their foreign policy positions.

Evidence from the American National Election Studies

The American National Election Studies contains four sets of questions that are particularly useful for understanding how voters' foreign policy preferences shape their views of presidential candidates.[1] These questions asked voters to say whether they think defense spending should be increased or decreased (the ANES has included this question in surveys since 1980), whether the United States should adopt a more confrontational or a more cooperative relationship with the Soviet Union (asked in 1980–1988), whether the United States should intervene more or less extensively in Central America (asked in 1984, when this was arguably the most controversial aspect of US foreign policy under President Ronald Reagan), and the extent to which the United States should seek to solve international problems using diplomacy versus military force (asked in 2004). For each of these issues, ANES respondents placed their own preferences and presidential candidates' policy positions on seven-point scales. These data allow me to create indices of preference alignment. Higher values of this index indicate that voters believe their preferences lie closer to the views of the Republican presidential candidate on a given policy debate.[2]

We will see that these measures of preference alignment predict presidential vote choice. Yet, the key question for the purposes of this chapter is how voters weight those preferences relative to perceptions of presidential candidates' foreign policy competence. The best measure that the ANES offers for assessing this trade-off is a question that appeared in surveys from 1980 to 2008, asking respondents to use four-point scales to rate the extent to which they believe each presidential candidate would "provide strong leadership."[3] I used these data to create a leadership strength index, which reflects the difference in how each voter rated the Republican and Democratic presidential candidates. Positive values of this index indicate that a respondent said the Republican candidate would be a stronger leader.

I standardized the preference alignment and leadership strength indices in order to facilitate head-to-head tests of the extent to which these measures predict presidential voting. A one-unit increase in either index reflects a one-standard deviation shift in the Republican candidate's favor. I entered both variables into statistical models predicting the chances that ANES respondents voted for Republican presidential candidates.[4] Following standard practice in scholarship on presidential voting, each statistical model controlled for respondents' partisanship, ideology, gender, and race.

Figure 2.1 shows that leadership strength predicts more variation in presidential vote choice than any measure of preference alignment on foreign policy issues.[5] These comparisons support the claim that foreign policy preferences matter at the ballot box, but that voters assign greater priority to assessing presidential candidates' leadership qualities. If taking unpopular foreign policy positions would help presidential candidates to craft an image of leadership strength, then it appears to be in their interest to do so.

EXTENDING PROMINENT STUDIES OF ISSUE VOTING

ANES data on defense spending, US-Soviet relations, intervention in Central America, and the use of force provide fine-grained measures of the extent to which voters believe presidential candidates share their policy views. Yet, these are a small subset of the foreign policy issues that could plausibly shape presidential voting. The remainder of this section therefore expands the scope of my analysis to cover a broader range of topics. To do that, I followed the lead of three prominent studies of issue voting in US foreign policy: John Aldrich, John Sullivan, and Eugene Borgida's "Foreign Affairs and Issue Voting"; Shana Gadarian's "Foreign Policy at the Ballot Box"; and Sowmya Anand and Jon Krosnick's "Impact of Attitudes toward Foreign Policy Goals on Public Preferences among Presidential Candidates."[6]

Each of these studies exploits the fact that foreign policy issues frequently possess partisan orientations. For example, Gadarian explains that Repub-

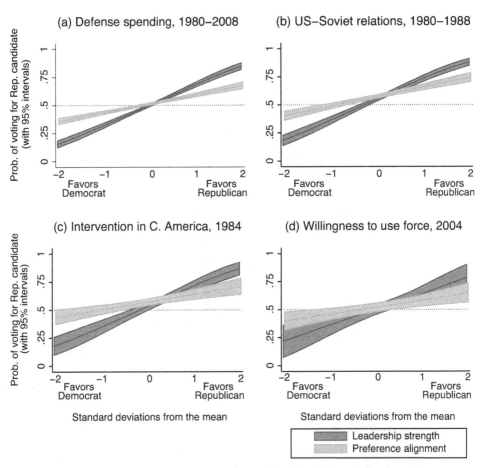

Figure 2.1. Issues and images in presidential voting. These graphs show that perceptions of whether a presidential candidate is a strong leader explain roughly twice as much variation in presidential vote choice relative to preference alignment on foreign policy issues. Each model is a logit regression that predicts the probability that an ANES respondent votes for the Republican presidential candidate. All models control for respondent party, ideology, gender, and race. See appendix for full results.

licans typically support higher levels of defense spending than Democrats do. She infers that voters who support higher levels of defense spending should be more likely to think that a Republican presidential candidate shares their foreign policy preferences. If foreign policy preferences matter at the ballot box, then voters who prefer increased defense spending should also be more likely to support Republican presidential candidates. Gadarian confirmed this hypothesis by analyzing twenty-four years of ANES data. Anand and Krosnick used a similar procedure to demonstrate that voters'

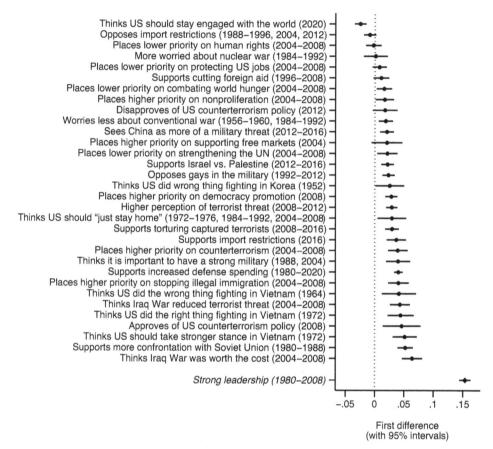

Figure 2.2. Foreign policy preferences, leadership strength, and presidential voting. This figure shows that thirty-two foreign policy preferences all predict less variation in presidential vote choice than perceptions of whether presidential candidates are strong leaders. "First differences" reflect the increased probability of voting for a Republican presidential candidate associated with shifting an independent variable by one standard deviation in the direction that favors Republicans. All models control for party, gender, and race.

foreign policy priorities predicted their candidate preference during the 2000 presidential election. Aldrich, Sullivan, and Borgida's use of this technique to examine voting patterns in the 1980 and 1984 presidential elections is the most widely cited study of issue voting and US foreign policy.

I applied this method to examine every foreign policy preference that the ANES reports in its cumulative data file. The resulting analysis spans thirty-two issues. I ordered each preference scale so that higher values reflect views that were more likely to be held by Republicans. (The appendix describes this process for readers interested in the details.) Figure 2.2 lists these issues, articulated in a manner that reflects the typical Republican's preferences. Figure 2.2 also describes the extent to which each foreign policy preference predicts presidential voting. Each data point in figure 2.2 reflects the output from a separate statistical model.[7] These models estimate the extent to which shifting a respondent's preferences by one standard deviation toward the Republican position changed the predicted probability of that respondent voting for the Republican presidential candidate.[8] As with this section's earlier analysis, each statistical model controls for partisanship, gender, and race.

Figure 2.2 shows that citizens' foreign policy preferences consistently predict their behavior in the voting booth: of the thirty-two sets of foreign policy preferences that I analyzed in these models, twenty-five bear a statistically significant relationship to presidential vote choice.[9] Yet, none of these preferences explains voters' behavior even half as well as perceptions of presidential candidates' leadership strength. These findings once again suggest that leaders have incentives to take unpopular policy positions on nearly any foreign policy issue if doing so would help them to craft or maintain a favorable personal image.

LIMITATIONS OF ANALYZING CLOSED-ENDED SURVEY DATA

Caution is always warranted when analyzing political surveys. We can never know whether survey responses reflect genuine beliefs as opposed to respondents rationalizing support for candidates whom they like for other reasons.[10] Later, I will therefore present experimental data that allow me to draw clearer causal inferences about how voters evaluate presidential candidates. Those experiments will confirm that voters prioritize selecting leaders who seem competent over leaders who take appealing foreign policy positions.

Another limitation with the analysis presented in this section is that ANES measures of leadership strength do not specifically pertain to handling foreign policy issues. Hence, I will present original data that I gathered to confirm that this section's findings are consistent with how voters evaluate presidential candidates' expected performance in the foreign policy domain.

One last caveat to this section's analysis is that survey questions often ask voters to express their attitudes in artificial terms. When surveys ask voters to say what they think about US foreign policy in Central America, or to rate the quality of a presidential candidate's leadership strength on a four-point scale, they may elicit top-of-the-head reactions to unfamiliar ideas rather than engaging the considerations that citizens actually have on their minds when they step inside the voting booth.[11] I will address this concern by analyzing open-ended questions that allow voters to say, in their own words, what they like and dislike about presidential candidates.

Evidence from Open-Ended Candidate Evaluations

In every presidential election since 1952, the ANES has asked voters to say whether there is anything in particular they like or dislike about the presidential nominees. Voters can mention up to five positive attributes and five negative attributes for each candidate. The ANES refers to these judgments as "mentions data." The mentions data provide a detailed portrait of how voters have perceived the strengths and weaknesses of presidential nominees for more than half a century.

ANES researchers have classified these statements into more than seven hundred categories called "master codes."[12] Some master codes capture broad considerations, such as "I know more about him" or "he has kept his campaign promises." Other master codes are quite specific, such as references to Hubert Humphrey's service as vice president or reactions to Dwight Eisenhower's handling of the 1956 Suez Crisis. Master codes are available for ANES surveys conducted from 1952 to 2004. These data span 172,864 judgments offered by 27,286 voters.[13]

I asked a team of six research assistants to classify these data into four categories, which are neither mutually exclusive nor exhaustive. Following the definition advanced in the book's introduction, competence reflects a leader's ability to achieve strategic goals or to implement policy choices effectively. Examples include statements such as "capable," "hard-working," or "he will take care of things." When voters approve or disapprove of a leader's strategic goals or policy views in their own right, then I consider their responses to reflect assessments of issues rather than assessments of competence. Examples include "favors withdrawal in Vietnam" or "favors expanding unemployment compensation." When these statements referred specifically to domestic or foreign policy issues, I asked researchers to note those distinctions.

Assessments of competence reflect a subset of personal traits that voters can potentially value in their leaders. ANES respondents also frequently justify their opinions about presidential candidates with respect to physical appearance, charm, or other personal attributes that have little direct bearing on the ability to govern. Examples include "dignified," "has a good family life," or "looks good on TV." I use the term likability to capture any personal trait besides competence. A fourth category for classifying candidate evaluations is experience. For the purposes of this chapter, considerations of experience include any judgment that depends on a leader's prior political or military service. That includes descriptions of experience as a criterion in its own right (for example, "he has diplomatic experience") as well as evaluations of a leader's past performance in office (such as references to George H. W. Bush's handling of the 1991 Gulf War).

Open-ended statements in the ANES data often map neatly onto the four categories I just described.[14] For example, when voters refer to a leader as someone who is "a good negotiator" or as someone who "knows how to handle world politics," these statements clearly fit the book's definition of competence. When voters say that they like a candidate's positions on the Arab-Israeli peace process or on defense spending, then they are clearly invoking foreign policy issues.

Other statements are more ambiguous and categorizing them is inherently subjective. For example, when voters criticize a presidential candidate for having handled a foreign crisis poorly, it is hard to say whether that reflects an evaluation of the candidate's policy choices, leadership qualities, or both. That is why I asked six researchers to categorize every statement in the ANES data set, rather than relying on a single person or algorithm to provide the right answers for how to interpret that information.[15]

I employed a bootstrapping procedure in which I randomly sampled data points from the classifications recorded by each member of the research team. Thus, if all six researchers reported that a statement reflected an assessment of competence, then the code would always carry that designation in my statistical analysis. If the researchers were evenly divided as to whether a master code reflected an assessment of competence, then the code would carry that designation only half of the time. The statistics reported in the remainder of this section reflect patterns that span one thousand bootstrapped data sets.[16] This procedure allowed me to avoid passing judgment about the correct way to classify any open-ended statement. Instead, my statistical analysis incorporates the ambiguity surrounding every data point that I examine.

RESULTS

The first column of table 2.1 describes the frequency with which voters invoked different considerations when evaluating presidential candidates. Twenty-six percent of voters' statements reflect assessments of competence, while only 8 percent of these statements reflect assessments of foreign policy issues.[17] These findings confirm the expectation that assessments of presidential candidates' competence are significantly more salient to voters than assessments of those candidates' foreign policy platforms.[18]

Our next question is how well these judgments predict presidential vote choice. To answer that question, I transformed the data into a series of indices that describe the extent to which voters' judgments were more favorable to Democratic versus Republican candidates.[19] I examined how well these measures correlate with voting patterns. I use a statistic called "pseudo-R^2" to measure the degree to which different kinds of open-ended judgments correlate with voting behavior.[20]

Table 2.1 shows that assessments of presidential candidates' competence explain 25 percent of variation in presidential vote choice. By contrast, assessments of foreign policy issues explain just 10 percent of variation in presidential

Table 2.1 Salience and explanatory power of open-ended judgments

	Frequency of judgments across ANES mentions data	Explanatory power, univariate regression	Explanatory power, multivariate regression, relative to baseline
Competence	0.26 (0.03)	0.25 (0.03)	+0.09 (0.01)
Foreign policy issues	0.08 (0.01)	0.10 (0.02)	+0.03 (0.01)
Domestic issues	0.23 (0.02)	0.23 (0.02)	+0.07 (0.01)
All issues	0.39 (0.02)	0.36 (0.02)	+0.08 (0.01)
Likability	0.38 (0.03)	0.24 (0.02)	+0.09 (0.01)
Experience	0.22 (0.03)	0.22 (0.03)	+0.01 (0.01)
Leadership strength	0.06 (0.02)	0.07 (0.02)	+0.07 (0.01)
Good judgment	0.09 (0.03)	0.12 (0.03)	+0.08 (0.02)

Explanatory power statistics are pseudo-R^2 values in logit models that predict presidential vote choice. The multivariate model controls for partisanship, gender, and race. Means and standard errors estimated across one thousand bootstrap samples.

vote choice.[21] Table 2.1 also presents results from multivariate analyses that include information on voters' partisanship, gender, and race. A baseline model featuring those three factors explains 42 percent of the presidential vote. That value climbs by nine percentage points if we add assessments of competence to the model, but by just three percentage points if we add assessments of foreign policy issues.[22] All of these results are consistent with the book's claim that voters place a higher priority on personal images rather than policy positions when they decide which presidential candidates are most qualified to be commander in chief.

STRONG LEADERSHIP AND GOOD JUDGMENT

These open-ended data also provide a useful opportunity to examine how voters' evaluations of presidential candidates map onto the book's concepts of strong leadership and good judgment. In particular, we can see whether either one of these attributes appears to play a larger role than the other in shaping candidate evaluation. As I explained in chapter 1, this question is relevant to asking why the commander-in-chief test tilts in favor of candidates who use hawkish foreign policy positions to communicate leadership strength. I have argued that this is because leadership strength is easier for voters to evaluate than good judgment. If voters simply think that the first of those attributes is more important than the second, then that could also explain why foreign policy hawks have an advantage at the ballot box, but that would not be what my theory argues.

The ANES data indicate that voters do not prioritize leadership strength over good judgment when evaluating presidential candidates. To test this claim, I asked the research team to identify statements that (a) specifically related to foreign policy and that (b) were relevant to the concepts of either leadership strength or good judgment as this book defined those terms. Table 2.1 shows that voters were more likely to base their candidate evaluations on good judgment relative to leadership strength. I also found that assessments of good judgment had more explanatory power when explaining presidential vote choice.

These findings should be interpreted with some caution: ANES mentions data can be vague, and that makes it difficult to parse voter responses in detail. For example, voters who think one candidate would "do a good job of handling the Middle East" are clearly referencing competence, but there is no way to tell whether the voter has based that assessment on perceptions of strength, judgment, or both. Nevertheless, these data suggest that voters do not inherently prioritize strength over judgment when evaluating a commander in chief. If anything, it appears that the opposite is true.

Experimental Evidence

This section analyzes two preregistered survey experiments that examine how voters evaluate leaders' fitness to be commander in chief. I fielded these experiments through a YouGov survey administered to a nationally representative sample of one thousand Americans in September 2020.[23]

Survey experiments help researchers avoid many of the pitfalls that surround the study of public opinion. When we ask voters to evaluate presidential candidates whose attributes vary at random, we can draw precise conclusions about voters' priorities. Designing these experiments myself also means that I could ask voters to evaluate the kinds of attributes, such as strong leadership and good judgment, that matter most for the book's argument. Of course, asking voters to evaluate hypothetical leaders raises questions about the extent to which experimental findings reflect real-world voter behavior.[24] But that is why this chapter analyzes experiments along with sixty years of observational survey data. We will see that both methodologies generate similar results, showing that voters prioritize personal images over policy positions when deciding which leaders are fit to be commander in chief.

EXPERIMENT A: DESIGN

The first experiment asked respondents to compare two presidential candidates at a time.[25] Table 2.2 shows how each profile included information about candidates' background, information about candidates' policy positions, and information about candidates' personal traits. This information appeared in random order.

The background information in each profile described a candidate's gender (man, woman), race (Asian American, Black, Hispanic, white), party (Democrat, Republican), years of political experience (zero to thirty), and

Table 2.2 Sample comparison, experiment A

	Candidate A	Candidate B
Gender	Man	Woman
Race	White	Hispanic
Party	Democrat	Republican
Years in politics	10 years	16 years
Years of military service	5 years	None
Military spending	Would keep about the same	Would increase
US troop levels in Afghanistan	Would decrease	Would decrease
Cooperation with allies	Would increase	Would decrease
Would be a strong leader	Probably	Probably not
Would use good judgment	Probably not	Definitely

years of military experience (zero to thirty). Each profile described the candidates' positions on three policy issues: military spending, US troop levels in Afghanistan, and cooperation with allies. I selected these policy issues because they reflect the book's core focus on defense expenditures, military interventions, and unilateralism. The survey described each candidate as planning to handle those issues by increasing existing efforts, decreasing existing efforts, or keeping existing efforts about the same.[26]

Each profile also included information on presidential candidates' personal traits, describing the chances that each candidate would "be a strong leader" and the chances that each candidate would "use good judgment" when handling foreign policy issues. These attributes reflect the two core elements of foreign policy competence that I articulated in chapter 1. The survey described each candidate as "definitely," "probably," or "probably not" possessing each attribute.

The survey asked respondents to evaluate presidential candidates in two different ways. Half of respondents were asked to say which candidate they would prefer to vote for in a presidential election. The other half of respondents received a more specific question about which candidate would do a better job of handling US foreign policy and national security. If these questions had elicited substantially different reactions from respondents, then that would have raised doubts about the electoral significance of voters' foreign policy attitudes. However, both questions elicited similar findings, so I pool those data in all analysis that follows.

EXPERIMENT A: RESULTS

Figure 2.3 summarizes the probability that respondents preferred one candidate over the other, conditional on that candidate possessing a specific attribute.[27] For example, figure 2.3 shows that study participants preferred 54 percent of candidates who said that they would decrease US troop levels

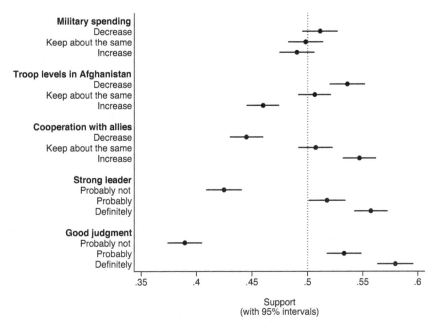

Figure 2.3. Policy positions, personal traits, and candidate support (experiment A). The outcome variable "support" reflects the chances that a candidate was preferred to his/her opponent, conditional on possessing a given attribute.

in Afghanistan, whereas they preferred only 46 percent of candidates who said that they would increase US troop levels in Afghanistan.[28] Candidates' support for cooperation with allies had an even larger impact on respondents' preferences.[29]

These results show that voters take foreign policy issues into account when evaluating presidential candidates. Yet the overarching question in this chapter is not whether voters care about foreign policy issues at all. Rather, experiment A was designed to compare the priority that voters place on foreign policy issues relative to the priority that voters place on selecting leaders who possess appealing personal traits. And the data shown in figure 2.3 are clear about that: on average, levels of support for presidential candidates were roughly twice as sensitive to descriptions of the candidates' personal traits relative to the candidates' policy positions.

In principle, it could be the case that voters individually value leaders' policy positions more than their personal attributes, and that voters' policy preferences simply cancel each other out in large populations. But that is not what drives the experiment's findings. If I divide the data according to any subset of respondents' foreign policy preferences—for instance, if I only examine respondents who said they preferred to cut defense spending—then the data still show that respondents placed less emphasis on that policy issue than on leaders' personal traits.

A last item worth noting in figure 2.3 is that, when respondents considered which presidential candidates would do a better job of handling foreign policy, they appeared to care more about which candidates had good judgment as opposed to which candidates would be stronger leaders. This finding provides additional reasons to believe that voters do not simply equate foreign policy competence with leadership strength. In principle, voters want a commander in chief who can balance the attributes of strength and judgment. The book's subsequent chapters will nevertheless show that this is easier said than done, and explain why presidential candidates generally find it easier to tilt their foreign policy agendas in favor of signaling leadership strength.

EXPERIMENT B: DESIGN

My first survey experiment supported the book's claim that voters prioritize personal images over policy issues when evaluating presidential candidates. However, that experiment examined a relatively small number of policy positions and personal traits. In order to probe the generalizability of those findings, I conducted a second experiment that employed a different research design.

This experiment asked respondents to evaluate one presidential candidate at a time. In each case, the survey asked voters to say how well they thought a candidate would handle US foreign policy and national security, using a scale that ranged from zero to one hundred. Each profile contained randomly ordered information about candidates' background, policy positions, and personal traits.[30] Since this experiment did not require participants to compare candidates on the basis of identical attributes, it could accommodate a much broader range of information. Box 2.1 provides an example of what these profiles looked like. Each respondent rated five profiles.

Presidential candidates were described as endorsing anywhere from zero to six policy positions. These positions spanned twenty-five issues, which I have listed in the appendix.[31] A subsequent survey module elicited respondents' preferences regarding those exact same foreign policy issues.[32] The data from that module allowed me to estimate the proportion of study participants who supported each policy position that appeared in the experiment. I used these data to estimate the aggregate popularity of each candidate's foreign policy platform. Aggregate popularity reflects the average proportion of respondents who agreed with each of a candidate's foreign policy proposals. Thus, if the candidate endorsed one policy with 25 percent popular support and another policy with 75 percent support, then the aggregate popularity of that platform would be 50 percent.[33]

Candidates were described with respect to thirty-five personal traits, which I have also listed in the appendix. These traits span all twenty-five of

---

Box 2.1. *Sample profile, experiment B*

Candidate A

- Male
- Republican
- 18 years of experience in politics
- Did not serve in the US military

- Would increase spending on national defense
- Opposed the Iran nuclear agreement
- Thinks the US does too much to help solve world problems
- Thinks the US should decrease its commitment to NATO

- Appears to be a strong leader
- Appears to be knowledgeable about US foreign policy
- Does not appear to have a close relationship with the military

---

the performance-related attributes that I described in chapter 1 when I documented how political pundits describe a competent commander in chief. These traits include terms like being "decisive," "sensible," and "working well under pressure." The other ten traits included in this experiment were attributes that I would *not* expect most people to associate with foreign policy competence, such as being "articulate" or "good looking."[34] Adding these nonperformance traits to the study provides leverage for testing the chapter's thesis. If I were to find that voters value performance and nonperformance traits equally, then this would indicate that voters are drawn to leaders who seem likable, or who are portrayed in generally positive terms. But my theory is more specific than that. Since I have argued that voters place special value on assessing leaders' competence, I expected participants in this experiment to largely ignore nonperformance traits when evaluating a presidential candidate's fitness to be commander in chief.

The experiment described each candidate as possessing up to three traits. The experiment also described each candidate as *not* appearing to possess up to three traits. This allowed the survey to present positive traits and disputed traits using identical language.

EXPERIMENT B: RESULTS

Figure 2.4 shows that perceptions of competence played a significant role in shaping perceptions of candidates' ability to manage US foreign policy and national security. Candidate ratings increased by 2.4 points, on average, for

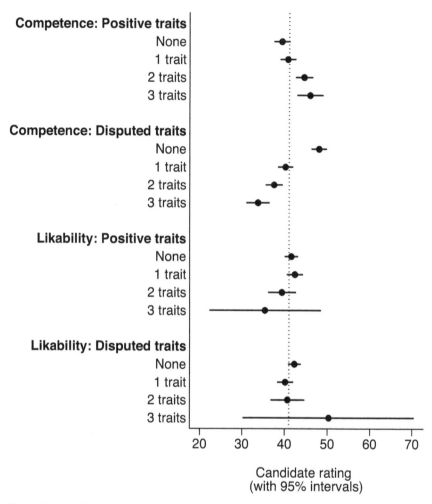

Figure 2.4. Results of experiment B: Personal traits. Average candidate ratings based on five thousand candidate profiles, with standard errors clustered for one thousand respondents. The vertical dotted line reflects the mean candidate rating of forty-two.

every performance-related trait that those candidates appeared to possess.[35] Candidate ratings decreased by 4.9 points, on average, every time a candidate was described as not appearing to possess a performance-related trait.

These results did not simply reflect study participants being drawn to candidates who were described in positive terms. Indeed, there was no consistent relationship between candidate ratings and the number of *non*performance traits that the candidate was described as possessing.[36] The fact that study participants essentially ignored information about nonperformance traits shows that they were looking for specific indications of foreign policy competence when they evaluated a potential commander in chief.[37]

By comparison, candidates' policy positions had a relatively weak impact on perceptions of their ability to handle US foreign policy. On average, a candidate who proposed a series of policy positions that received support from one-third of voters received an average rating of forty. Candidates who proposed a series of policy positions that received support from two-thirds of voters received an average rating of forty-five. Moving from a two-to-one ratio of voters who oppose a candidate's foreign policy platform to a two-to-one ratio of voters who support a candidate's foreign policy platform obviously reflects a gargantuan shift in public opinion. But the difference in the ratings that accompanies that kind of a shift in public opinion—five points—is roughly the same size as the effect associated with adding a single disputed trait to a candidate's profile.

This comparison vividly captures the book's claim that voters prioritize supporting leaders who seem competent at foreign policy decision making over leaders who take appealing foreign policy positions. Of course, in an ideal world, these things would go together. And, in some cases, leaders may find that adopting popular policy positions just so happens to be the thing that maximizes their personal images. But that need not be the case. If leaders ever find themselves in a situation where they thought that taking an unpopular policy position would help them to convey an impression of foreign policy competence, then this section's findings suggest that it would be in their interest to make that trade-off. Indeed, the results from the experiments presented in this section suggest that presidents and presidential candidates could plausibly decide to sacrifice the popularity of their entire foreign policy platforms if that helps them to convey just a few appealing personal traits.

Evidence from the 2020 Presidential Election

This section presents results from another YouGov survey that I administered to a nationally representative sample of one thousand respondents.[38] The survey sampled voters prior to the 2020 presidential election, and then followed up after Election Day to see how respondents voted.[39] The survey asked voters to rate Republican president Donald Trump and his Democratic challenger, former vice president Joe Biden.

The survey's distinctive feature was that it asked voters to draw explicit distinctions in how well they expected Trump and Biden to handle foreign versus domestic policy issues. This design feature fills one of the major gaps in the chapter's analysis of the American National Election Studies. While the ANES asks voters to rate presidential candidates' strengths and weaknesses overall, my survey directly asked voters to assess leaders' fitness to be commander in chief. Consistent with the book's theory, I will show that voters were much more likely to base these judgments on assessments of presidential candidates' personal attributes as opposed to their policy positions.

DATA

The survey asked three sets of questions about former vice president Biden and President Trump.[40] The first set of questions asked voters to say which candidate they thought would do a better job as president of handling foreign policy and national security, and which candidate they thought would do a better job of handling domestic policy.[41] Forty percent of respondents said that they expected Trump to do a better job of handling foreign policy, with 45 percent favoring Biden in this area.[42]

The survey's second set of questions asked voters to explain, in their own words, why they thought that one candidate would do a better job of handling foreign policy and why they thought that one candidate would do a better job of handling domestic policy and the economy.[43] Following the same procedure that I developed for analyzing open-ended data earlier in the chapter, I worked with six research assistants to code the content of voters' statements. Each member of the research team coded responses as reflecting competence, issues, and/or experience. These categories were identical to the classifications that I employed when analyzing open-ended data from ANES surveys.[44] The appendix once again provides information about interrater reliability.

The survey's third set of questions asked respondents to select from a prespecified list of options to explain why they thought that Joe Biden or Donald Trump would do a better job of handling each policy domain.[45] This amounted to asking voters to categorize their own beliefs. I captured the category of competence with the statement "He has better judgment for handling foreign [domestic] policy issues." I captured the category of issues with the statement "He has better policy proposals for handling foreign [domestic] policy issues." And I captured the category of experience with the statement "He has better experience handling foreign [domestic] policy issues."[46]

RESULTS

Table 2.3 shows that competence was by far the most frequent consideration that respondents invoked when explaining why one candidate would do a better job of handling foreign policy, accounting for nearly two-thirds of open-ended explanations.[47] These remarks include the following:

- "Trump wouldn't allow other countries to take advantage of the US. Biden would let other countries walk all over him."

- "Trump doesn't back down or want to appease others. Puts America first, as he promises. It's refreshing to be the 'ugly American' once in awhile!"
- "He's [Trump] tough and don't care what people think and don't need nobody speaking for him like Biden does."
- "He's [Biden] an intelligent rational adult and not a poster child for malignant narcissism like Trump."
- "Donald Trump doesn't think things through and has little experience in the area. He makes decisions based on his emotions."
- "Biden is more trustworthy than Trump. I don't have to be concerned about what Biden is doing with a foreign dictator."

By contrast, survey respondents invoked policy issues in roughly one-quarter of their open-ended explanations. For example, Biden's supporters mentioned potentially reducing defense spending, rejoining the Paris Climate Agreement and the Iran nuclear deal, and taking steps to restore relationships with allies. Trump's supporters were more likely to mention raising defense spending, revising trade deals, and restricting immigration. These responses show that the candidates' policy views were by no means irrelevant to what voters thought about them. But the data clearly indicate that policy issues were not the main thing on voters' minds when they considered which presidential candidate was most fit to be commander in chief.

One potential concern when interpreting open-ended responses is that some respondents might have used these statements to express animosity toward political rivals rather than engaging with the substance of why one candidate would do a better job of handling foreign policy issues. In order to investigate this issue, I asked the research team to note any responses that primarily reflected criticism of an opponent rather than praise for a favored candidate. This characterized 38 percent of voters' statements. As expected, some of these statements were not particularly friendly. For example, one Biden supporter explained that "dryer lint would do a better job than that lying pocket of pus in the Oval [Office]." Another respondent noted that Biden "isn't a complete lunatic who capitulates to dictators because of his daddy issues, unlike Trumpenfuhrer." Similarly, Trump supporters made frequent references to Biden's supposed "dementia," having "clips in his brain," being in thrall to communists, or associating with the devil himself.

Table 2.3 Frequency of explanations

	Open-ended data	Open-ended data, criticism removed	Closed-ended data
Competence	0.62 (0.02)	0.59 (0.02)	0.40 (0.02)
Issues	0.27 (0.01)	0.29 (0.02)	0.20 (0.02)
Experience	0.34 (0.01)	0.38 (0.01)	0.27 (0.02)

Table 2.3 shows the proportion of respondents who invoked different considerations when explaining why they thought Biden or Trump would do a better job of handling foreign policy.

These statements lend themselves to multiple interpretations. Some might reflect performative partisan loathing. Others could reflect legitimate doubts about the candidates' fitness to be commander in chief. I addressed this ambiguity by reanalyzing the data after removing judgments that the research team characterized as being primarily critical of one candidate.[48] Table 2.3 shows that this change did not significantly change this section's statistical results.

The survey's closed-ended data provide another tool for validating the research team's classifications. Since the closed-ended responses required respondents to select just one option, whereas the research team's codings were not mutually exclusive, the overall magnitude of response proportions declines relative to the open-ended data. But the patterns in relative response rates are largely identical across question formats. Once again, we see that assessments of competence are twice as common as assessments of policy issues when voters assess which candidate would be a better commander in chief.[49]

STRONG LEADERSHIP AND GOOD JUDGMENT

Finally, I repeated the chapter's prior analysis of whether voters' open-ended assessments of presidential candidates were more likely to invoke perceptions of strong leadership or good judgment. I found that voters in the 2020 election were equally likely to discuss those attributes when explaining why they thought that either Joe Biden or Donald Trump would do a better job of handling foreign policy issues: both categories comprise 17 percent of voters' responses. These data provide an additional reason to believe that voters do not inherently prioritize strength over judgment when deciding which leaders would do a better job of managing international affairs. Chapter 3 will nevertheless show that voters find the first of those attributes easier to evaluate. This gives presidents and presidential candidates special reasons to focus on crafting images of leadership strength when trying to convince voters that they would be an effective commander in chief.

DISCUSSION AND CHAPTER SUMMARY

This section has shown that voters do not generally assess leaders' fitness to be commander in chief by analyzing their policy positions. Instead—and consistent with the book's theory—we see that voters primarily judge a leader's ability to handle foreign policy on the basis of their personal traits.

If the chapter had only presented these descriptive statistics, then it would provide weak foundations for understanding how voters administer the commander-in-chief test. Since the data in this section are descriptive, they cannot directly sustain causal claims about voters' priorities. But that is why the chapter presented two preregistered survey experiments, both of which confirmed that voters prioritize selecting competent leaders over leaders who take appealing foreign policy positions.

Another concern with the data in this section is that they might reflect the idiosyncratic dynamics of the 2020 presidential campaign. Partisanship is deeply entrenched in today's political discourse and Donald Trump is an unusually polarizing figure. One might therefore worry that this section's findings only apply to a specific historical moment. But that is why I analyzed more than half a century of survey data, showing that my argument generalizes across presidential politics writ large.

The fact that voters appear to prioritize personal images over policy issues when conducting the commander-in-chief test offers three main implications for the study of US foreign policy. First, the chapter's findings suggest that existing scholarship understates the degree to which foreign policy shapes presidential politics. The vast majority of scholarship on foreign policy and presidential voting focuses on voters' policy preferences. By treating foreign policy issues as the fundamental building blocks of the relationship between foreign policy and presidential voting, existing scholarship neglects a substantial component—indeed, this chapter suggests, the primary component—of how foreign policy shapes presidential politics.

A second and related implication of this chapter's analysis is that issue-based polling is not well suited to capturing the relationship between public opinion and US foreign policy. If voters prioritize selecting leaders who seem competent over leaders who take appealing foreign policy positions, then it does not make sense for scholars to devote the bulk of their attention to studying voters' policy preferences. Instead, this chapter suggests that scholars and journalists should focus polling questions and survey experiments on studying the personal attributes that voters associate with a competent commander in chief.

Finally, the chapter's findings offer new insights for understanding political strategy. If the relationship between public opinion and US foreign policy revolves solely around voters' policy preferences—or even if it revolves primarily around voters' policy preferences—then leaders would have incentives to make popular policy choices. But, if the relationship between public opinion and US foreign policy revolves primarily around personal images, then that is what we should expect leaders to maximize. This means that disconnects between voters' aggregate preferences and leaders' policy choices do not necessarily indicate that leaders are neglecting public opinion. Instead, these choices may often reflect leaders seeking to cultivate mass public opinion by conveying personal attributes that voters prioritize over their policy preferences. Chapter 3 provides a closer look at how that process works and how it steers US foreign policy in a direction that voters would not otherwise choose.

The Hawk's Advantage

How Foreign Policy Issues Shape Leaders' Personal Images

"Only Nixon could go to China." This adage reflects the idea that President Richard Nixon's reputation for being a hardline Cold Warrior helped him convince the US public that it was wise to establish diplomatic relations with communist leaders in Beijing. Foreign policy analysts frequently invoke this example to convey broader ideas about how leaders can leverage their personal images to shape voters' perceptions of important foreign policy issues.[1] This chapter explores the opposite of that phenomenon: I explain how the positions leaders take on foreign policy issues also shape their personal images.

My analysis of this topic offers two principal insights. First, I show that leaders do not need to take popular foreign policy positions in order to improve their personal images. Second, I demonstrate that the politics of image-making favor foreign policy hawks. Consistent with my theory, I show that voters associate hawkish foreign policy positions with leadership strength, that voters associate dovish foreign policy positions with good judgment, and that the first of these effects is stronger than the second.

I support these claims by analyzing three decades of survey data from the American National Election Studies (ANES) and an experiment in which I asked voters to evaluate hypothetical presidential candidates. These different forms of evidence complement each other to sustain inferences that neither could support on its own. The ANES data show that foreign policy hawks enjoy electoral advantages that revolve around the unique association that voters draw between foreign policy hawkishness and leadership strength. Yet, ANES surveys examine a relatively small number of foreign policy issues, and it is inherently difficult to draw causal inferences from conventional polling data. The survey experiment asks voters to evaluate hypothetical candidates rather than real leaders, but it confirms the causal link between foreign policy positions and personal images and reveals that this relationship generalizes across a broad range of issues. Chapters 4 and 5 will then use archival records to show how leaders perceive and react to issue-image trade-offs in a manner that shapes political strategy.

The Hawk's Advantage in Presidential Voting

In every presidential election year since 1980, the ANES has asked voters to state their preferences for military spending on a seven-point scale, and then to use that same scale to describe how they think presidential candidates would handle the defense budget. On average, 29 percent of ANES respondents prefer to cut military expenditures, 41 percent want to increase those expenditures, and 30 percent want to hold defense spending constant. The median voter has preferred the latter position in every presidential election in the ANES data set, save for 1980, where the median ANES respondent preferred a slight increase in military expenditures (a "five " on the survey's seven-point scale).[2]

ANES surveys also ask voters to say where they think presidential candidates stand on defense spending. Figure 3.1 shows that these perceptions

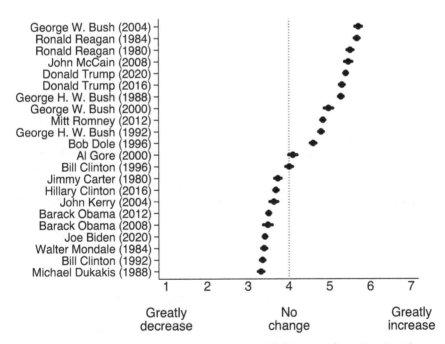

Figure 3.1. Voter perceptions of candidate positions on defense spending. Average values with 95 percent intervals.

are fairly accurate. For instance, voters generally believe that Republicans are willing to spend more money on defense than Democrats. Voters understood that Ronald Reagan and John McCain were significantly more hawkish on defense spending than more moderate Republicans such as Mitt Romney or George H. W. Bush. Voters similarly understood that Michael Dukakis and Walter Mondale were significantly more dovish on defense spending than centrist Democrats such as Al Gore and Jimmy Carter.[3]

I used these data to construct an index that I call the defense spending differential. The defense spending differential represents the difference that an individual voter perceives in two presidential candidates' positions on military expenditures.[4] This index ranges from a minimum of zero if voters perceive no difference between two candidates' positions on defense spending, to a maximum of six if the respondent thinks that one candidate would greatly raise defense spending while the other candidate would greatly reduce defense spending.[5]

From 1980–2008, ANES surveys asked voters to rate presidential candidates' personal traits using four-point scales.[6] One of those traits is the extent to which candidates seem like "strong leaders."[7] I used these data to construct an index, called leadership strength differential, that captures the leadership score for the candidate who seemed more hawkish on defense spending, minus the leadership score for the candidate who seemed more dovish on defense spending. If a voter perceived no difference between the candidates' positions on military expenditures, then I randomly assigned one candidate to be the hawk.

VOTERS ASSOCIATE HAWKISHNESS WITH LEADERSHIP STRENGTH

These data reveal that voters generally associate hawkishness on military spending with leadership strength. In cases where voters believed that one candidate would spend more money on defense than the other, the more hawkish candidate received a leadership strength rating that was 0.34 points higher than that of his opponent, on average.[8] Yet, this raw difference in leadership scores could reflect many things. For example, figure 3.1 showed that voters generally see Republicans as taking more hawkish positions on defense spending. If voters typically believe Republicans are stronger leaders anyway, then we would see a positive correlation between candidates' positions on defense spending and perceptions of candidates' leadership strength, even if those factors were not causally related.

In order to account for these concerns, I constructed a statistical model that controls for several factors. I will refer to this list of variables throughout my analysis as the "baseline model." The baseline model includes information about each voter's partisanship, ideology, gender, and race. It controls for preference alignment—in this case, whether voters identified

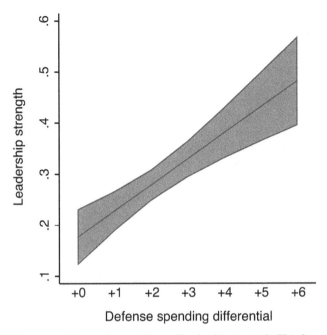

Figure 3.2. Defense spending and perceptions of leadership strength. This figure shows that voters reliably associate hawkishness on defense spending with leadership strength, even when controlling for partisanship, ideology, gender, race, preference alignment, incumbency, and year fixed effects.

their preferences for defense spending as lying closer to one candidate or the other—to address the concern that voters develop positive perceptions of candidates simply because they agree with those candidates' policy positions. I include information about whether presidential candidates are incumbents, and I account for potentially idiosyncratic elements of individual presidential campaigns.[9] There are 8,480 respondents for whom the ANES records data on all variables in the baseline model.

Figure 3.2 shows how this analysis indicates that a one–standard deviation shift in the defense spending differential is associated with a 0.07-point change in perceptions of the candidates' leadership strength. This is a substantively important shift: it amounts to more than half of the average gap in leadership strength ratings between candidates in the data set (0.12). It is worth repeating that this relationship holds even when controlling for party, ideology, and voters' policy preferences, and even though most voters oppose raising military expenditures. This discrepancy between issues and images— the fact that voters associate positive personal qualities with leaders whose policy positions they oppose—is consistent with the argument that the politics of defense spending present voters with an issue-image trade-off.

DO VOTERS ASSOCIATE HAWKISHNESS WITH OTHER PERSONAL ATTRIBUTES?

It is now important to show that hawkish positions on defense spending *uniquely* shape perceptions of leadership strength. If we found that voters drew similar associations between hawkishness and other personal traits—for example, if candidates who planned to increase defense spending were just as likely to come across as being more decent or more compassionate—then we might conclude that the findings in figure 3.2 are confounded by other factors.

Figure 3.3 confirms that presidential candidates' positions on defense spending are uniquely associated with perceptions of their leadership strength. Each data point in figure 3.3 reflects a separate "defense spending coefficient." I generated these coefficients by using the baseline model to analyze the extent to which voters associate hawkishness on defense spending with each of the personal traits that the ANES data capture.[10] Larger values of these coefficients indicate stronger positive associations between candidates' positions on defense spending and voters' perceptions of those candidates' personal qualities.

Figure 3.3 shows that the association between defense spending hawkishness and perceived leadership strength is more reliable than the association between defense spending hawkishness and any other candidate trait. Only one other trait in the ANES data—morality—bears a statistically significant relationship to candidates' positions on defense spending. The statistical significance of that finding also depends on voters' perceptions of George W. Bush during the 2004 election,[11] and it is smaller than the association between defense spending and leadership strength.[12] This analysis is consistent with the idea that hawkish foreign policies serve a unique function in the politics of image-making, helping presidential candidates to craft impressions of leadership strength.[13]

THE HAWK'S ADVANTAGE AT THE BALLOT BOX

So far, we have seen that voters associate hawkishness on defense spending with leadership strength. But do these perceptions actually matter at the ballot box?

If my theory is correct, then we should find three patterns in the ANES data. First, we should see that voters are more likely to support presidential candidates who take more hawkish positions on defense spending. Second, we should see that this "hawk's advantage" depends on perceptions of leadership strength. Third, we should find evidence that the hawk's advantage is *not* as reliably associated with perceptions of other personal attributes. Confirming these predictions would support the idea that candidates who take more hawkish positions on defense spending enjoy electoral advantages that are uniquely associated with perceptions of leadership strength.

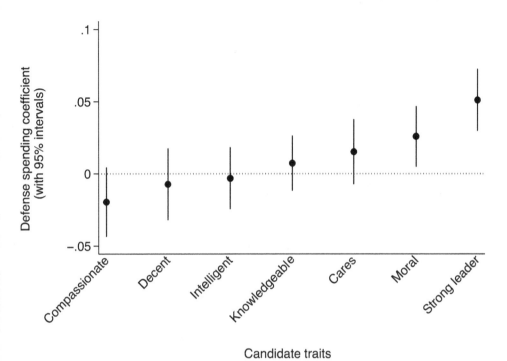

Figure 3.3. How candidates' positions on defense spending relate to perceived personal traits. Each data point represents a separate model examining the association between presidential candidates' positions on defense spending and voters' perceptions of a personal trait. All models control for partisanship, ideology, gender, race, preference alignment, and year fixed effects.

In order to test the claim that presidential candidates who take more hawkish positions on defense spending also tend to win more votes, we can replace the baseline model's outcome variable with vote share, defined as the probability that ANES respondents vote for the candidates they identify as taking more hawkish positions on defense spending. Figure 3.4 confirms that voters are more likely to support presidential candidates whom they expect will take more hawkish positions on military expenditures.[14] It is again important to note that the model controls for preference alignment, thereby showing that candidates who seem hawkish on defense spending enjoy electoral advantages that are statistically unrelated to what voters think about the merits of raising the defense budget.

Our next question is whether this hawk's advantage depends on voters' perceptions of leadership strength. To test this hypothesis, I employed Imai, Keele, Tingley, and Yamamoto's method for analyzing the degree to which the relationship between an independent variable (hawkishness) and a dependent variable (vote share) is mediated by a third factor (perceptions of

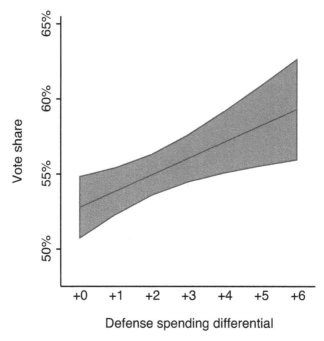

Figure 3.4. Defense spending and vote share. This figure shows that voters are more likely to support candidates who appear willing to spend more money on national defense, even when controlling for preference alignment, partisanship, ideology, gender, race, and year fixed effects.

Table 3.1 Estimating the degree to which perceptions of personal traits mediate the hawk's advantage in ANES data

Attribute	Pct. of total effect mediated (95% confidence interval)
Leadership strength	0.49 (0.24, 2.42)
Cares about people like me	0.07 (0.04, 0.15)
Morality	0.04 (0.02, 0.19)
Knowledgeable	0.02 (0.01, 0.07)
Intelligent	−0.05 (−0.13, −0.03)
Compassionate	−0.18 (−0.76, −0.10)
Decency	−0.18 (−2.22, 1.95)

leadership strength).[15] This analysis indicates that 49 percent of the hawk's advantage shown in figure 3.4 is attributable to the fact that more hawkish candidates also generally seem like stronger leaders, with the entirety of the observed relationship between hawkishness and vote share falling inside the model's 95 percent confidence interval. By contrast, table 3.1 shows that no other personal trait plausibly explains more than 15 percent of the hawk's advantage. This analysis confirms the expectation that the hawk's advantage at the ballot box is uniquely associated with the way that voters associate hawkish policy positions with leadership strength.

EXTENDING THE ANALYSIS TO OTHER AREAS OF FOREIGN POLICY

So far, we have examined the relationship between defense spending, leadership strength, and voting behavior. Yet, this finding does not hinge on analyzing defense spending to the exclusion of other foreign policy issues.

In chapter 2, we saw that ANES surveys have also asked voters to state their personal preferences and presidential candidates' positions with respect to US-Soviet cooperation (1980–1988), intervention in Central America (1984), and willingness to use military force (2004). I combined these data with voters' attitudes on defense spending to create an index of foreign policy hawkishness. This index averages voters' perceptions of candidates' stances on every foreign policy issue that the ANES included in a given year, such that higher values reflect more hawkish positions.[16] I created a similar index of foreign policy preference alignment, capturing the extent to which voters tended to agree with one candidate's foreign policy positions more than the other.[17] Rerunning my analysis with these data replicates all of this section's findings.

LIMITATIONS OF ANALYZING OBSERVATIONAL SURVEY DATA

This section has demonstrated that voters associate hawkish foreign policies with leadership strength, even when we control for what voters think of those policies on the merits. I showed that this pattern cannot be attributed to partisanship, ideology, individual presidential candidates, or the idiosyncratic dynamics of individual elections. I found that voters do not draw similar associations between hawkish foreign policies and other aspects of a candidate's personal image. I demonstrated that candidates who take more hawkish positions on foreign policy issues actually do better at the ballot box and that—statistically speaking—this hawk's advantage can be entirely explained by the fact that these candidates seem like stronger leaders. I documented this pattern using thirty years of data on public attitudes toward defense spending, and I replicated those findings using broader measures of foreign policy attitudes.

The most plausible threat to this analysis is the fact that ANES data capture voters' perceptions of where presidential candidates stand on foreign policy issues. It is always possible that these perceptions reflect factors that are unrelated to partisanship, ideology, or other variables for which I controlled. For instance, voters might simply assume that presidential candidates who seem like strong leaders will also support raising military expenditures. This would mean that candidates' personal images shape voters' perceptions of where they stand on policy issues, whereas this book argues that the causal logic works the other way around.

It is impossible to refute these kinds of concerns decisively using nonexperimental survey data. Yet, that explanation would be surprising given what we know about political attitudes. Political scientists generally expect that voters will align their policy preferences with the views of candidates whom they support for other reasons.[18] If anything, voters' tendency to minimize cognitive dissonance should make it harder to show that leaders gain electoral benefits from taking foreign policy positions that do not reflect voters' policy preferences. I will further document the causal nature of the relationship between foreign policy hawkishness and perceptions of leadership strength using experimental evidence.

A second drawback with this section's analysis is that ANES data ask voters to say whether presidential candidates seem like strong leaders, but not to say whether presidential candidates appear to possess good judgment. This means that the ANES data do not allow me to test two of the book's core claims: that hawkish foreign policy positions undermine perceptions of good judgment and that this effect is dominated by the association that voters draw between hawkishness and leadership strength. Of course, the hawk's advantage at the ballot box suggests that the upsides of taking hawkish policy positions outweigh the downsides of taking those positions. But this section did not document the book's description of how that mechanism works.

A final drawback with this section's analysis is that the ANES only examines four foreign policy issues in a manner that allows me to test the book's claims about how leaders' policy positions shape perceptions of their personal traits. Defense spending is generally seen as a proxy for voters' broader foreign policy attitudes,[19] and the other foreign policy issues that I analyzed in this section surely reflect voters' broader orientations toward international affairs. The ANES would not have asked about these issues otherwise. Yet, it is obviously not ideal to test a theory of public opinion on such a narrow set of issues.

The rest of the chapter presents a preregistered survey experiment that I designed to plug the gaps in this section's analysis. The experiment asked respondents to rate presidential candidates who took positions on a broad range of foreign policy issues. I randomized candidates' policy positions to facilitate causal inference. And I measured respondents' perceptions of those candidates' personal attributes in ways that directly reflect the book's concepts of strong leadership and good judgment. The experiment thus tests the causal foundations of the book's theoretical framework in a manner that observational surveys cannot support.

Experimental Evidence

This survey experiment, which I administered to one thousand respondents via Qualtrics, asked participants to rate two hypothetical presidential candidates.[20] The experiment described each candidate with a profile like the one shown in box 3.1.[21] The first paragraph of each profile described the candidate's background. This paragraph presented randomized information on the candidate's party, gender, experience in politics (zero to thirty years), and experience in the military (zero to thirty years).[22]

Each profile then presented five policy positions that the candidate had taken on foreign policy issues. The experiment selected each candidate's policy platform at random from a list of fifty-two policy positions distributed across twenty-six policy areas. I developed this list by reviewing recent surveys that studied Americans' foreign policy preferences.[23] Box 3.1 provides some examples of how these positions spanned military, economic, and diplomatic issues. The appendix provides the full list of policy positions that appeared in the experiment.

All policy positions that appeared in the experiment involved contemporary US foreign policy. I thus excluded questions such as "Do you support President Trump's decision to assassinate Qassem Suleimani?" Since these questions refer to prior foreign policy decisions, they are not necessarily relevant to predicting a presidential candidate's future behavior. These

---

Box 3.1. *Sample candidate profile*

Allen

Allen is a Democratic candidate for president. She has worked in politics for twenty-five years. She did not serve in the US military.

While campaigning for president, Allen has taken the following positions on foreign policy issues.

- Allen supports withdrawing US troops from Afghanistan.
- Allen thinks we should avoid publicly criticizing European allies, even if they do not meet their obligations to support collective defense.
- Allen would cut overall levels of military spending.
- Allen opposes maintaining long-term military bases in the Middle East.
- Allen thinks it is not generally justifiable to use military force against countries that have not attacked us first, even if those countries pose a serious threat to US national security.

---

topics will also likely be confounded by voters' beliefs about prior leaders: mentioning Trump's decision to assassinate Suleimani would surely elicit views of Trump himself, and not just what voters thought about the merits of killing a hostile foreign leader.[24]

Candidates' profiles presented their policy positions in a straightforward and factual manner, absent the kinds of normatively charged rhetoric with which leaders typically surround their policy proposals. This presentational style is useful, because it allows the experiment to zero in on how voters intuitively react to the content of leaders' policy positions. We will see that, without any special prodding, respondents reliably associated foreign policy issues with leaders' personal images in a manner that confirms the book's unique theoretical predictions.

We can summarize each candidate's hawkishness as the number of hawkish positions that appeared in a candidate's profile. The experiment then contained six questions designed to examine how hawkishness influenced voters' perceptions of presidential candidates.[25] I measured preference alignment by asking, "To what extent do you agree with [name]'s foreign policy positions?" I elicited these views using a seven-point scale, because this is the level of granularity that ANES surveys use to measure preference alignment.[26]

I used two questions to measure respondents' perceptions of the extent to which a candidate would be a strong leader. The first question asked, "If [name] were elected President, what is your best guess about how likely [s/he] would be to vigorously promote US interests?"[27] The second question asked how likely the candidate would be to "back down when challenged."[28] These questions employ the exact language that I used to define the book's concept of leadership strength in chapter 1. This ensures that the experiment's measures of leadership strength map directly to the book's theory, and that they are not confounded by other ways that respondents might interpret phrases like "strong leadership." I elicited these ratings on four-point scales, because this is the level of granularity that ANES surveys use to measure candidate traits. I combined these ratings to create an index of leadership strength.[29]

I used two additional questions to construct an index of good judgment. The first question asked respondents how likely the candidate would be to "avoid taking unnecessary risks when making foreign policy decisions."[30] The second asked respondents how likely the candidate would be to "make major foreign policy mistakes."[31] As with my measures of leadership strength, these questions employ the exact same language that I used to define the book's concept of good judgment in chapter 1.

These data show that respondents' assessments of preference alignment, leadership strength, and good judgment varied independently. The correlation between leadership strength and good judgment was just 0.15; the correlation between leadership strength and preference alignment was 0.22; and the correlation between good judgment and preference alignment was 0.38. These patterns are consistent with the idea that voters' assessments of leaders' personal attributes are not a straightforward reflection of the extent to which voters agree with leaders' policy positions on the merits.

HOW POLICY POSITIONS SHAPE PERSONAL IMAGES

Figure 3.5a confirms that presidential candidates who take more hawkish foreign policy positions also come across as being stronger leaders. On average, candidates who took five hawkish policy positions received leadership strength ratings that were 0.41 points higher than candidates who took five dovish policy positions.[32] That amounts to more than a half a standard deviation in leadership strength ratings across the experiment as a whole (0.69).[33]

The relationship between hawkishness and leadership strength in this experiment is also notable given that respondents did not generally support hawkish foreign policies on their merits. Figure 3.5b demonstrates that point by showing that leaders' hawkishness had no impact on the degree to which voters approved of their foreign policy platforms.[34] The contrast between figures 3.5a and 3.5b confirms the book's description of how voters use foreign policy debates to draw inferences about leaders' personal traits in a manner that does not simply reflect voters' policy preferences.

My theory assumes that hawkish foreign policy positions undermine perceptions of leaders' judgment. Figure 3.5c shows that the experiment confirmed this prediction, too. Figure 3.5 additionally shows that candidates' hawkishness had more of an impact on ratings of leadership strength than on perceptions of good judgment. The difference between these estimated effects is substantively large—nearly a factor of three.[35]

These experimental results provide clear support for my theory of how foreign policy positions shape leaders' personal images. They show that (i) voters associate hawkishness with leadership strength, (ii) voters associate dovishness with good judgment, (iii) the first of those relationships is stronger than the second, and (iv) both effects are independent of voters' policy preferences.

GENERALIZABILITY ACROSS ISSUE AREAS AND RESPONDENT DEMOGRAPHICS

I designed the survey experiment to cover twenty-six foreign policy issues, in contrast to the relatively narrow range of foreign policy issues discussed in my earlier analysis of ANES data. This breadth of coverage allows me to show that my findings are not being driven by idiosyncratic policy positions that just so happen to influence respondents in a manner that is consistent with the book's theoretical framework.

In order to test the generalizability of my argument across foreign policy issues, I replicated my analyses for each of the twenty-six issues that the

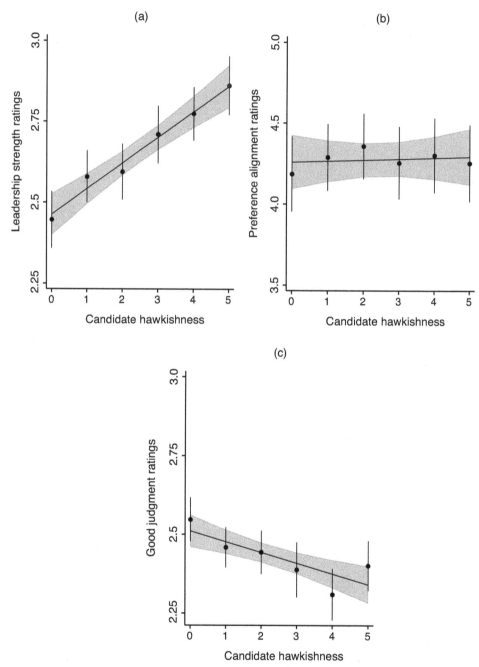

Figure 3.5. Experimental results. How candidates' hawkishness influenced evaluations of (a) leadership strength, (b) preference alignment, and (c) good judgment. Results presented with 95 percent intervals.

experiment examined.[36] For example, one policy issue in this experiment is whether or not candidates favored withdrawing US troops from Afghanistan. I found that candidates who wanted to keep US troops in Afghanistan received preference alignment scores that were 0.30 points lower, on average, than candidates who wanted to withdraw US troops from Afghanistan. I found that candidates who wanted to keep US troops in Afghanistan received leadership strength scores that were 0.20 points higher, on average, than those of their counterparts. And I found that candidates who took the more hawkish position on this issue received good judgment scores that were 0.12 points lower, on average, than those of the doves. Each of these effects is consistent with the chapter's overall argument. We see that taking a hawkish foreign policy position on keeping US troops in Afghanistan boosted perceptions of leadership strength, even though respondents did not actually support the idea on its merits; we see that taking hawkish foreign policy positions generally depressed perceptions of good judgment; and we see that the first of those effects was larger than the second.

I replicated that analysis for all twenty-six policy issues that appeared in the experiment. Figure 3.6 presents results. Each data point in this figure reflects the degree to which taking the hawkish position on a policy issue

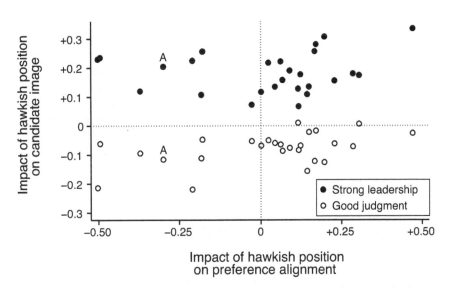

Figure 3.6. Generalizability across issues. Each data point reflects the degree to which taking the hawkish position on a single policy issue influenced evaluations of candidates' leadership strength (shown in solid circles) and good judgment (shown in hollow circles). The data points labeled with an "A" on the left side of the figure describe effects associated with candidates who said they would keep US troops in Afghanistan, relative to candidates who supported withdrawing from that conflict.

changed respondents' perceptions of presidential candidates. The horizontal axis in figure 3.6 shows how taking hawkish positions affected preference alignment. The vertical axis in figure 3.6 shows how hawkish policies shaped perceptions of candidates' personal attributes.

These data reveal that every hawkish position that appeared in the experiment overall improved perceptions of candidates' leadership strength. It is also apparent that the degree to which a hawkish policy position boosted perceptions of a candidate's leadership strength was unrelated to respondents' policy preferences.[37] This pattern reinforces the book's argument that voters intuitively associate hawkishness with leadership strength, even when they disagree with hawkish foreign policy positions on their merits.

Figure 3.6 also shows that hawkish policies consistently undermined perceptions of candidates' judgment. This pattern holds for twenty-four of twenty-six foreign policy issues that appeared in the experiment.[38] These effect sizes are also generally smaller in magnitude than the associations that respondents drew between hawkishness and leadership strength. For twenty-three out of the twenty-six policy positions that appeared in the data set, hawkish positions had a greater impact on perceptions of leadership strength than on perceptions of good judgment.[39] The results in figure 3.6 thus confirm that the empirical patterns I documented in this section generalize across foreign policy issues.

This section's findings hold if we limit the analysis to presidential candidates who are men, women, Democrats, Republicans, or who share the respondent's political party (as would be the case in a presidential primary). The section's findings also hold if we limit the analysis to respondents who are men, women, white, Hispanic, Democrat, Republican, independent, college educated, or non–college educated, as well as respondents who score at either high or low levels on a battery of questions measuring knowledge of foreign policy.[40] The fact that the experiment's results hold across such a diverse range of demographic groups adds credibility to the claim that issue-image trade-offs are deeply embedded in the politics of foreign policy, and that this dynamic is not driven by an idiosyncratic subset of voters who hold unusual attitudes toward international affairs.

Implications of the Book's Quantitative Evidence

This chapter used a combination of survey and experimental evidence to document several claims about how foreign policy positions shape leaders' personal images. I found that voters reliably associate foreign policy hawkishness with leadership strength, even when voters do not agree with the substance of those policy positions. I demonstrated that this association between hawkishness and leadership strength consistently outweighs the tendency for hawkish foreign policies to undermine perceptions of good judgment or other personal attributes. And I showed that the association between hawkishness and leadership strength explains why foreign policy hawks consistently outperform their counterparts at the ballot box.

Along with the statistical evidence presented in chapter 2, these findings offer new insights for understanding the relationship between public opinion and US foreign policy. Most existing analysis of public opinion and US foreign policy assumes that voters evaluate leaders based on their policy positions and support elected officials whose views resemble their own. Chapters 2 and 3 have shown that this relationship reflects only part—and, perhaps, a minor part—of how voters determine leaders' fitness to be commander in chief. If voters assess foreign policy leadership on the basis of personal images rather than policy issues, then that has two primary implications for political strategy.

First, the book's findings suggest that the politics of foreign policy will often revolve around efforts to shape leaders' images in ways that have nothing to do with the substance of major foreign policy issues. A good example of this phenomenon came during the 1976 presidential campaign, when President Gerald Ford committed what was arguably the most famous gaffe in the history of presidential debates by saying that Eastern Europe was not dominated by the Soviet Union. What Ford meant to say was that the United States did not *accept* Soviet domination in Eastern Europe.[41] Ford's campaign quickly clarified this point, and most voters agreed with the substance of Ford's position. Ford's polling numbers nevertheless collapsed following this debate, with many voters explaining to pollsters that the president appeared to be ignorant of world affairs. This is an example of how optics that bear virtually no relation to the substance of US foreign policy can impact voters' perceptions of foreign policy competence.

This chapter's statistical findings also show how political leaders can use *unpopular* foreign policy positions as tools for building mass public support. This logic runs directly opposite to conventional ideas of how democratic politics operate. In particular, the book's theoretical framework and empirical evidence suggest that leaders who make unpopular foreign policy decisions are not necessarily neglecting what voters want. Behavior that seems disconnected from public opinion may actually reflect leaders' attempts to cultivate mass public appeal. The next four chapters present case studies that show how the book's argument helps to reframe the history of US foreign policy.

Peace through Strength

John F. Kennedy, Ronald Reagan, and the Politics of Defense Spending

> The primary objective for Kennedy in dealing with specific foreign affairs issues is to enhance his image by demonstrating his knowledge and competence.
>
> —Ithiel de Sola Pool, campaign adviser
> to John F. Kennedy

This chapter explains how presidential candidates in the 1960, 1980, and 1984 elections viewed debates about military spending as tools in the politics of image-making. Consistent with my theory, I show that presidential candidates in these elections advocated military buildups to boost impressions of their leadership strength in a manner that did not also expose themselves to criticism for possessing poor judgment.

The 1960 election pitted Democratic senator John F. Kennedy against Republican vice president Richard Nixon. In 1980, the former Republican governor of California, Ronald Reagan, squared off against incumbent president Jimmy Carter. In 1984, Reagan fended off a challenge from Carter's former vice president, Walter Mondale. These elections meet the book's case selection criteria because foreign policy issues were unusually salient at the time.[1] When voters pay more attention to foreign policy issues, presidential candidates should have greater incentives to take positions that align with voters' policy preferences. We will nevertheless see that every presidential candidate in these elections saw debates about defense spending as a proving ground for crafting impressions of leadership strength, regardless of what voters thought about the merits of raising military expenditures.

Studying these elections together allows me to demonstrate that the book's argument generalizes across important variations in the political environment.

Kennedy was a Democrat while Reagan was a Republican. Defense spending was highly unpopular in 1960 and 1984, whereas 1980 is the only presidential election on record in which voters supported raising military expenditures. Kennedy carried the popular vote in 1960 by a slim margin while Reagan won both of his election contests handily. Kennedy and Reagan were nonincumbents in 1960 and 1980, respectively, whereas Reagan ran for reelection as a sitting president in 1984. Despite these variations, the chapter will show that Kennedy and Reagan used their positions on the defense budget in a manner that is consistent with the book's logic of image-crafting. The chapter's concluding section expands on these findings to make a broader argument about how public opinion shapes the politics of defense spending, even if this relationship is not as straightforward as leaders giving voters the policies they want.

John F. Kennedy and the 1960 Presidential Campaign

This case study revolves around campaign memoranda that describe how Kennedy's advisers designed their political strategy, along with fifty-four private surveys that Kennedy commissioned from pollster Louis Harris.[2] At the time, Harris's surveys were the most systematic polling effort that a presidential campaign had ever conducted.[3] Collecting and analyzing these documents allows me to describe mass public opinion as Kennedy's campaign saw it throughout the 1960 presidential race.

I use these sources to substantiate four claims. First, I explain how Kennedy's advisers believed that foreign policy was their primary political vulnerability. Second, I show that Kennedy's campaign viewed combating their vulnerability on international affairs as a matter of establishing an image of foreign policy competence. In fact, Kennedy's advisers explicitly rejected the idea that they should worry about the popularity of their positions on individual foreign policy issues. This finding shows that Kennedy's advisers prioritized crafting an appealing personal image over appealing to voters' policy preferences.

Third, I explain how Kennedy's advisers determined that proposing to raise the defense budget offered unique advantages in terms of conveying leadership strength without raising questions about Kennedy's judgment. This finding shows not only that the Kennedy campaign viewed the politics of defense spending as an issue-image trade-off, but that they believed this strategy would work for the exact reasons that the book's theory expects. Finally, I provide evidence that Kennedy's strategy did, in fact, help him to win the 1960 presidential election.

KENNEDY'S VULNERABILITY ON INTERNATIONAL AFFAIRS

Heading into the 1960 election, Kennedy's staff believed that their main weakness lay with foreign policy. Kennedy was knowledgeable about world politics and had served with distinction in the US Navy during World War II, but he had little high-level experience dealing with international affairs. By contrast, Richard Nixon had risen to national prominence by leading anti-communist investigations in Congress, he had confronted Soviet premier Nikita Khrushchev in the nationally televised "kitchen debate," and he had spent eight years as vice president under Dwight Eisenhower, who remained the country's most trusted voice on global issues. Nixon's foreign policy experience was widely expected to be an asset in 1960, given how the Soviets had recently developed the world's first intercontinental ballistic missile (ICBM), launched the Sputnik satellite, and shot down a US spy plane. These events caused many people in the United States to worry that they were losing the Cold War.[4]

Kennedy's top speechwriter, Theodore Sorensen, thus concluded at the start of the campaign that "world affairs will occupy the center of men's minds. Our primary task is to convince the voters of the candidate's and party's ability to make progress in these areas."[5] John Kenneth Galbraith, a Harvard economist who played a key role in shaping Kennedy's campaign strategy, similarly warned that "Nixon's claim to vast experience in a period of trouble and peril is going to be one of our most difficult and perhaps our most difficult issue."[6] Ithiel de Sola Pool, an MIT professor of political science who advised Kennedy on public opinion research, argued that "the foreign affairs issue is the number one question on the minds of voters" and that "this issue is Kennedy's area of greatest weakness."[7]

The private polls that Kennedy commissioned from Louis Harris reinforced his vulnerability on foreign affairs. Figure 4.1 shows how Harris tabulated the proportion of voters in each state who were concerned with various issues. While the exact mix of issues in each survey varied from poll to poll, Harris almost always reported voters' level of concern in eight areas: ageing, civil rights, economics, education, farming, states' rights, taxes, and war and peace. Table 4.1 summarizes these data across the fifty-four surveys that I found in the JFK Presidential Library's archives.[8] I use the term "issue salience" to capture the proportion of voters who said that an issue was one of their primary concerns.

The Harris data confirm that war and peace issues were the electorate's priority by a wide margin. On average, 55 percent of Harris' respondents mentioned some aspect of international affairs as being an issue of concern. (The second-ranked issue across those surveys was taxes, which Harris recorded as being a priority for just 33 percent of voters.)[9] And, while Harris's data showed that Kennedy and Nixon supporters disagreed about the im-

SUMMARY OF ISSUES OF CONCERN IN OHIO

	October			September		
	Total Voters	Voting for: Kennedy	Nixon	Total Voters	Voting for: Kennedy	Nixon
	%	%	%	%	%	%
War and Peace	51	49	53	47	47	47
Rebuild U.S. prestige in world	13	12	14	12	12	12
Get tough with Russia	13	11	16	9	7	10
Cut foreign aid	8	10	7	12	14	10
Beef up nation's defenses	8	8	7	7	7	8
Do something about Cuba	6	5	7	4	4	4
Find way to avoid war	3	3	2	3	3	3
Economic Bite	43	53	30	33	42	25
Unemployment	23	28	17	13	17	10
High cost of living	18	23	12	17	21	14
Small business problems	1	1	1	2	3	1
Need new industry	1	1	--	1	1	--
Taxes and Waste in Government	33	33	33	33	28	37
Taxes too high	12	11	14	12	10	14
Too much waste and spending in Washington	7	5	9	9	7	10
Taxes inequitable	5	6	5	7	6	8
Property tax too high	5	7	2	--	--	--
Federal income tax too high	4	4	3	5	5	5
Education	32	40	25	24	28	20
More, better schools	20	24	17	16	20	12
Better paid teachers	8	12	4	6	8	4
Cut frills in education	4	4	4	2	--	4
Old Age Problems	28	31	25	28	32	23
Medical care for aged	17	20	14	16	21	11
Extend and increase social security	11	11	11	12	11	12
Farm Problems	25	24	27	24	27	24
Get rid of surplus	6	7	4	5	6	6
Remove price supports	5	3	7	5	6	5
Get rid of Benson	3	3	4	5	6	5
Cost-price squeeze	9	10	8	8	9	8
Raise parity	2	1	4	--	--	--
Civil Rights	15	17	12	16	15	16
Pro-integration	10	12	8	12	13	11
Anti-integration	5	5	4	4	2	5
States' Rights	5	1	10	7	--	10
Unions Too Powerful, Corrupt	4	3	6	7	5	8
Need Stronger Leadership	4	3	6	3	--	5
Cut Imports	3	--	4	--	--	--

Figure 4.1. Example of Harris data on "issues of concern." © Louis Harris and Associates.

portance of some issues, both sets of voters saw war and peace issues as being their highest priority by a wide margin.

The Harris polls also confirmed that war and peace issues played to Kennedy's disadvantage, in the sense that voters who said that they were concerned with international affairs were also more likely to say that they planned to vote for Nixon. To show this, I tabulated the proportion of voters in each survey who said that they planned to vote for Kennedy, conditional on also identifying a particular policy area as being one of their priorities. I refer to those proportions as Kennedy's vote share among voters concerned with a given issue.

Table 4.1 Analysis of Harris polling data through September 1960

Issue area	Issue salience among all voters	Issue salience among Kennedy voters	Issue salience among Nixon voters	Kennedy vote share through 9/60
Ageing	24.2% (0.9)	28.6% (1.1)	19.7% (1.0)	59.3% (1.9)
Civil rights	16.2% (1.3)	17.4% (1.3)	14.9% (1.5)	54.9% (2.4)
Economics	30.5% (1.7)	37.4% (2.2)	23.5% (1.2)	59.4% (1.5)
Education	21.7% (1.3)	25.3% (1.9)	17.6% (0.8)	55.7% (1.8)
Farming	19.7% (1.5)	18.9% (2.0)	21.0% (1.3)	43.2% (3.5)
States' rights	7.5% (0.9)	3.5% (0.6)	11.8% (1.3)	16.5% (3.2)
Taxes	33.2% (1.0)	30.3% (1.2)	36.5% (1.2)	46.8% (1.4)
War and peace	54.8% (2.4)	53.5% (2.8)	56.2% (2.2)	47.9% (1.2)

"Issue salience" is the proportion of voters who said that an issue reflected one of their primary concerns. "Vote share" is the overall proportion of voters concerned with each issue who also said that they supported Kennedy for president. All data are weighted according to states' electoral vote count. Standard errors in parentheses.

Table 4.1 reports Kennedy's vote share within each of Harris's eight policy domains through September 1960, which was the first full month of the national presidential campaign. The data show Kennedy trailing Nixon by four points among voters who listed war and peace issues as an area of concern.[10] The only issues where Kennedy fared worse were states' rights, farming, and taxes but table 4.1 shows that those issues mattered to much smaller segments of the electorate. These data confirm that war and peace was not just the most common area of concern for voters, but also an area in which Kennedy was unusually vulnerable.

STRONG LEADERSHIP, GOOD JUDGMENT, AND THE MISSILE GAP

Conventional theories of democratic politics suggest that Kennedy should have addressed his vulnerability on foreign affairs by taking policy positions that were more popular than those of his opponent. But Kennedy's advisers explicitly rejected the notion of appealing to voters' policy preferences. Public opinion analyst George Belknap summarized the campaign's views of this matter by writing that "a large percent of people express a concern over 'keeping the peace,' but specific foreign affairs issues [are] not of great importance to them." Instead, Belknap wrote, most voters had a tendency to "personalize" foreign policy debates, using issues as litmus tests for the strength of a presidential candidate's prospective leadership. And, unfortunately for Kennedy, Nixon had a long-standing reputation for being tough on Communism. Belknap thus warned that "Nixon may be able to make the claim that 'toughness-softness' is the crucial difference between himself and his Democratic opponent in the public mind."[11] These statements are all consistent with the book's argument that leaders prioritize crafting images of foreign policy competence over taking foreign policy positions that appeal to voters on the merits, and that the politics of image-making are particularly associated with perceptions of leadership strength.

These ideas recurred throughout the Kennedy campaign's deliberations. Public opinion analyst Alexander Klein thus boiled down the key question on voters' minds as: "Whom would you want at the White House talking on the phone with Khrushchev?"[12] Speechwriter Richard Goodwin argued that Nixon's strongest lines of attack revolved around questioning "whether Kennedy can 'stand up to' or 'sit down with' Khrushchev."[13] Ithiel de Sola Pool described this dynamic in a manner that concretely reflects the book's core argument. "Particular postures on issues," he wrote, "will not directly affect many votes. The primary objective for Kennedy in dealing with specific foreign affairs issues is to enhance his image by demonstrating his knowledge and competence."[14] When Pool described how "the foreign affairs issue is Nixon's greatest source of strength," he similarly explained that "the most important aspect of the Nixon personality is his image of competence, experience, and self-confidence. Here is Nixon's great vote catching asset, particularly when it is applied to dealing with the Russians."[15]

In order to undermine Nixon's reputation for foreign policy competence, Kennedy needed to identify some area in which he could plausibly challenge Nixon's leadership abilities, or where he could criticize the Eisenhower administration's foreign policy more generally. He did this by arguing that the United States was experiencing a "historic decline in American prestige" during which the "balance of world power is slowly shifting to the Soviet-Red Chinese bloc."[16] Kennedy attributed these problems to the Eisenhower administration's fiscal conservatism. Eisenhower feared that the country would become a garrison state if it did not curb the growth of military expenditures, and he had gone to great lengths to limit defense spending throughout his two terms in office.[17] This stance gave Kennedy an opportunity to draw clear contrasts with the outgoing administration on the issue of military expenditures, and to connect his position on that issue to broader concerns about the United States' global status.

Kennedy's staff settled on that strategy as early as May 1959, when Harvard historian and campaign adviser Arthur Schlesinger argued that a defense buildup should be the key foreign policy initiative for Kennedy's broader promise to "get America moving again."[18] Schlesinger and his colleagues designed Kennedy's campaign around that slogan as a way to portray their candidate as providing fresh, vigorous leadership.[19] In Schlesinger's view, Kennedy's support for expanding the country's defense program indicated "new initiative in foreign policy" that would accompany the campaign's promise to produce a "moral and political revival at home."[20]

This strategy allowed Kennedy to project leadership strength without inviting criticism for how he might handle specific foreign policy issues. For example, consider how Kennedy described his international agenda in a

December 1959 interview, which the campaign later featured in a book describing Kennedy's foreign policy platform. Note how Kennedy avoids drawing clear policy contrasts with Nixon, and instead uses his proposed defense buildup to justify a broader claim about how he would provide stronger foreign policy leadership than his predecessors:

Q: *To sum up, Senator, what would you say are the main points of difference between your views on foreign policy and those of the Eisenhower-Nixon administration?*

KENNEDY: The basic differences are not so much in broad policy objectives as in basic attitudes which affect our day-to-day decisions around the globe—our neglect of Latin America, our vacillation in the Middle East, our timidity in Eastern Europe, our shortsightedness in India, and tied in with all of these, our emphasis on budgetary considerations over security considerations.[21]

In addition to amplifying his own image of leadership strength, Kennedy used his position on defense spending to portray Nixon as being complacent in the face of a rising Soviet menace. Walt Rostow, who was the Kennedy campaign's top national security adviser, articulated this strategy in a memorandum in which he argued that "nothing is more likely to swing votes than the conviction that the Republicans have endangered the nation's safety."[22] Kennedy exploited that vulnerability by claiming that the Eisenhower administration had "move[d] from crisis to crisis" because "we have not been paying the price" that was necessary to ensure US national security, while accusing Eisenhower and Nixon of placing "a balanced budget ahead of a balance of power."[23] By contrast, Kennedy promised to be "a vigorous proponent of the national interest . . . a man capable of acting as the commander-in-chief of the Great Alliance, not merely a bookkeeper who feels that his work is done when the numbers on the balance sheet come even."[24]

Kennedy justified his call for increased defense spending by invoking an alleged missile gap with the Soviet Union. Fears of the missile gap had emerged in 1957, when the President's Science Advisory Committee warned that the Soviets had a superior capacity for producing ICBMs.[25] Throughout the campaign, Kennedy warned that the missile gap gave the Soviets a "shortcut to world domination." Kennedy claimed that this revealed how Eisenhower and Nixon had been "gambling our survival" to balance the budget. By contrast, Kennedy promised to launch a "crash" missile program to bolster the country's defenses.[26]

Kennedy's claims about the missile gap were exaggerated. By 1960, the US intelligence community knew that, even if the Soviets had the capacity to produce more ICBMs than the United States, they were not actually doing that. Moreover, even if the Soviets chose to produce more ICBMs than the United States, that was just one element of the overall nuclear balance, which also included bombers, submarines, and intermediate-range missiles. Thus, in addition to the fact that the missile gap did not exist, it was doubtful that such a gap would have undermined the country's strategic deterrent.[27]

Kennedy almost certainly knew that he was misleading the public about the threat of a missile gap. As a US senator who served on the Foreign Relations Committee, Kennedy had access to the relevant intelligence reporting. CIA Director Allen Dulles briefed Kennedy on these issues during the 1960 campaign. And, while Kennedy might have said that he simply disagreed with the available intelligence, that skepticism faded fast after Election Day. Just two weeks after Kennedy's inauguration, Secretary of Defense Robert McNamara surprised reporters by telling them that they should not talk about missile gaps anymore, because "there is no missile gap." The next day, Kennedy said in a press conference that "it would be premature to rush a judgment as to whether there is a gap or is not a gap."[28]

However, the primary question for the purposes of this case study is not whether Kennedy believed that a military buildup was in the national interest, but rather why he thought those statements would be politically useful when running for president. As noted earlier, part of that value came from the fact that Kennedy could use his stance on defense spending as evidence that he would offer stronger foreign policy leadership than what Eisenhower and Nixon had provided. And Nixon could not easily rebut this logic. The notion that the projected balance of forces should rely on assessments of intentions and not just capabilities was a nuanced matter that Kennedy dismissed as wishful thinking: "another symptom of our national complacency . . . our willingness to confuse the facts as they were with what we hoped they would be."[29] Furthermore, Kennedy did not need to prove his claims about the missile gap beyond a reasonable doubt. He only needed the public to see the missile gap as a credible risk in order to link that issue to broader notions of how he would exercise more vigilant leadership on national security. "Those who oppose such an effort," he argued, "are taking a chance on our national survival. And today the only real question is which chance do we take—our money or our survival?"[30]

Expressed in terms of the book's theoretical framework, Kennedy's stance on closing the missile gap allowed him to send a vivid message of leadership strength without raising evaluable concerns about his foreign policy judgment. When Harris summarized the value of Kennedy's attacks on this issue during a presidential debate, he thus wrote, "Most significant is that it represents Kennedy on the offensive almost totally and Nixon on the defensive. The best that Nixon can register through on is that all is well, that we haven't really lost anything in the world."[31] Walt Rostow similarly noted that Kennedy's stance on closing the missile gap allowed him to "seize the initiative and move things toward positive American goals," without leaving Nixon clear grounds for rebuttal.[32]

NIXON'S CONSTRAINTS ON DEFENSE SPENDING

Why, then, did Nixon not simply match Kennedy's hawkishness on defense spending? Several Republican leaders—most notably New York governor Nelson Rockefeller—urged him to do just that. However, accepting Rockefeller's advice would have required Nixon to repudiate Eisenhower's long-standing efforts to restrain the growth of military expenditures. Rostow described these cross pressures as being one of the main reasons why Kennedy should hammer Nixon on military expenditures.[33] As Rostow explained it, this line of attack "may well yield a clear break in the Republican position for the following reason: Nixon is already torn between presenting himself as the man who will simply carry forward the Eisenhower formulae or presenting himself as a young man of independence and vigor."[34] In other words, Kennedy's stance forced Nixon to choose between maintaining his image of being an energetic Cold Warrior and keeping Eisenhower in his corner, both of which were key elements of Nixon's claim to foreign policy competence.

Kennedy's strategy played out as intended. Heading into the Republican National Convention in July, Nixon met with Rockefeller to draft a policy platform that would unify their respective wings of the party. That platform initially proposed "new efforts" for producing bombers, missiles, and submarines, and it asserted that "there must be no price ceiling on America's security." These statements were obvious attempts to repudiate Eisenhower's caps on military expenditures, and Eisenhower demanded that Nixon remove them. The final Republican Party platform thus emphasized the "*continued* development" of existing weapons programs and stated that "there *is* no price ceiling on America's security."[35] Furthermore, even though the final platform stated that "the United States can and must provide whatever is necessary to insure its own security," it added the caveat that "to provide more would be wasteful." These statements effectively doubled down on the budget-conscious approach that Kennedy was criticizing.[36]

Kennedy and his aides understood that the political value of their stance on defense spending was uniquely well suited to diminishing Nixon's image of foreign policy competence. When Arthur Schlesinger originally recommended that Kennedy orient his foreign policy platform around increasing the defense budget, he warned that this strategy would not work if the Republicans selected Rockefeller as their presidential nominee. Since Rockefeller was not part of the Eisenhower administration, Schlesinger argued, he could match Kennedy's position on military expenditures, critique Eisenhower for being complacent, and offer his own promises to reinvigorate the United States' defense posture.[37] According to Ted Sorenson, Kennedy agreed with that assessment: "Had the Republicans, he felt, nominated Nelson Rockefeller, who would not need to defend the administration and who often sounded like Kennedy on defense and economic growth, the New

York Governor might have been able to outflank the Kennedy position and win the race."[38]

These quotes capture two points that are relevant to the chapter's argument. First, Kennedy appears to have believed that the success of his presidential campaign depended on taking a stance on defense spending that voters overwhelmingly opposed. Second, Kennedy's statement suggests that, if Nixon had not received the Republican nomination in 1960, then *both* presidential candidates would have been likely to advocate increased military expenditures as a way to craft impressions of leadership strength. The fact that the public did not actually want to raise the defense budget in 1960 was irrelevant to the politics of the issue as Kennedy and his advisers saw it. The crucial thing was that promising to raise the defense budget helped to construct an appealing personal image, and Kennedy expected any other candidate to see it the same way.

DID KENNEDY'S STRATEGY WORK?

While it is always challenging to assess the role that any one issue played in a presidential election, the polls that Kennedy commissioned from Louis Harris show that Kennedy successfully neutralized his vulnerability on foreign policy issues over the course of the 1960 campaign. We have seen that voters who were concerned with war and peace issues were initially more likely to support Richard Nixon. By the end of the presidential campaign, however, Kennedy had reversed those proportions, taking the lead among voters who prioritized international affairs. On average, the Harris data show that Kennedy increased his vote share among voters who were concerned with war and peace issues by 0.7 percentage points per week.[39] The book's appendix shows that this effect holds when controlling for Kennedy's overall popularity, and that Kennedy's gains on war and peace issues outstripped his performance in any other policy area that Harris surveyed. These patterns are consistent with the claim that Kennedy made unique progress in convincing voters that he was competent to handle foreign policy issues. Given how Kennedy's strategy for dealing with foreign affairs during the 1960 campaign revolved around taking an unpopular position on defense spending, these data support the book's argument about how leaders can win mass public support by taking policy positions that voters oppose.

At the broadest level, Kennedy's behavior in the 1960 presidential campaign goes to show that the relationship between public opinion and foreign policy is not as straightforward as "giving voters what they want." Traditional theories of democratic politics assume that leaders build public appeal by taking popular policy positions. Seen through that lens, Kennedy's advocacy for increased military spending seems starkly undemocratic. Indeed, President Eisenhower used his farewell address to warn about how a growing "military-industrial complex" was pressuring elected officials to expand defense outlays that voters neither wanted nor needed at the time.[40]

Yet, this book's theory explains how voters evaluate presidential candidates on the basis of their personal images, not just on the content of their policy positions. We have seen that Kennedy and his advisers believed that a hawkish position on defense spending offered unique advantages for convincing voters that Kennedy would be a competent commander in chief. And the data suggest that this strategy worked. The 1960 presidential election thus provides a prime example of how foreign policies that seem disconnected from public opinion may actually reflect leaders attempting to win mass public support by making issue-image trade-offs.

A corollary to this argument is that leaders who take popular policy positions may not be trying to appeal to voters' policy preferences, either. Even when leaders act in ways that appear to be consistent with conventional theories of democratic politics, their behavior might actually be intended to send broader messages about their personal fitness to be commander in chief. The ideal way to evaluate this claim would be to identify a case that scholars have treated as a paradigmatic example of leaders attempting to win public support by taking popular policy positions, and then to use the archival record to show that these leaders were in fact primarily motivated by the logic of image-making. That is the purpose of the book's next case study, which examines the politics of defense spending during the 1980 presidential campaign.

The Politics of Ronald Reagan's Defense Buildup

The 1980 election is the only presidential contest since World War II in which a majority of people in the United States supported raising military expenditures. According to that year's American National Election Studies (ANES) survey, 71 percent of voters thought the US defense budget was too small. Incumbent president Jimmy Carter was also vulnerable to criticism for his handling of foreign affairs, given how the 1980 election occurred during the Iranian hostage crisis. It therefore seems as though the book's theory should be unnecessary for explaining why Ronald Reagan chose to place defense spending at the center of his foreign policy platform. If Carter already seemed like a weak commander in chief, then Reagan might not have needed to spend much effort making this argument. And if defense spending was popular, then that fact alone could be sufficient to explain why Reagan supported a military buildup. Indeed, scholars have frequently treated Reagan's position on defense spending as a clear example of how leaders respond to voters' policy preferences.[41]

This section will nevertheless show that debates about defense spending in 1980 were closely tied to the politics of image-making. First, we will see that, even though voters doubted Carter's foreign policy competence, they worried about whether Reagan would be an effective commander in chief. In general, voters saw Reagan as being a stronger leader, but they also worried that Reagan possessed poor judgment, and would thus get the United States involved in an unnecessary war. Both campaigns believed that the outcome of the 1980 presidential contest depended on whether Reagan could exploit his reputation for leadership strength without seeming as though he would make excessively risky decisions.

We will also see that Reagan's advisers believed that a proposed military buildup was the ideal tool for solving their candidate's image problem. Following a strategy similar to the one John F. Kennedy had employed when running for president two decades earlier, Reagan's team saw a hawkish stance on defense spending as a useful vehicle for bolstering impressions of leadership strength—and for accusing their opponent of complacency—without raising evaluable concerns about Reagan's judgment. Voters' policy preferences thus appear to have played a minor role in Reagan's decision to orient his foreign policy platform around raising the defense budget. The section concludes by showing how Reagan indeed continued to use a hawkish position on defense spending as a tool in the politics of image-making when running for reelection in 1984, despite the fact that only one-quarter of voters supported that position.

THE 1980 PRESIDENTIAL ELECTION AS A CONTEST OF PERSONAL IMAGES

Ronald Reagan's 1980 campaign strategy drew heavily on public opinion surveys conducted by pollster Richard Wirthlin. At the start of the campaign, Wirthlin's data showed that Reagan held a substantial advantage over Carter in terms of being viewed as a "strong, decisive leader."[42] Wirthlin's surveys also revealed that voters' demands for leadership strength were especially relevant to the domain of foreign affairs. After testing a series of potential themes for Reagan's campaign, Wirthlin found that the most effective message was as follows: "*A Strong Leader*: We are tired of suffering insults at the hands of other nations. We need a President who will stand up for America even if the rest of the world doesn't approve."[43]

Wirthlin additionally found that Reagan's main vulnerability was that voters worried that he possessed poor judgment. According to Wirthlin's data, "Reagan's principal negative image perceptions focus on (a) a simplistic and naïve approach to the issues; (b) frequent misuse of information and the confusing use of facts; and (c) a rashness that could lead to disaster if he had control of the country."[44] Once again, Wirthlin found that these concerns were closely related to international affairs, with surveys showing that voters were especially worried about whether Reagan "can be trusted not to start a nuclear war if he were president."[45] This argument was reinforced by a series of focus groups that the Reagan campaign conducted, which revealed that voters did not feel as though they knew much about the candidate other than his reputation for decisiveness, and showed that Reagan's lack of experience and perceived "risk of war" were voters' principal apprehensions about his candidacy.

Reagan's advisers thus built their general election strategy around balancing perceptions of leadership strength and good judgment—the strategic challenge that lies at the core of this book's discussion of what it takes to pass the commander-in-chief test.[46] When it came to foreign affairs, Wirthlin articulated Reagan's primary objective as "resolv[ing] the perceptual dilemma that large numbers of voters now wrestle with: on the one hand, Reagan would be a strong and decisive leader in foreign affairs . . . but on the other hand he would be too quick to push the nuclear button."[47]

Carter's advisers viewed the campaign in similar terms. Carter's top pollster, Patrick Caddell, found that Carter's main vulnerability was being viewed as a weak leader: "passive, defensive, always overwhelmed by events, rarely leading, always reacting." But Carter's main asset was that he seemed safer than Reagan, particularly since Carter had kept the United States out of war during his presidency.[48] "He has proven," Caddell wrote, "that he will not blow the world sky high."[49] By contrast, Caddell's polling showed that Reagan's main weakness was the perception that he "shoots from the hip too much without thinking things through."[50] Caddell thus articulated his theory of victory in 1980 in terms of preventing Reagan from passing a "minimum threshold of relative acceptability."[51] In a June memo outlining strategy for the general election, Caddell defined the campaign's central message as being: "when you vote for President—vote like your whole world depends on it."[52] In his convention speech, for example, Carter argued that Reagan lived in "a make-believe world, a world of good guys and bad guys, where some politicians shoot first and act questions later."[53]

Carter's strategy succeeded in putting Reagan on the defensive.[54] In June, for example, Wirthlin's surveys found that voters overwhelmingly agreed that Reagan was a stronger leader: he dominated voters' perceptions of this attribute by forty percentage points (53 to 13 percent).[55] Voters were more likely to say that Reagan was the candidate who would "start an unnecessary war," but this margin was a relatively small seven percentage points (33 to 26 percent), and voters were more likely to say that Carter would be the more "dangerous" president (22 to 19 percent). By October, however, Reagan was seen as the more dangerous candidate (by a margin of 27 to 16 percent) and his deficit on the "unnecessary war" question had ballooned to twenty-five percentage points (41 to 16 percent), which was now larger in magnitude than Reagan's advantage on perceived leadership strength (42 to 26 percent).[56]

Since Reagan ended up beating Carter by nine percentage points in the popular vote, it is easy to underestimate the degree to which Reagan's advisers felt that Reagan's image problems could keep him out of the White

House. By late October, Wirthlin's surveys showed Reagan leading Carter in the national race by a single percentage point.[57] A *New York Times* poll even found Carter one point ahead less than two weeks from election day.[58]

The Reagan campaign's concern for their candidate's image was the main reason why it agreed to debate Carter on October 28. When Reagan was comfortably ahead in the early fall, his advisers had thought that debating the president was all downside, running the risk that Reagan would make a gaffe and let Carter sneak back into the race. But by mid-October, Reagan's advisers felt that they needed a debate in order to brake Carter's momentum, particularly as this would grant Reagan a national forum for defusing the perception that he would be a dangerous commander in chief.[59]

These documents show how the Reagan and Carter campaigns viewed the politics of foreign policy during the 1980 presidential election in a manner that closely parallels this book's theoretical framework. Rather than focusing on how they could take the most popular positions on policy issues, both candidates saw their main task as navigating the politics of image-making. In particular, both campaigns viewed the election as hinging on the question of whether Reagan could exploit his reputation for leadership strength without raising unacceptable concerns about the quality of his judgment. Next I explain how Reagan's stance on defense spending played a key role in striking that balance.

DEFENSE POLICY AS A TOOL IN THE POLITICS OF IMAGE-MAKING

Reagan's advisers expressly encouraged him to "use [his] issue positions as vehicles for conveying positive image traits."[60] The way that Reagan approached this challenge closely resembled the approach that John F. Kennedy had taken to the politics of defense spending two decades earlier.

Reagan generally followed Kennedy's example in avoiding discussions of how he would handle foreign policy crises any differently from the incumbent president. For instance, even though voters were generally dissatisfied with how President Carter had handled the Iranian hostage crisis, any attempt to criticize Carter for being too soft on this issue was liable to raise fears about Reagan's itchy trigger finger. In his campaign plan, Wirthlin warned that, while voters were "dissatisfied with the US slippage in world leadership and . . . willing to take a firmer stand in foreign policy," they were still "willing to take minimal risks to be restored to a position of leadership in the world which has been lost during the Carter term."[61] In other words, Reagan had to find foreign policy issues on which he could criticize Carter for being weak without also suggesting that Reagan would do anything dangerous as president.

Taking a hawkish position on defense spending was an ideal tool for this purpose. Calling Carter weak on defense served Reagan's goal of "dramatizing the loss of American power and prestige abroad suffered since 1976."[62] To this end, Reagan criticized Carter's decision to delay or to cancel several weapons programs, including the B-1 bomber, the neutron bomb, the Trident submarine, and the MX missile. Reagan argued that these decisions reflected the "weakness, indecision, mediocrity, and incompetence" of a president who chose to "live in the world of make-believe" rather than confronting the Soviet threat head on.[63] Reagan charged that Carter had allowed the Soviets to go unchallenged in conducting "the greatest military buildup in the history of mankind," thereby taking the lead in "virtually every category of military strength."[64] The Republican Party platform used this issue to portray Carter as a weak and complacent leader, arguing that "the evidence of the Soviet threat to American security has never been more stark and unambiguous, nor has any President ever been more oblivious to this threat and its potential consequences."[65]

Just as importantly, Reagan's proposed defense buildup allowed him to make promises about restoring the United States' international position without wading into controversial debates about the use of military force. Indeed, Reagan claimed that building military strength would discourage adversaries from challenging the United States at all. As Wirthlin explained it, "Governor Reagan should point out repeatedly that long-term prospects for real and enduring peace in the world depend directly on our economic and military strength and the prestige of America abroad."[66] Campaign manager Bill Casey argued that this theme would inoculate Reagan against charges of being reckless, because he could respond to all questions related to war by claiming that "I am proposing nothing more than American firmness and American strength."[67] Reagan conveyed these themes by arguing that his defense program would build a "margin of safety," while the central theme of his foreign policy platform was the concept of pursuing "peace through strength." As Reagan put it in his convention speech, "War comes not when the forces of freedom are strong, but when they are weak."[68]

Carter tried to deflect Reagan's criticisms by portraying himself as a hawk on defense matters, too. Carter's campaign hastened to note that he had raised real military expenditures in all four years of his presidency; that Carter planned to continue increasing the defense budget by 4 percent per year in his second term; and that he had significantly upgraded several components of the United States' ground, naval, and strategic forces.[69] But Carter's ability to take a hawkish stance on this issue was constrained by his prior commitments to restraining the budget deficit and to pursuing arms control. In particular, Carter had renounced the idea that the United States should seek military superiority over the Soviet Union, instead arguing that Washington should orient its defense policy around preserving "strategic equivalence" with Moscow. In order to defend that stance, Carter's team stressed that military objectives had to be balanced against "competing, legitimate needs for the budget dollar," arguing that Carter's defense package was "steady, strong, and sane," while claiming that Reagan's proposed defense buildup would trigger a potentially destabilizing arms race.[70] In other words, Carter's position on defense spending was largely oriented around highlighting the quality of his judgment, in order to compensate for the fact that Reagan was widely perceived as being a stronger supporter of military readiness.

Carter's proposal for implementing a moderate defense buildup to preserve strategic equivalence was defensible on its merits. It was also likely consistent with voters' policy preferences. The 1980 American National Election Studies survey found that the median voter preferred only a "slight increase" in military expenditures.[71] Yet, the question of exactly how much extra defense capability the United States needed was a complex matter on which few voters could be expected to hold firm opinions. Carter thus faced an uphill battle in convincing voters that Reagan's more hawkish stance on defense spending was not "sane." And, instead of engaging with the substance of this debate, Reagan simply lobbed charges that Carter was being weak and complacent, which was exactly how he wanted to frame the contest. Thus, in an August speech, Reagan asked, "Since when has it been wrong for America to aim to be first in military strength? How is American military superiority dangerous?"[72]

Reagan's use of the "peace through strength" mantra to maintain a reputation for leadership strength without raising evaluable concerns about his judgment was particularly apparent during his national debate with Carter on October 28. As noted earlier, both campaigns believed that the outcome of the debate—and perhaps the election itself—hinged on Reagan's ability to seem like a strong leader while also defusing questions about whether he would get the United States involved in an unnecessary war. The debate's very first question honed in on this issue, asking Reagan how he differed from Carter on the use of military force. Reagan simply dodged the substance of the question, pivoting to his standard message of how expanding the country's military resources would bring peace through strength:

Q: *You have been criticized for being all too quick to advocate the use of lots of muscle, military action, to deal with foreign crises. Specifically, what are the differences between the two of you on the uses of American military power?*
REAGAN: I don't know what the differences might be, because I don't know what Mr. Carter's policies are. . . . I'm only here to tell you that I believe with all my heart that our first priority must be world peace. . . . And to maintain that peace requires strength."[73]

Throughout the remainder of the debate, Reagan parried Carter's attempts to portray him as a dangerous leader by claiming that the president had mischaracterized his positions. For instance, after Carter argued that Reagan had made some "extremely dangerous and belligerent" statements about arms control, Reagan responded: "I know the President's supposed to be re-plying to me, but sometimes, I have a hard time in connecting what he's saying with what I have said or what my positions are." Of course, that was largely because Reagan avoided making his foreign policy positions explicit. So long as he stuck to his focus on defense spending, Reagan could portray himself as being a strong leader without wading into controversies that might undermine perceptions of his judgment.

REPRISING "PEACE THROUGH STRENGTH" IN 1984

This section has argued that, even though a majority of Americans sup-ported raising military expenditures in 1980, that was not the central reason why Ronald Reagan made a defense buildup the centerpiece of his foreign policy platform. Instead, we have seen that Reagan's campaign viewed the defense spending issue as a vehicle for bolstering perceptions of leadership strength without raising clear concerns about Reagan's judgment. Thus, even if a defense buildup had *not* been popular in 1980, it is reasonable to expect that Reagan would still have found this position to be a strategic asset.

Of course, we cannot rerun history to examine this counterfactual directly. But the 1984 election offers something close to that. By the end of Reagan's first term in office, only 20 percent of voters thought that the defense bud-get was too low.[74] And, by that point, Reagan had already implemented the largest military buildup that the United States had ever conducted during peacetime. If Reagan had seen his stance on defense spending as a way of appealing to voters' policy preferences, then we would expect him to have moderated that position heading into 1984—perhaps by arguing that he had already succeeded in solving the military deficiencies that Carter had left him. By contrast, if Reagan saw the political value of defense spending pri-marily in terms of bolstering his personal image, then we would expect him to keep that hawkish stance front and center in his campaign strategy. Rea-gan's approach to the politics of defense spending in 1984 was, in fact, al-most identical to how he had treated that issue four years earlier.

The 1984 presidential election had one of the most lopsided outcomes in US history: Ronald Reagan defeated former vice president Walter Mondale by winning 59 percent of the popular vote. Yet, as the general election cam-paign ramped up in July, Reagan's private polling showed that most voters disapproved of how he had handled international affairs.[75] Reagan's chief pollster, Richard Wirthlin, warned that "a disturbing plurality of Americans [47 percent] continue to feel that the world is less safe now than it was four years ago."[76] When Wirthlin asked voters to say what worried them most about Reagan being reelected, 51 percent of responses focused on foreign policy, with 38 percent of respondents specifically citing fears that Reagan would get the country involved in a war.[77]

These fears were stoked by Reagan's hawkishness and escalating Cold War tensions. During his first term, Reagan had implemented a massive defense buildup, he had invaded Grenada, and he had supported Nicaragua's anticommunist insurgency. Reagan had also deployed US soldiers to Lebanon who suffered 241 fatalities in an October 1983 terrorist attack. As historian David Ryan describes it, "Americans were worried about the hard-line aspects of Reagan's character. They feared that he just might be the candidate who would act on his aggressive rhetoric and get the United States involved in a regional conflict or that he might press the Soviet Union too hard."[78] Wirthlin's polling substantiated this concern. For instance, when Wirthlin's September 1984 survey asked voters to say which candidate would be more likely to get the United States involved in a war, responses identified Reagan as riskier than Mondale by a margin of 42 to 18 percent.[79]

Reagan nevertheless consistently dominated Mondale on questions relating to which candidate would be a stronger leader. Thus, when Wirthlin's September survey asked voters to choose which candidate that attribute best described, Reagan came out on top by a whopping forty percentage points (64 to 24 percent).[80] Voters' perceptions of Reagan and Mondale were thus consistent with this book's argument about the relationship between policy issues and personal images: the hawkish candidate seemed like a stronger, but riskier, commander in chief.

In order to address concerns about his judgment, Reagan took several steps to moderate his foreign policy leading up to the 1984 election. The Reagan White House referred to these initiatives as "the Year of Peace." The Year of Peace involved withdrawing US troops from Lebanon, visiting China, avoiding confrontation with Moscow after the Soviet Union shot down a Korean passenger jet, and organizing a presidential meeting with Soviet foreign minister Andrei Gromyko to discuss arms control. Reagan's political advisers believed that this behavior would defuse the charge that Reagan was too "trigger-happy."[81] Reagan's Year of Peace initiative is thus consistent with the book's description of how dovish foreign policies help leaders to convey good judgment.

If Reagan had moderated his foreign policies so much that they had become more dovish than the views of the mass public as a whole, then that would contradict the book's argument about how the relationship between issues and images in foreign policy generally favors hawks. Yet, while Reagan tempered his policies at the margin, his views remained more hawkish than what voters wanted at the time. For example, the 1984 American National Election Studies asked three questions that allowed voters to compare their views with the candidates' policy positions. Those issues pertained to whether the United States should spend more or less money on national defense, whether the United States should cooperate more or less with the Soviet Union, and whether the United States should intervene more or less extensively in Central America. The ANES data reveal that voters saw Reagan as being more hawkish than Mondale on all three issues—and that, in each case, voters also reported that their policy preferences lay closer to Mondale's views.[82]

It was particularly clear that voters did not agree with Reagan's continued advocacy for raising the defense budget. Public polling data showed that just 20 percent of Americans thought that US military spending was too low in 1984.[83] The Reagan campaign's own surveys showed that proposals to continue Reagan's military buildup were not a winning issue on the merits. For example, when Wirthlin asked voters to indicate which issue would have the most impact in driving their votes, he found that the most common response was being "against [the] arms race" (5 percent), while just 1 percent of voters said that their vote depended on which candidate would do more to strengthen national defense.[84]

If the relationship between public opinion and foreign policy primarily revolved around satisfying voters' policy preferences, then Reagan should have abandoned his support for raising military expenditures heading into the 1984 election. Or, at least, he should have sought to lower the salience of that stance. Instead, Reagan placed special emphasis on this issue in his speeches and campaign advertisements. Reagan's best-known use of the defense spending issue was a television advertisement titled "Bear in the Woods." This ad depicted a bear roaming around while a narrator warned: "There is a bear in the woods. . . . Some people say the bear is tame. Others say it's vicious and dangerous. Since no one can really be sure who's right, isn't it smart to be as strong as the bear—if there is a bear?"[85]

The Bear in the Woods ad vividly captures the book's argument about why the commander-in-chief test favors foreign policy hawks. Reagan claimed that there was no way to know which candidate's position on defense spending made more sense, thereby muddling Mondale's ability to claim that a more dovish position reflected better judgment. Instead, Reagan argued that it was better to err on the side of safety—thereby portraying Mondale as being complacent—even if voters did not actually want to raise defense expenditures at the time.

The archival record makes clear that Reagan's team felt that the key to winning reelection revolved around exploiting their candidate's image as a strong leader. Thus, Wirthlin identified the "strategic campaign imperative" as showing that "Ronald Reagan will provide strong, effective leadership for America's future."[86] Reagan aide Richard Darman agreed that "the umbrella theme [of the campaign] will be leadership," and argued that Reagan's peace through strength mantra was the ideal slogan for capturing that message.[87] Reagan aide Michael Deaver agreed that "to have peace, we must have strength. This is the essential message of the Administration's national security policies."[88] Thus, even though 80 percent of Americans already thought that the US military was strong enough, Reagan's team believed that advocating for a further military buildup offered important advantages when it came to honing their candidate's image.

Mondale's campaign recognized early on that Reagan's image of leadership strength posed one of their primary obstacles to winning the White House. As early as September 1983—four months prior to Mondale declaring his candidacy—adviser Bill Galston wrote a memorandum arguing that "your central challenge is to show that you are a credible commander-in-chief."[89] Similarly, when Mondale's pollster Peter Hart described the candidate's three primary weaknesses in a November 1983 memorandum, two of them focused on foreign policy leadership: "not being strong enough or forceful enough which feeds into the questions about whether he would stand up to the Russians" and "being soft on national defense."[90] (Mondale's third weakness, according to Hart, was the perception that he "rel[ied] on old answers and worn-out solutions.") Mondale's public opinion research consistently showed Reagan's dominance on leadership strength and explicitly attributed that image to Reagan's hawkishness on foreign policy issues. For instance, an October 1984 focus group report concluded that "Reagan is perceived as the more decisive, more recognizable man, and respondents cite his 'standing up for the United States' as a compelling example of leadership. He has successfully adopted a posture of bravado, toughness, and optimism to which respondents respond well."[91]

Mondale attempted to defuse this problem by imitating Reagan's rhetoric about the importance of maintaining a strong national defense. For example, Mondale once ran an ad arguing that he would implement "a plan for peace which deals from strength." Mondale's policy platform carefully avoided language that suggested Mondale would cut defense programs. Yet, Mondale could not match Reagan's hawkishness on this issue. As a US senator, and then as Jimmy Carter's vice president, Mondale had been a vocal proponent of restraining increases in defense spending and of instituting a "nuclear freeze" to restrain the ongoing arms race between Washington and Moscow.[92] Even if Mondale had been willing to abandon these positions for political purposes in 1984, he was stuck with a reputation for being relatively dovish on defense spending, and abandoning that position would have exposed him to charges of hypocrisy.[93] Mondale's foreign policy platform ultimately called for "steady, sustainable defense growth" of 3 or 4 percent in real terms, which was roughly one-third of Reagan's proposed buildup.[94]

Given his relatively dovish positions on national defense, the book's theory predicts that Mondale would attempt to portray his qualifications for serving as the country's commander in chief primarily in terms of possessing good judgment. Thus, when Galston advised Mondale that demonstrating his credibility as commander in chief was the campaign's "central challenge," he proposed that Mondale make sure to approach foreign policy in a manner that seemed "measured rather than reckless," while demonstrating that "Reagan doesn't know what he's doing and blunders into dangerous situations."[95] Peter Hart similarly noted when reviewing survey data that, despite Reagan's strong job rating, he seemed "extremely vulnerable" on questions about "handling of an international crisis."[96] Hart thus concluded that Mondale's strategy for dealing with foreign policy issues required "show[ing] Mondale as a stable, competent leader who avoids unnecessary risks and knows what he is doing."[97]

Mondale's campaign speeches consistently reflected these messages. For example, in his first major foreign policy address in March, Mondale claimed that "of all the responsibilities of the President, the most important is obviously to ensure our nation's security and to lead us toward peace. To do that, you must have a sure-footed leader, someone who knows what he's doing and sees the world as it is."[98] As part of this judgment-oriented message, Mondale portrayed Reagan's defense buildup as wasteful spending that would provoke a destabilizing "limitless arms race" between Washington and Moscow.[99] This rhetoric reflects the book's argument about how, even if hawkish foreign policy positions help leaders to craft images of leadership strength, they also expose leaders to charges of possessing poor judgment.

Yet, Mondale struggled to convince voters that his prudence would generate foreign policy gains. The central problem, as Mondale's pollsters saw it, was that voters did not trust that the Soviet Union would reciprocate more moderate foreign policies. Indeed, Reagan argued throughout the 1984 campaign that his rapid arms buildup would make arms control *more* likely in the long run, by convincing Moscow that it was useless trying to outrun Washington in an arms race. Mondale pollster Peter Hart diagnosed this problem in a manner that closely aligns with this book's argument about how good judgment in foreign policy is inherently challenging for voters to evaluate. He said that convincing voters to trust Mondale on arms control demanded "sophisticated" reasoning that reconciled "seemingly conflicting public attitudes" in which voters worried about nuclear war but also believed that "Soviets treat conciliatory gestures as weakness."[100] By contrast, Mondale's research showed that he was "dogged by his association with the Carter administration and the perception that he somehow wouldn't or couldn't effectively 'stand up against' Soviet aggression or provocation."[101]

In other words, Reagan's hawkishness generated a clear image of leadership strength, whereas Mondale's more moderate stances were less useful for signaling good judgment. These conclusions closely align with the book's argument about how leadership strength is the more evaluable of those two attributes. The most authoritative political history of the 1984 campaign explains that Mondale's advisers eventually determined that "the real message of the polls was that people wanted a strong leader whether they liked his policies or not."[102] This interpretation matches the book's description of issue-image trade-offs: the primary political value of Reagan's campaign messaging lay with crafting an image of leadership strength, even when that involved departing from voters' policy preferences.

REAGAN'S DEFENSE BUILDUP AS AN EXERCISE IN IMAGE-MAKING

This section has described how Ronald Reagan used a hawkish stance on defense spending to craft impressions of leadership strength in the 1980 and 1984 elections. In the first of these cases, voters generally agreed that US military expenditures were too low. The archival record nevertheless demonstrates that Reagan and his team did not see the primary political value of proposing a military buildup as appealing to voters' policy preferences. Instead, Reagan used this position as a tool in the politics of image-making. This stance allowed Reagan to seem like a strong leader, to portray Jimmy Carter as a complacent commander in chief, and to do so without exposing Reagan to clear criticism for possessing poor judgment. In 1984, Reagan reran that playbook even though voters no longer agreed that the defense budget was too small. Once again, the archival record reveals how Reagan's campaign organized its strategy around showing that their candidate was a strong leader—even if that involved raising the salience of policy stances with which most voters disagreed.

The 1984 presidential campaign also demonstrates that the politics of issue-image trade-offs do not solely apply to presidential challengers. When John F. Kennedy ran for president in 1960, and when Reagan won his party's presidential nomination in 1980, both men had limited foreign policy experience and voters knew relatively little about them. In principle, this could indicate that presidential challengers have special incentives to make issue-image trade-offs in order to demonstrate that they are competent to serve as the country's commander in chief. The fact that Reagan placed his hawkish position on defense spending front and center in his 1984 reelection bid shows that, even as an incumbent, Reagan still believed it was useful to raise the salience of unpopular policy positions if that helped to reinforce his image of leadership strength. Reagan's approach to this issue worked so well that every subsequent Republican nominee for president has incorporated the peace through strength theme into his official platform.[103]

Defense Spending and Democratic Responsiveness

There are many other examples of how the politics of defense spending revolve around personal images rather than voters' policy preferences. For example, one of the most enduring visuals from the 1988 presidential campaign was Democratic nominee Michael Dukakis smiling awkwardly while riding in a battle tank (see figure 4.2). The Dukakis campaign ran this advertisement to promote a policy message: that, even though Dukakis wanted to cut the size of the United States' nuclear arsenal, he still supported building conventional armaments, such as tanks.[104] The 1988 American National Election Studies showed that voters saw Dukakis's position on defense spending as being more closely aligned with their personal preferences than the position of Dukakis's opponent, Vice President George H. W. Bush.[105] Bush's campaign nevertheless relentlessly exploited Dukakis's stance on defense spending to argue that he was weak on defense, and the "tank ride" advertisement's goofy optics only reinforced the perception that Dukakis was out of his depth on military issues. As Norman Ornstein and Mark Schmitt put it, Dukakis's stance on defense spending might have appealed to voters on its merits, but "Bush managed to shift the debate back to strength versus weakness, defining the issue much as it had been defined by Reagan in 1980."[106] This interpretation is consistent with the book's logic of issue-image trade-offs—though I would note that the true originator of that strategy was John F. Kennedy, not Ronald Reagan.

Rather than listing additional examples of how leaders treat debates about defense spending as a proving ground for leadership strength, this section concludes by explaining how my theory sheds new light on the broader politics of foreign policy. In particular, I argue that the book's theory can help

Figure 4.2. Michael Dukakis's "tank ride." © Associated Press, reproduced with permission.

to explain a long-standing puzzle of how the US defense budget appears responsive to public opinion—even if voters almost never support raising military expenditures.

Since the question of how to handle the defense budget is a perennial issue, there is a rich body of data that tracks public opinion on this subject over time. Figure 4.3 presents results from 439 surveys since World War II that have asked voters to say whether they would prefer to see military expenditures increased, decreased, or kept about the same.[107] These data show that the median voter almost never supports raising the defense budget. Since World War II, there have been only two years in which a majority of Americans favored increasing military expenditures: 1980 and 1981. In the average year, just one-quarter of voters believe that the defense budget is too small.[108]

These data suggest that the politics of defense spending in the United States are not democratically responsive: nearly any increase to the defense budget since World War II has violated the median voter's preferences. And that observation has generated a substantial body of scholarship asking how such a large component of government spending can be so divorced from public opinion. Prominent works in this field attribute the long-term growth of the US defense budget to factors such as a "military-industrial complex," members of Congress using military spending to bring funds back to their districts, or national security elites pursuing a policy agenda that they believe is in the national interest, regardless of voters' policy preferences.[109]

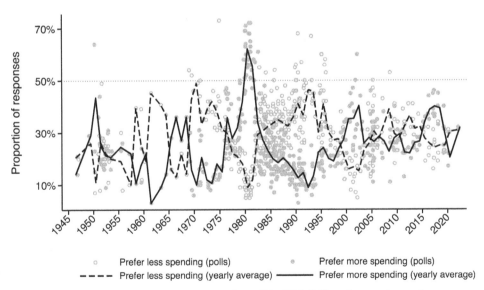

Figure 4.3. Public opinion on defense spending, 1946–2022. Polling data are drawn from 439 surveys. See appendix for details.

Other scholars argue that the US defense budget is, in fact, closely tied to public opinion. This view relies on the fact that public support for military spending is a reliable "lead indicator" for actual expenditures. This means that higher levels of support for increased military spending in one year consistently predict the defense budget's real growth rate in the next year.[110] This finding poses a problem for anyone who believes that public opinion plays little role in the politics of defense spending. Yet, the data shown in figure 4.3 reveal that this relationship is not as simple as giving voters what they want, because nearly every change in defense spending over the past seventy years has conflicted with the median voter's preferences.

The book's theory and evidence help to resolve this puzzle. Chapter 1 explained how politicians can use hawkish positions on the defense budget to craft images of leadership strength. Chapter 2 showed that voters attach a higher priority to electing strong leaders than to electing leaders who share their policy preferences on defense spending. Chapter 3 confirmed that presidential candidates who promise to raise defense spending do, in fact, come across as being stronger leaders. And this chapter's case studies showed that this is exactly what John F. Kennedy and Ronald Reagan were doing when they advocated defense buildups during their presidential campaigns. By treating foreign policy debates as exercises in political image-making, the book's theoretical framework can therefore explain why there is a robust relationship between public opinion and defense spending *and* why that relationship is not a straightforward function of voters' policy preferences. Chapter 5 shows how the book's theory offers similar insight about the relationship between public opinion and the Vietnam War.

Campaigning in a Quagmire

Lyndon Johnson, Richard Nixon, and the Politics of the Vietnam War

What is important in the campaign is not what you say but the impression you convey by saying it.

—Samuel Huntington, campaign adviser
to Hubert Humphrey

This chapter examines the politics of the Vietnam War during the 1964, 1968, and 1972 presidential elections. These elections fall within the book's case selection criteria because they each featured an unusually high percentage of voters who considered foreign policy issues to be the country's most important problems.[1] Examining these elections together also better shows how the book's argument applies to a variety of contexts. We will see that the politics of image-making help to explain the origins (1964), the continuation (1968), and the ending (1972) of the Vietnam War. The book's argument applies to one extremely close election (1968) and to two lopsided elections (1964 and 1972). It applies when the war was a relatively minor factor in national politics (1964) and when it was at the center of public discourse (1968 and 1972). It holds when Democrats occupied the White House (1964 and 1968) and with a Republican incumbent (1972). Altogether, this chapter shows how the politics of image-making shaped the life cycle of one of the United States' most controversial foreign wars.

Goldwater, Johnson, and the Origins of the Vietnam War

The 1964 presidential election pitted incumbent Democrat Lyndon Johnson against Republican senator Barry Goldwater. President Johnson believed that Goldwater's ultraconservative domestic agenda rendered him unelectable. Yet, Johnson also set himself the goal of winning the largest popular vote margin in history, both to establish a strong mandate for his legislative program and to cement his personal political legacy.[2] Johnson thus placed a high priority on cultivating mass public opinion, and he commissioned an extensive volume of private polling to help him maximize public support.

Johnson's research showed that international affairs was his primary policy weakness at the start of the 1964 presidential campaign.[3] This message was particularly clear in a series of studies that the public relations firm Doyle Dane Bernbach conducted for Johnson in June. These studies listed policy issues as being either "favorable" or "unfavorable" to the president in all fifty states. The firm concluded that foreign policy was unfavorable to Johnson in twenty-eight states, and favorable to him in none.[4] No other issue area raised anything close to this level of alarm.[5]

Johnson hired pollster Oliver Quayle to deliver a more detailed portrait of public opinion in the specific states that Johnson planned to target during the campaign. I found twenty-six of Quayle's polls in the LBJ Presidential Library's archives.[6] Though Johnson maintained excellent overall favorability ratings across these surveys (an average of 69 percent), most voters (an average of 57 percent) said they disapproved of how Johnson was handling US involvement in Vietnam. Johnson's Vietnam policies received majority disapproval in twenty of Quayle's twenty-six state polls, and it was Johnson's single most unpopular policy issue in fourteen of the twenty-six states that Quayle surveyed.[7] In speaking with his mentor, Senator Richard Russell, Johnson therefore predicted that "the Republicans are going to make a political issue out of it [Vietnam], every one of them." Russell agreed that "it's the only issue they've got."[8]

The fact that Johnson saw Vietnam as his primary foreign policy weakness is an insight that only appears in the archival records. Most public polling at the time showed that the Vietnam War had relatively low salience among voters. For instance, when an April Gallup poll asked voters to say what the United States should do next in Vietnam, 73 percent of voters said either that they had not given this question much thought or that they did not know. When a May Gallup poll asked voters to say how much attention they were paying to developments in South Vietnam, more than 60 percent answered "little or none." Scholars frequently treat these figures as an indication that the politics of the Vietnam War had little significance for the 1964 presidential election.[9] The documents reveal that Johnson and his advisers saw things differently.

It is also important to note that Johnson knew voters did not support escalating US involvement in Vietnam. For instance, the April Gallup poll found that voters who had opinions about what to do in Vietnam were divided among support for withdrawing US forces (15 percent), continuing the present policy (10 percent), applying nonmilitary pressure (16 percent), military escalation (15 percent), and other "miscellaneous" options (27 percent). Johnson accurately summarized the results of this poll to National Security

Advisor McGeorge Bundy by saying that "the majority think we're mishandling it [Vietnam]. But they don't know what to do."[10]

This section nevertheless shows that Johnson and Goldwater both determined it was in their political interest to recommend escalating the Vietnam War. Goldwater believed that taking a hawkish stance on Vietnam would help him to portray Johnson as a weak leader; Johnson chose to parry Goldwater's attacks by obtaining open-ended authorization to use military force in Vietnam. In both cases, we will see that Johnson and Goldwater used foreign policy debates as vehicles for shaping their personal images, even if this required steering the country toward a war that voters did not want.

THE PRIMACY OF IMAGES OVER ISSUES IN THE 1964 PRESIDENTIAL ELECTION

Goldwater argued throughout the 1964 campaign that Johnson had adopted a timid "Why win?" approach to the conflict in Vietnam.[11] The basis for this charge was that Johnson—and the Kennedy administration before him—had limited US involvement in the war. By contrast, Goldwater advocated taking "strong, affirmative action" to achieve victory in Vietnam, particularly by stepping up efforts to bomb communist supply routes. Goldwater even suggested that he would go to war with China if that were necessary to stop communists from controlling Saigon.[12]

If the politics of foreign policy revolved around satisfying voters' policy preferences, then Goldwater's hawkish stance on Vietnam should have been a political liability, and he should have downplayed his unpopular views on the subject.[13] Yet, Goldwater's campaign actually thought Vietnam was one of their most favorable foreign policy issues, because they saw it as a vehicle for raising broader questions about Johnson's ability to provide strong leadership in global affairs.[14] Goldwater thus laced his stump speeches with claims that Johnson had gotten the United States "bogged down in an aimless, leaderless war," or that Vietnam was "soaked with American blood while being sacrificed to this Administration's indecision," or that the conflict represented a "Soft Deal for communism."[15] Meanwhile, Goldwater's staff released statements with titles such as "Sen. Goldwater Charges Failure of Leadership in Viet Nam" and "Sen. Goldwater Lashes Democratic Leaders' Indecision."[16] Goldwater used a nationally televised conversation with President Eisenhower to place concerns about leadership strength at the center of national discourse: "I look upon our problem in getting peace in the world, so as to maintain all of our strength, our spiritual strength, our moral strength, our economic, our political, our psychological strength, and our military strength. . . . That's why possibly I've laid more stress upon strength than on other parts of the campaign."[17]

Johnson's advisers knew exactly what Goldwater was doing, and they feared that it would work. For example, Johnson's special assistant Bill

Moyers explained in a July memorandum that the primary impact of Goldwater's statements on Vietnam was to make it seem as if Johnson was concealing the extent to which the war had deteriorated on his watch.[18] Here, Moyers wrote that the main threat that Goldwater's arguments posed involved "forcing you to talk about Viet-Nam and also, in effect, actually admitting that Viet-Nam is a political issue." Note the degree to which this statement clashes with conventional ideas about how the politics of foreign policy depend on drawing policy contrasts that appeal to voters' policy preferences: even though voters overwhelmingly disagreed with Goldwater's position on escalating the war in Vietnam, Moyers believed it was in Johnson's interests to avoid discussing that issue.

Johnson's advisers believed that their main political challenge in handling Vietnam policy was to find a way to assure voters that Johnson was a strong leader, and not simply to take positions that voters supported on their merits. Moyers articulated this logic in a memorandum that explicitly prioritized cultivating Johnson's personal image over appealing to voters' policy preferences. Moyers wrote:

> If the choice for the United States is seen by most of the public in terms of a scale running from hard to soft, it is difficult for a government official—and particularly for a candidate—to get much mileage out of being for peace. In answer to inquiries he will make assurances that he is not soft, and by taking a firm position on many outstanding issues demonstrate that he is not for "yielding." Such responses are likely both to undercut any clear image of working for peace and to tie an administration's hands in the negotiation of existing differences.[19]

In other words, Moyers argued that it was crucial to avoid treating the politics of Vietnam as a matter of satisfying voters' preferences, even though that is what conventional theories of democratic politics assume. Moyers furthermore explained that the reason it was politically unwise to seek a popular position on Vietnam was that any stance moderate enough to satisfy voters' collective preferences would also exacerbate charges that Johnson was "soft." The Johnson and Goldwater campaigns thus saw debates about Vietnam in similar ways: as a trade-off between maximizing the popularity of their policy positions and crafting personal images of leadership strength.

NUCLEAR WEAPONS AND THE "DAISY AD"

Vietnam was not the only battlefield on which Johnson and Goldwater contested each other's personal images. Johnson placed particular emphasis on arguing that Goldwater could not be trusted with his "thumb on the nuclear button." This controversy was most famously captured by a television advertisement in which a girl plucking daisies in a field was enveloped by a mushroom cloud, after which a narrator instructed viewers to vote for President Johnson because "the stakes are too high for you to stay home." The "Daisy Ad" was a masterpiece of political theater, and a prime example of how the politics of foreign policy revolve around personal images, not just policy positions.[20]

Concerns about Goldwater's fitness to manage the US nuclear arsenal played more of a role in the 1964 election than the candidates' discussions of Vietnam. But the documents reviewed so far in this section demonstrate that Johnson still saw the Vietnam conflict as a political vulnerability. This meant that, despite whatever advantages Johnson already possessed in the politics of image-making, he still felt pressured to neutralize Goldwater's argument that he was being too soft on communism in Southeast Asia. The remainder of the section showed how Johnson responded to those pressures in a manner that shaped the origins of the Vietnam War.

THE GULF OF TONKIN CRISIS

By May 1964, Johnson's team determined that the best way to deal with the politics of the Vietnam War was to ask Congress to pass an open-ended authorization for the use of military force. William Bundy—the assistant secretary of state for East Asian and Pacific Affairs who was responsible for organizing staff efforts on the congressional resolution—wrote that the primary goal of this exercise was to provide "a continuing demonstration of US firmness" while maintaining "complete flexibility in the hands of the Executive in the coming political months."[21] This stance provided a vehicle for addressing Johnson's image problem without requiring the president to defend any specific policy choices.

Yet, Johnson's advisers also believed this gambit would succeed only if Congress passed the desired resolution without extensive debate, because that was the only way that Johnson could avoid explaining what he actually intended to do with his proposed legal authority.[22] By mid-June, Johnson's staff had concluded that they could only rush the resolution through Congress in the presence of an "acute emergency."[23] As Secretary of State Dean Rusk explained during a National Security Council meeting, "We should ask for a resolution only when the circumstances are such as to require action, and, thereby, force Congressional action."[24] In the absence of such an emergency, Johnson's staff believed it was best simply to avoid discussing Vietnam wherever possible.[25]

These discussions are consistent with the book's theory of how the politics of image-making shape foreign policy. Though Goldwater had taken an unpopular position in favor of escalating the Vietnam War, Johnson and his advisers viewed that position as a political threat. Rather than attempting to draw a favorable policy contrast with Goldwater on this issue, they sought to lower the salience of debates about Vietnam until a crisis emerged. And instead of trying to identify a position on Vietnam that was consistent with voters' collective preferences, Johnson's staff determined that their optimal strategy would be to use an open-ended congressional resolution to rebut charges that the president was weak and indecisive. Johnson's staff was also explicit in arguing that the value of the open-ended resolution lay with communicating leadership strength in a way that did not also generate concerns about Johnson's judgment. The book's theoretical framework thus captures the nature, the timing, and the reasoning behind Johnson's approach to Vietnam.

Johnson found the opportunity he was looking for on August 2, when the North Vietnamese Navy fired on a US destroyer in the Gulf of Tonkin. Two days later, the US military incorrectly reported a second Vietnamese naval attack. The Johnson administration immediately understood that these events provided the kind of emergency that would allow them to justify asking Congress for an open-ended authorization of military force with minimal debate. Congress passed the resolution on August 7 with just two dissenting votes in the Senate and none in the House of Representatives. The Gulf of Tonkin Resolution ultimately served as the legal basis for US military operations in Vietnam until its repeal in 1971.[26]

Following the playbook that his advisers had developed three months earlier, Johnson argued that his sole purpose in pursuing the Gulf of Tonkin Resolution was to demonstrate the United States' firmness and resolve.[27] Johnson assured Senator J. William Fulbright, who was one of the Senate's principal skeptics of escalating the war, that he would seek additional approval from Congress before sending ground troops to Vietnam. Given this promise—which Johnson subsequently broke—Fulbright took the lead in shepherding the Gulf of Tonkin Resolution through Congress with minimal debate. Fulbright privately assured skeptical Democrats, "You pass this thing and it gives Lyndon a tool in the campaign."[28]

The state polls that Johnson commissioned from Oliver Quayle showed that the proportion of voters who disapproved of how Johnson was handling the war fell by fourteen percentage points following the Gulf of Tonkin Resolution.[29] Pollster Louis Harris documented a similar trend in a different series of surveys that he analyzed for Johnson's private use.[30] Prior to the Gulf of Tonkin Resolution, Harris's research found that 58 percent of voters disapproved of Johnson's handling of the Vietnam War, and that 59 percent of voters thought Johnson would do a better job of handling Vietnam than Goldwater. Since the latter statistic was below Johnson's 64–36 lead at that stage of the presidential race more generally, Harris had previously argued that Vietnam was "clearly an issue working for Goldwater." After the Gulf of Tonkin episode, Harris found that 72 percent of voters supported Johnson's handling of Vietnam, and that 71 percent of voters thought that

Johnson would do a better job of handling that issue. "In a single stroke," Harris concluded, Johnson had "turned his greatest political vulnerability in foreign policy into one of his strongest assets."[31]

TURNING FOREIGN AFFAIRS FROM A LIABILITY TO A STRENGTH

How did Lyndon Johnson turn foreign affairs in general—and Vietnam in particular—from a liability to a strength? If the politics of foreign policy revolved around satisfying voters' policy preferences, then this shift should have resulted from Johnson taking policy positions that were more popular than those of his opponents. But that is not what happened during the 1964 election, when Johnson avoided explaining where he stood on Vietnam and then asked Congress to authorize a war that voters did not want. I showed that Johnson behaved in this manner because he viewed debates about Vietnam primarily in terms of how they shaped public perceptions of which candidate would be the more competent commander in chief. Johnson and his advisers explicitly articulated their political strategy in terms of crafting an appealing personal image that balanced strong leadership and good judgment, and they candidly rejected the notion of trying to take policy positions that maximized voters' preferences.

Of course, to say that the politics of Vietnam during the 1964 campaign were mostly about images rather than issues does not mean those debates were illegitimate. Barry Goldwater frequently spoke about military matters in an off-the-cuff manner that suggested he might make reckless foreign policy decisions.[32] Even Goldwater admitted that he might not be cut out for the presidency, once telling a journalist, "You know, I haven't really got a first class brain."[33] If the United States was bound to escalate the Vietnam War under either candidate's leadership, voters would at least be better served by placing responsibility for escalation in the hands of a leader whom they trusted.

Yet, voters did not get an opportunity to choose whether or not to escalate the war in Vietnam, and this exposes a crucial difference between the book's theoretical framework and conventional ideas of how democracy works. If the politics of foreign policy revolved around satisfying voters' policy preferences, then Johnson should have staked out firm opposition to Goldwater's unpopular stance on escalating US involvement in Vietnam. Instead, Johnson focused primarily on cultivating an appealing personal image, and he determined that the best way to craft that image lay with pursuing legal authority to conduct a war that most voters opposed. The 1964 presidential election thus provides a vivid example of how the politics of image-making can guide US foreign policy in a direction that is more hawkish than what voters actually want.

Humphrey, Nixon, and the Bombing Pause

By the spring of 1968, the Vietnam War had become so unpopular that Lyndon Johnson declined to seek reelection. The resulting presidential contest set the sitting vice president, Hubert Humphrey, against former Republican vice president Richard Nixon. Throughout the campaign, voters consistently ranked Vietnam as the country's most important problem. Yet voters also lacked consensus on how to handle the war. Since no proposed revision to US strategy in Vietnam was likely to gain popular support, Humphrey and Nixon largely refrained from drawing major policy contrasts on that issue. If the politics of foreign policy revolved around appealing to voters' policy preferences, then the Vietnam War should have played little role in the 1968 presidential election.

Yet, that is not how the 1968 presidential election played out. Instead, I explain how Humphrey's association with a failing military strategy made him seem incompetent. Humphrey felt that it was important to break from Johnson's Vietnam policies in order to demonstrate his strength and independence, even if that required advocating policies that voters opposed. Humphrey's advisers explicitly told him to ignore voters' policy preferences and to take positions on the war that were solely intended to improve his personal image. Humphrey eventually decided that the best way to do this was to propose a bombing pause in Vietnam. The bombing pause was strategically insignificant and extremely unpopular. Humphrey's decision to support the bombing pause nevertheless mitigated his image problem in a manner that was so effective that it nearly won him the election.

This section's description of the 1968 presidential campaign thus provides another demonstration of how the politics of foreign policy revolve around personal images and not just policy issues. Even if Humphrey and Nixon endorsed virtually identical strategies for fighting the war in Vietnam, their personal images were very different. The way that Humphrey and Nixon contested those images played a crucial role in making Nixon the country's thirty-seventh president.

THE PRIMACY OF IMAGES OVER ISSUES IN THE 1968 ELECTION

Throughout the 1968 presidential campaign, Richard Nixon promised to deliver "peace with honor" in Vietnam. Yet, Nixon never explained how he planned to do that. Nixon hinted that "I do have some specific ideas about how to end the war," but he also said it would be inappropriate to reveal these ideas to the public, on the grounds that doing so might undermine ongoing peace negotiations.[34] Nixon is thus widely remembered as having campaigned on a "secret plan" to win the Vietnam War. Though Nixon never used that exact phrase, it accurately reflects his evasive approach to the issue.[35] As Nixon reportedly admitted to one of his speechwriters, "I've come to the conclusion that there's no way to win the war. But we can't say that, of course. In fact, we have to seem to say the opposite."[36]

This behavior is inconsistent with conventional ideas of how the politics of foreign policy revolve around satisfying voters' policy preferences. How could Nixon use an issue to his advantage if he never told voters where he stood on it? The answer to this question is that Nixon believed the public's frustrations with Johnson's handling of the Vietnam War had more to do with Johnson's image than with his policies. By the summer of 1968, it was clear that Johnson had routinely exaggerated the extent to which the United States was making strategic progress in Vietnam.[37] These revelations exacerbated Johnson's so-called credibility gap on Vietnam War policy. And, since Humphrey had defended Johnson's Vietnam War policy in his capacity as vice president, he now lacked credibility, too.[38] Nixon therefore did not need to draw clear policy contrasts with Humphrey in order to convince voters that he would exercise more competent leadership on Vietnam.

Humphrey's image problem was well known at the time. His campaign was continually interrupted by hecklers who criticized the candidate for being a Johnson sellout. One protester's sign asked, "Why Change the Ventriloquist for the Puppet?"[39] Humphrey's campaign manager, Lawrence O'Brien, argued that shaking this image would be Humphrey's foremost political challenge. In his 1968 campaign plan, O'Brien wrote, "Humphrey must clearly, sharply, and decisively divorce himself from Lyndon Johnson [if] he has any hope of winning this election. Under no circumstances can [Humphrey] be elected if voters think of him as Lyndon's boy."[40]

Humphrey's private polling confirmed that he had a major image problem. These surveys showed that Nixon consistently beat Humphrey on survey questions that asked voters to say who was more independent, who was more decisive, and especially who would be the stronger leader.[41] Another campaign study found that "substantially more people judge Nixon than Humphrey to be strong, firm, and decisive. . . . Overwhelmingly, they believe Nixon—not Humphrey—could best keep this nation out of another war and keep the country strong."[42] A series of private polls that targeted undecided voters found that "the two most frequent accusations made by the respondents in regard to Humphrey were that he will be too weak, soft, or indecisive; and that he will be a repetition of Johnson."[43] The report continued, somewhat incredibly: "We asked our respondents to associate the candidates with animals. The majority of undecided voters compared Humphrey with sheep, lambs, kittens, or puppies. Our investigation reveals that Humphrey is perceived as weak and indecisive."

Polling data showed that Humphrey was seen as being particularly incompetent on the issue of Vietnam. Gallup, for example, conducted five surveys during the general election asking voters who would do a better job of handling the Vietnam War. Nixon led Humphrey on that question by an average of twenty percentage points.[44] Harvard political scientist Samuel

Huntington, who led Humphrey's Vietnam Task Force, cited these data in arguing that "the Vietnam War is clearly your most difficult issue in this campaign. . . . Given this lopsided distribution of opinion, Nixon's strategy is clearly to exploit the war by remaining silent on it."[45] Democratic public opinion analyst Gerald Hursh offered a similar perspective, writing, "Nixon seems to be succeeding by saying very little about Vietnam. He is capitalizing on public frustration with the war. . . . To exploit frustration, and anxiety, it is often politically sufficient simply to give the illusion of change, strength, and decisiveness. Mr. Humphrey suffers from a public image of no change and of indecision."[46]

Thus, even though voters saw Nixon and Humphrey as offering similar policy positions on Vietnam,[47] this did not mean that Vietnam was irrelevant to presidential politics in 1968. Humphrey's mere association with Johnson's Vietnam War policies undermined his personal image, convincing many voters that Humphrey could not handle that issue as president. As a result, Nixon did not need to establish a policy contrast on Vietnam in order to make that issue work to his benefit.

THE BOMBING PAUSE

By July, Humphrey's campaign decided that the best way to manage his image problem was for Humphrey to support a bombing pause over North Vietnam. Samuel Huntington's Vietnam Task Force prepared a paper for Humphrey that articulated this position, which Humphrey then presented to Johnson at the White House on July 25.[48] Johnson emphatically rejected the idea and, in Humphrey's words, "told me that he'd tell the nation that I was irresponsible in regard to the negotiations if I did this."[49] Humphrey made a second attempt to clear a bombing pause with Johnson when visiting the president's Texas ranch on August 8, when Johnson again rejected the idea on similar grounds.[50] Humphrey's third, and most consequential, clash with Johnson over the bombing pause involved debating the Vietnam plank in the Democratic National Convention's official party platform. Before the convention, Humphrey secured approval for the bombing pause from both National Security Advisor Walt Rostow and Secretary of State Dean Rusk. Yet Johnson refused to accept Humphrey's proposal and he forced the platform committee to endorse the administration's position that a bombing pause would only be acceptable in response to North Vietnamese concessions.[51]

Caving to Johnson during these confrontations only reinforced the perception that Humphrey was a weak leader, resulting in a series of newspaper headlines such as "How President Forced a Tough Plank on Vietnam: Softer Proposal Killed in Secret," "Johnson Altered Vietnam Plank," or "Bowing to Dixie Demands Costs [Humphrey] Chance of Making Peace with Doves."[52] Humphrey aide Ted Van Dyk later recounted that "the sole

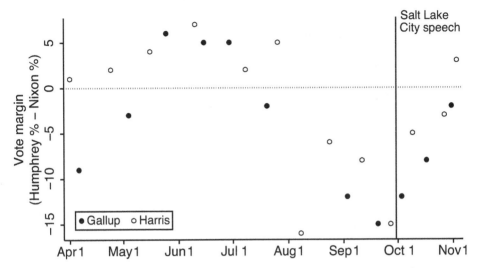

Figure 5.1. Nixon-Humphrey standing, April–November 1968. The figure's vertical axis captures the difference between the proportion of voters who said they planned to vote for Humphrey and Nixon, respectively. Source: Archibald Crossley and Helen Crossley, "Polling in 1968," *Public Opinion Quarterly* 33, no. 1 (1969): 12–13.

issue of the campaign for the first month [after the convention] became the VP's position on Vietnam."[53] As aide William Connell put it, "Humphrey found it was impossible to get on TV and attack Nixon because every press conference and every other moment of communication was filled with questions about bombing North Vietnam."[54] Antiwar demonstrations became increasingly disruptive at Humphrey's campaign events, to the point of sometimes forcing Humphrey to interrupt his stump speech so that hecklers could take the microphone.

Figure 5.1 demonstrates how Humphrey's standing in the polls deteriorated throughout the summer of 1968. By the end of September, the Gallup and Harris surveys both found that Humphrey lagged Nixon by fifteen percentage points. Humphrey's aides finally convinced him to go public with his proposed bombing pause, over Johnson's objections, in a nationally televised address delivered from Salt Lake City on September 30.

It is important to note that Humphrey's proposed bombing pause did not represent a major departure from Johnson's handling of the war. Johnson had already said he would order a bombing halt if North Vietnam made reciprocal concessions. Humphrey simply argued that the communists had already met that condition through a recent lull in fighting. Johnson's director of policy planning at the State Department, Walt Rostow, told the president that "an objective analysis shows that there is little significant difference among any of these proposals or the current policy of the US government."[55] David Ginsburg, the Humphrey aide who was responsible for representing the campaign during the Democratic National Convention's debate over the Vietnam plank, later said that "the differences between these drafts, over which we struggled and fought, as we see them now are so small as to be laughable."[56] Indeed, Johnson wound up ordering a bombing pause himself on October 31.

Humphrey also knew that voters opposed the bombing pause. Among the Humphrey campaign's state polls that I found at the Minnesota Historical Society, eight asked voters to describe their preferences for handling the Vietnam War. On average, just 25 percent of voters supported a bombing pause or other military concessions, and that proportion never exceeded 29 percent in any poll. By contrast, 65 percent of voters across these state polls supported continuing or expanding US military operations in Vietnam, and that proportion never fell below 61 percent. As Humphrey pollster Evron Kirkpatrick thus explained, "The public has no enthusiasm for a bombing pause. . . . There is *far more* popular support for a tougher policy" (emphasis in original).[57] The Democratic National Committee's private polling even showed that a majority of Humphrey's supporters opposed making unilateral concessions to North Vietnam.[58] Thus, forced with a need to break from the president—and running against an opponent who refused to state his own position—Humphrey decided to support a policy that he knew the public did not want.[59]

Why would Humphrey's campaign devote so much of their energy to a strategically insignificant proposal that voters opposed? How could they let this become "the sole issue of the campaign"? This behavior makes no sense if we think that the politics of foreign policy revolve around voters' policy preferences. In fact, Humphrey's aides urged him to ignore voters' policy preferences entirely, and to evaluate the political benefits of the bombing pause solely in terms of how it influenced his personal image.

Thus, in defending his recommendations on the bombing pause as chair of Humphrey's Vietnam Task Force, Samuel Huntington wrote that "what is important in the campaign is not what you say but the impression you convey by saying it."[60] When Evron Kirkpatrick summarized his polling data to Humphrey's policy committee three days before the Salt Lake City address, he argued that "a strong and vigorous policy, no matter what it is, will be better than the present one."[61] The Humphrey campaign's survey of undecided voters reached a similar conclusion: "Our investigation indicates that *any* decisive stand, *regardless* of what it is, will do Humphrey more good than harm" (emphasis in original).[62] In the words of campaign manager Lawrence O'Brien, "The great majority of people . . . don't give a damn about [Humphrey] having a position on any issue distinct from LBJ—what matters is the image of independence.[63]

The results of the Salt Lake City speech appear to have vindicated this logic. Figure 5.1 shows that Humphrey's polling numbers rapidly improved after his address.[64] On the eve of the election, Gallup and Harris both said the race was too close to call. Nixon ultimately won the popular vote by just 0.7 percentage points. Given how Humphrey's public support increased so sharply and so consistently from the Salt Lake City speech through Election Day, it is not implausible to argue that Humphrey might have won the presidency if he had taken his advisers' advice and announced the bombing pause sooner.[65]

RETHINKING THE ROLE OF VIETNAM IN THE 1968 ELECTION

The way that the Nixon and Humphrey campaigns viewed the politics of Vietnam departs from two conventional ideas of democratic politics.[66] First, it is widely assumed that leaders need to draw sharp policy contrasts in order to gain electoral advantages from foreign policy issues. Yet, the fact that Humphrey and Nixon took virtually identical positions on the Vietnam War did not prevent this issue from playing a critical role in the 1968 presidential election. Instead, we have seen that voters' concerns about Vietnam largely revolved around questions about which candidate would provide more competent wartime leadership. This was primarily a matter of evaluating candidates' personal images rather than parsing differences in their policy platforms.

Second, conventional notions of democratic politics also assume that voters should be more likely to support leaders whose views resemble their own. But the book's theoretical framework has explained why leaders can benefit from taking *un*popular policy positions, so long as those positions help to cultivate a favorable personal image. That is exactly how Humphrey and his advisers saw the political value of supporting a bombing pause in Vietnam. Public opinion data show that this strategy paid off handsomely, even if it was not enough to win the election.

The main way this case study deviates from the book's argument is that Humphrey used a dovish foreign policy position—the bombing pause—as a way to improve perceptions of his leadership strength. This was largely due to the fact that Humphrey's image of weakness was the product of his relationship with President Johnson, rather than his views of foreign policy per se. Humphrey's advisers thus believed that any break with Johnson's policies would help to demonstrate Humphrey's independence. This meant that Humphrey had no special reason to take a hawkish policy position. (If anything, breaking from Johnson in a dovish direction helped to court support among the Democrats' antiwar base, though the documents show that Humphrey's advisers believed that the bombing pause would help to improve Humphrey's image across the electorate as a whole.)

Yet, even if the politics of image-making led Humphrey to make a dovish proposal at the tactical level, the broader dynamics of the case remain consistent with the book's claim that the commander-in-chief test enables open-ended military interventions. Even though voters considered the Vietnam

War to be by far the country's most important problem in 1968—and even though Johnson's Vietnam War policy had driven him out of office—neither candidate attempted to identify a better and more popular course of action. The irony was that this behavior did not result from candidates ignoring public opinion, but rather from the fact that both candidates sought to *culti-vate* public opinion by contesting their personal images rather than debating the substance of policy issues. This process allowed Richard Nixon to enter the White House unconstrained by any promises about how he would end the war, which would last for four more years and claim the lives of twenty thousand additional US soldiers.

Nixon, McGovern, and the Paris Peace Negotiations

Voters continued to identify Vietnam as the country's most important problem throughout Richard Nixon's first term as president.[67] This political challenge was partly of Nixon's own making, given how he had pledged to deliver "peace with honor" when running for president in 1968. The fact that Nixon did not make peace during his first presidential term raised questions about Nixon's ability to deliver on his promises. The remainder of this section explains how these concerns dominated debates about Vietnam during the 1972 presidential election and how they ultimately led Nixon to prolong the United States' commitment to a failing, unpopular war.

This section presents two distinct arguments about how the politics of image-making caused Nixon to prolong US military involvement in Vietnam. The first of these arguments is that, starting in 1970, Nixon deliberately strung out the conflict in order prevent South Vietnam from collapsing before the next presidential election—and ideally to ensure that Saigon could survive for a "decent interval" of time after US withdrawal, at which point it would be harder to blame Nixon for the collapse of an ally.[68] Since this controversy took place outside of a presidential campaign, it does not meet the case selection criteria that I laid out in the book's introduction. Engaging arguments about the decent interval nevertheless adds to the chapter's analysis by showing how the politics of image-making plausibly extended the Vietnam War for at least two years. The archival record from this period also reveals how Nixon and his aides viewed the politics of the Vietnam War almost exclusively through the lens of image-making rather than maximizing voters' policy preferences. If nothing else, this material serves as a useful precursor for understanding how the Nixon administration approached the politics of Vietnam heading into the 1972 election.

After examining controversy over the decent interval, I explain how the politics of image-making impacted Nixon's handling of the Vietnam War during the 1972 presidential campaign. I show that, even though Nixon had the opportunity to make peace with Hanoi in October 1972, he deliberately delayed that settlement until he had defeated George McGovern on Election Day. I begin this discussion by explaining how the peace terms that Nixon could have obtained in October 1972 were far more popular—and, indeed, objectively better—than the concessions McGovern had proposed. Conventional theories of political strategy imply that Nixon should have had strong incentives to exploit this policy contrast. I instead demonstrate that Nixon avoided signing a peace agreement, preferring to create a vague aura of progress. I further show that this strategy was the product of Nixon's belief that specifying his intended peace terms could undermine his reputation for foreign policy competence. For the third presidential election in a row, neither presidential candidate attempted to articulate a policy for Vietnam that maximized voters' preferences, while the winning candidate campaigned on the basis of unnecessarily extending a military commitment that voters opposed.

THE "DECENT INTERVAL"

By the end of 1970, Nixon realized that he could not force Hanoi to abandon its military presence in South Vietnam. From that point on, Nixon publicly claimed that his objectives were to retrieve the US prisoners of war (POWs) and to leave the Saigon regime in a position to defend itself without assistance from US combat forces.[69] In order to achieve those objectives, Nixon was willing to accept a "cease-fire in place" that allowed North Vietnamese troops to remain in the South. A cease-fire in place would leave the Saigon regime in a precarious position. As South Vietnamese president Nguyen Van Thieu put it, "Have you ever seen any peace accord in the history of the world in which the invaders had been permitted to stay in the territories they had invaded?"[70]

Many scholars argue that Nixon knew it was impossible to prevent the fall of South Vietnam, and that he simply sought to ensure that Saigon collapsed long enough after US withdrawal such that this event did not make it look like Nixon was surrendering to communism. This thesis is consistent with the book's logic of issue-image trade-offs, because it claims that Nixon prolonged an unpopular war to preserve his reputation for foreign policy competence. There is indeed a substantial volume of evidence suggesting that the Nixon administration viewed the politics of the Vietnam War along those very lines. Here and throughout the remainder of this section, I focus primarily on describing the views of the two men who played the largest role in shaping US policy toward Vietnam: President Nixon and his national security advisor, Henry Kissinger.

It is clear that Nixon and Kissinger did not expect US withdrawal to end the fighting in Vietnam. When discussing options for withdrawal in March 1971, Nixon admitted, "of course there will still be war out there."[71] In July of that year, Nixon accepted that the fighting in Vietnam was "doomed always just to trickle out the way it is."[72] When discussing negotiations with North Vietnam in 1972, Kissinger told the president that, "If they're willing to leave Thieu in place while we get out, [then] let them go at each other afterwards."[73] As those negotiations moved toward a final settlement, Kissinger candidly informed Nixon that "assuming [this agreement] got signed, I believe the practical results will be a cease-fire, an American vindication, and return of prisoners . . . and they'll go at each other with Thieu in office."[74]

The documentary record also confirms that Nixon and Kissinger had little faith in Saigon's ability to defend itself when war resumed following US withdrawal. Debating South Vietnam's future in 1971, Nixon explained, "It's a chancy thing to know whether South Vietnam can survive. Who knows?"[75] By the summer of 1972, Nixon's assessment had grown even more pessimistic: "I look at the tide of history out there," he told Kissinger, and "South Vietnam probably can never survive anyway."[76] Heading into the final stages of peace negotiations in fall 1972, Kissinger admitted to Nixon, "I think that Thieu is right, that our terms will eventually destroy him."[77] When Nixon's top domestic policy advisor, John Erlichmann, asked Kissinger how long he expected Saigon to survive after the Paris Peace Accords went into effect, Kissinger replied, "I think that if they're lucky they can hold out for a year and a half."[78]

The documentary record further reveals that Nixon and Kissinger believed it was a political priority to defer Thieu's collapse until after the 1972 presidential election. Kissinger warned Nixon against trying to settle the war in 1971, on the grounds that "trouble can start mounting in '72 that we won't be able to deal with, and which we'll have to answer for at the elections."[79] Kissinger similarly told Nixon in March 1971 that "we can't have them knocked over brutally, to put it brutally, before the election."[80] Nixon accepted and encouraged that sentiment, telling Kissinger that, when it came to negotiating a cease-fire with North Vietnam, "you've got to remember that everything is domestic politics from now on. . . . Everything's domestic politics."[81] In a later conversation, Nixon spelled it out further: "if the ARVN [South Vietnam's military] collapses," then "a lot of other things will collapse around here."[82]

These documents support the claim that, starting around the end of 1970, Nixon sought to prolong an unpopular war in order to preserve his political image through Election Day. As historian Ken Hughes described it, "The president had more to lose by doing the popular thing (bringing American soldiers home by the end of 1971) than by doing the unpopular thing (keeping them fighting and dying in Vietnam into 1972)."[83] This logic is consistent with the book's argument about how issue-image trade-offs steer US foreign policy in an unnecessarily hawkish direction.

The most plausible defense of Nixon and Kissinger's behavior during this period is that North Vietnam was not necessarily willing to negotiate peace with the United States prior to 1972. Before 1972, Hanoi claimed it would only return US prisoners of war once Nixon had replaced Thieu with a "coalition government" that the communists would dominate. This proposal amounted to asking Nixon to overthrow an ally, and it is hard to believe that Nixon would have done that. It is, of course, possible that Nixon could have convinced Hanoi to drop this demand sooner if he had placed a higher priority on negotiations. But the most thorough account of Hanoi's decision making during this period concludes that "peace never had a chance in 1971."[84] For that reason, it is difficult to know just how much public opinion shaped Nixon's Vietnam War policies before 1972.

The documentary record is nevertheless clear about *what kind* of public opinion the Nixon administration cared about when handling the politics of the Vietnam War, and this is the central question when it comes to evaluating the book's argument. When Nixon and his top advisers debated ending the war, they did not focus on maximizing voters' policy preferences. Instead, their discussions primarily revolved around preserving Nixon's reputation for foreign policy competence, even if that required extending a war that voters no longer wanted to fight. The remainder of this section shows how similar dynamics shaped Nixon's handling of the Vietnam War as he ran for reelection.

NIXON, MCGOVERN, AND THE PARIS PEACE NEGOTIATIONS

The Democratic nominee for president in 1972, Senator George McGovern, promised a complete military withdrawal from Vietnam, Laos, and Cambodia within the first ninety days of his presidency. McGovern said that he "expected" North Vietnam to return US prisoners of war, but that he would not require Hanoi to make this concession prior to US withdrawal. McGovern also promised to cease future military aid to South Vietnam, to renounce the possibility of coming to Saigon's defense in the future, to replace Thieu with a coalition government that guaranteed a communist takeover, to end naval operations in areas adjacent to Vietnam, and to remove US forces from Southeast Asian countries such as Thailand.[85]

McGovern's proposals for handling the Vietnam War were extremely unpopular. For example, a May 1972 poll found that 75 percent of voters opposed McGovern's plan to withdraw from Vietnam without first securing an agreement for returning US POWs.[86] Surveys conducted in August showed that 64 percent of voters thought McGovern's proposals were "poorly thought out."[87] A majority of respondents (51 to 33 percent) said in a September survey that they disagreed with McGovern's plans for bringing troops home.[88] A plurality of voters (47 to 32 percent) said in October that it would be "wrong to accept" McGovern's proposed terms.[89]

Nearly every account of McGovern's campaign argues that his Vietnam policies were driven by personal convictions.[90] Yet, these proposals were not devoid of political logic. For one thing, appealing to the antiwar left helped McGovern to win the 1972 Democratic presidential nomination. McGovern also hoped that his moral clarity on Vietnam would highlight how Nixon had broken his 1968 campaign promise to end the conflict.[91] Meanwhile, McGovern sought to convince voters that Nixon was a warmonger who was bound to continue the war indefinitely if he were reelected. McGovern thus argued that the 1972 election presented voters with a choice between "four more years of war or four more years of peace."[92] Voters might have been uncomfortable with McGovern's proposed methods for ending US involvement in Vietnam, but at least they could be sure that he would stick to that promise.[93]

By October 1972, however, Nixon was not preparing for four more years of war. Instead, Nixon was entering the final stages of negotiating a peace treaty with North Vietnam. The draft treaty included concessions from Hanoi that were far more favorable to the United States than what McGovern had demanded. By October 8, Hanoi had agreed to return the POWs concurrently with US withdrawal, dropped its demand that the United States remove Thieu from power, revised its concept of a coalition government into a weaker institution that would not threaten Thieu's authority, allowed the United States to continue providing economic and military assistance to Saigon, and accepted a regional cease-fire that included Laos and Cambodia, without imposing additional restrictions on US naval activity or basing.[94] These terms avoided several unpopular concessions that McGovern had offered. Since North Vietnam did not require the United States to make any sacrifices that McGovern had not publicly accepted, it is fair to say that Nixon had negotiated a political settlement that was objectively better than what McGovern's had proposed.

Nixon and Kissinger also knew that it would be virtually impossible to extract further concessions from Hanoi. If anything, Nixon and Kissinger expected their negotiating position to deteriorate if they did not accept Hanoi's terms before Election Day, because the Congress that convened in January would almost certainly vote to terminate funding for the war.[95] Kissinger thus concluded that the October deal was "the best we're ever going to get."[96] Nixon, too, described the deal as "the best settlement we can get."[97]

Conventional ideas of democratic politics suggest that Nixon should have had strong reasons to accept this negotiated settlement. Nixon understood that the terms Hanoi offered in October 1972 were more popular than McGovern's proposals, he had no reason to believe he could extract a better deal in the future, and ending the Vietnam War would have allowed Nixon to claim that he had solved the country's most important problem. Yet, we will see that Nixon also worried that signing the deal would undermine voters' perceptions of his foreign policy competence. Thus, rather than using the Paris negotiations to draw favorable policy contrasts with his opponent, Nixon sought to keep those negotiations secret and to extend them past Election Day, with full knowledge that this delay would precipitate a new round of fighting. This episode provides another vivid example of how the politics of image-making can steer US foreign policy in a direction that is more costly and more expansive than what voters want.

"LET'S TRY OUR BEST NOT TO HAVE IT BEFORE THE ELECTION"

Nixon had two reservations about concluding a negotiated settlement before Election Day. Nixon's first concern was that he might look weak for making concessions to the communists. Nixon's second concern was that voters would not think that the deal's terms justified four years of fighting under his presidency. Nixon recounted these concerns in his memoirs, explaining that "the hawks would charge, however unfairly, that I had given away too much in order to meet a self-serving deadline, and the doves would claim, however erroneously, that I could have obtained the same terms in 1969."[98] Though Kissinger was eager to conclude a peace treaty, he accepted Nixon's logic, saying "the doves should not be able to say in October that what you did, they would have done in February of '69 and saved twenty thousand lives."[99]

These statements show that Nixon and Kissinger did not view the politics of Vietnam in terms of advancing policies that maximized voters' policy preferences: they were more concerned with how peace negotiations shaped voters' assessments of Nixon's foreign policy competence. Nixon and Kissinger's logic is also consistent with the book's explanation for why dovish foreign policies are difficult to deploy in the politics of image-making. Signing a peace treaty with North Vietnam would make it look like Nixon was backing down to an adversary without enhancing Nixon's ability to claim that he possessed good judgment.

Nixon thus instructed Kissinger not to make peace with Hanoi before November 7. "Let's try our best not to have it [a finished agreement] before the election," he said at the start of the October negotiating session. "The more that we can stagger it past the election the better."[100] Nixon made clear that this choice was solely a matter of electoral politics, telling his deputy assistant for national security affairs, Alexander Haig, that "the best of all worlds" would be "to put this damn thing off until the day after the election."[101] Nixon even considered concluding a peace deal but then asking Hanoi to keep that deal secret until after Election Day.[102] Nixon warned his aides to maintain an "absolute sphinx-like attitude on everything" associated with the negotiations, and Kissinger agreed that they should try to cultivate "four weeks of confusion" about the potential peace terms as Election Day approached.[103] Attempting to create such confusion is exactly the opposite of what Nixon should have done if his strategy revolved around showing voters that his policies matched their preferences more than McGovern's. Instead, Nixon deliberately obscured the fact that he had the opportunity to end the war on terms that were better than what McGovern had proposed.

Nixon's decision to defer peace negotiations carried predictable costs. Kissinger warned that this would result in the United States having to "bomb the bejesus out of them" only to accept a proposal that "we've always been in the position" to sign.[104] These predictions proved accurate. As negotiations stalled, Hanoi ordered its forces to expand their positions in South Vietnam to take maximum advantage of an eventual cease-fire in place. In response, the United States launched one of the most controversial military operations of the war: the so-called Christmas bombings.

The Christmas bombings were the most intense bombing campaign conducted since the Second World War. In twelve days, the United States dropped more tonnage over North Vietnam than all US bombing sorties from 1969 to 1971 combined.[105] These sorties killed more than one thousand Vietnamese civilians and incited major protests in the United States.[106] And, when the United States and North Vietnam signed the Paris Peace Accords in January 1973, those terms were virtually identical to those proposed in October.[107] Kissinger later claimed in his memoirs that the Christmas bombings helped to deflect accusations that the United States had imposed unacceptable peace terms on Saigon, but he nevertheless accepted that the changes to those peace terms were probably not significant enough to "justify the anguish and bitterness of those last months of the war."[108]

VIETNAM AS NIXON'S "GREATEST ADVANTAGE" IN THE 1972 ELECTION

Nixon ultimately succeeded in convincing voters that he would handle foreign policy issues more competently than McGovern. As the election approached, an overwhelming majority of voters (71 to 14 percent) said that they thought Nixon would do more than McGovern to keep the United States' defenses strong.[109] A similar proportion of voters (70 to 14 percent) said they thought Nixon would deal more effectively with China and the Soviet Union, and a wide majority of voters (57 to 26 percent) said that Nixon would be more likely to "move the world closer to peace."[110] These responses cannot be attributed solely to anti-McGovern bias, as McGovern polled well on several domestic policies and personal attributes.[111]

Perhaps most importantly, roughly two-thirds of voters believed Nixon was doing "all he can" to end the Vietnam War (64 percent agree, 22 percent disagree),[112] while a majority of voters consistently said that they approved of how Nixon was handling the conflict overall.[113] Thus, even as Nixon was attempting to prevent peace negotiations from succeeding, most voters trusted that he was working responsibly to bring that conflict to a close.[114] As Nixon aide Harris Teeter noted in an August 1972 polling summary, Vietnam was "the issue on which the President has the greatest advantage [over McGovern] in terms of his perceived ability to handle it," whereas McGovern's greatest weakness was his perceived "lack of competence."[115]

Of course, the costs of deferring peace negotiations until January 1973 were small compared to the costs of the war overall. But the case nevertheless stands out as a clear example of how the politics of image-making can distort US foreign policy. By the fall of 1972, Nixon had a clear path to ending the Vietnam War on terms that were better and more popular than what his opponent had proposed. Nixon understood that he could not negotiate a better settlement, and he knew that prolonging negotiations would precipitate a new round of fighting. And, when Nixon and his advisers decided to extend negotiations past Election Day, they candidly explained how their main priority was to preserve Nixon's personal image rather than to maximize voters' policy preferences.

How the Politics of Image-Making Shaped the Vietnam War

This chapter examined the politics of US involvement in Vietnam during the 1964, 1968, and 1972 presidential elections. Though it would be implausible to argue that public opinion was the sole or even the principal factor driving US policy towards Vietnam throughout this period, I have shown that the politics of image-making contributed to the escalation and continuation of a strategic disaster. There are three principal reasons why these cases support the book's argument.

First, the chapter explained how none of the six presidential nominees from 1964 to 1972 attempted to develop policy positions that appealed to voters on their merits. In 1964, Lyndon Johnson and Barry Goldwater both supported escalating US involvement in Vietnam, even though they knew that voters opposed escalation. In 1968, Richard Nixon deliberately avoided explaining how he would handle the Vietnam War while Hubert Humphrey endorsed an unpopular bombing pause. In 1972, George McGovern bucked voters' preferences by recommending unilateral withdrawal from Vietnam, and Richard Nixon deliberately prolonged the war even though he had already negotiated peace terms that were more favorable than what McGovern had suggested.

None of these leaders behaved in a manner that is consistent with conventional ideas about how political strategy revolves around drawing popular policy contrasts. Moreover, none of these behaviors can be explained by saying that leaders had no choice but to support unpopular policies in Vietnam. We saw that most voters did not support Lyndon Johnson's decision to go to war in Vietnam, that most voters did not support Humphrey's bombing pause, and that Nixon's decision to prolong the conflict through the 1972 election was simply unnecessary.

Instead, the chapter showed how five of the six presidential nominees dealt with the Vietnam War in a manner that was primarily driven by image considerations. Barry Goldwater hoped that his proposals to escalate US military involvement in Vietnam would help him to portray Lyndon Johnson as being a weak leader. Johnson pursued congressional authorization to use force in Vietnam in order to rebut charges that he was soft on communism. Richard Nixon refused to articulate his plan for handling Vietnam in 1968 because voters already thought that he was more competent than Hubert Humphrey. Humphrey advocated the bombing pause to demonstrate his decisiveness. And when Nixon ran for reelection in 1972, he avoided signing a negotiated settlement because he feared this settlement would raise doubts about his handling of the war. George McGovern was the only presidential nominee described in this chapter who plausibly oriented his Vietnam War platform around doing what he thought was in the national interest—and, by all accounts, McGovern's Vietnam policies contributed to his losing the 1972 election in a historic landslide.

Finally, the chapter supports the book's argument about how the politics of image-making enable open-ended military interventions. In 1964, Johnson sought to bolster impressions of his leadership strength by requesting authorization to fight a war that voters opposed. In 1968, Humphrey and Nixon both declined to offer substantive proposals for ending an unpopular war. In 1972, Nixon deliberately prolonged the conflict in order to prevent voters from questioning his foreign policy competence. Altogether, these patterns show how image-making can influence electoral strategy in a manner that conventional notions of democratic politics do not capture. Chapter 6 will show how similar dynamics surrounded debates about the conduct of the Iraq War.

Staying the Course

How George W. Bush Turned an Unpopular War into a Political Asset

Elections are usually about attributes, not issues.
—George W. Bush's 2004 campaign manager, Ken Mehlman

This chapter examines the politics of the Iraq War during the 2004 presidential election, in which President George W. Bush defeated Democratic senator John Kerry. In addition to meeting the book's case selection criteria of examining presidential elections where foreign policy issues had unusually high salience, this case provides a unique opportunity to test the book's argument with both qualitative and quantitative evidence. For qualitative evidence, the chapter draws on firsthand accounts from Bush's and Kerry's campaign advisers that explain how each team developed its strategy for debating the Iraq War. For quantitative evidence, the chapter examines data from the National Annenberg Election Study (NAES). The NAES spans more than eighty thousand interviews conducted over thirteen months. It was the largest academic survey ever conducted during a presidential campaign, and it provides exceptionally granular insights about the role that personal images and policy issues played in shaping voters' attitudes toward Bush and Kerry.

The chapter advances four claims. First, I show how Bush translated his hawkish positions on the Iraq War into a clear indication of leadership strength, even though voters generally disagreed with how Bush had handled the war. Second, I explain how Kerry tried to portray Bush's handling of the Iraq War as reflecting poor judgment, but also how this argument was too nuanced to be effective. Stated in terms of the book's theory, I therefore argue that Kerry's judgment-oriented message was less evaluable than Bush's claims about leadership strength.

The chapter's third claim is that voters' (generally positive) perceptions of Bush's leadership strength outweighed voters' (generally negative) perceptions of how Bush had handled the Iraq War in explaining the outcome of the 2004 presidential vote. Finally, I show that this trade-off between issues and images only broke in Bush's favor late in the campaign, in a manner that almost surely reflected the success of Bush's political strategy. The politics of the Iraq War during the 2004 presidential election thus provide another example of how issue-image trade-offs favor foreign policy hawks.

Firsthand Accounts from Campaign Advisers

The 2003 invasion of Iraq generated enormous controversy. Several of the United States' core allies objected to the war. President Bush based his public case for war on the claim that Iraq was developing weapons of mass destruction, but it quickly became clear that this claim was mistaken. And though the Bush administration publicly predicted that the conflict would be quick and cheap, it had to maintain a large-scale troop presence to stabilize the country.

Public opinion surveys throughout the summer and fall of 2004 show that voters generally disapproved of how President Bush had handled the Iraq War. The Roper Center's iPoll database contains fifty-three national polls on this topic that were administered from July 2004 until the presidential election on November 2. The proportion of voters who disapproved of Bush's handling of the war exceeded the proportion of voters who approved of Bush's handling of the war in forty-three of those surveys, by an average margin of 52 to 45 percent.[1] A similar margin of voters said throughout this period that they did not believe the Iraq War had been worth the cost.[2]

Conventional ideas of how public opinion shapes foreign policy suggest that the Iraq War should have hurt President Bush's prospects for reelection. If voters thought that Bush had not done a good job of handling that conflict, then how could the war have been a political asset for him? The answer to this question is that both campaigns treated the politics of the Iraq War as a vehicle for conveying foreign policy competence—and that those debates helped Bush convince voters that he was a strong leader.

This section relies on firsthand accounts provided by Bush's and Kerry's campaign strategists. Though political operatives often have incentives to conceal the true reasoning behind their decisions, there are four main reasons to believe that the arguments described in this section are credible. First, Bush's and Kerry's advisers agree on all of this section's key points. This makes it hard to believe that Bush's and Kerry's advisers constructed a narrative designed to suit partisan or personal ends. A second reason to doubt the claim that this narrative has been engineered after the fact is that the Bush campaign made its strategy explicit from the start. Shortly after Kerry secured the Democratic presidential nomination, Bush's advisers told the media that they would portray Kerry's positions on the Iraq War as indications of weak leadership. A third reason to believe the accounts described in this section is that they do not always present the campaigns' actions in a sympathetic light. Both campaigns explained how they deliberately pivoted voters' attention away from substantive policy questions in order to cultivate their candidates' personal images. Finally, the second half of this chapter will confirm that this section's key claims are consistent with survey data that capture political attitudes over the course of the 2004 presidential campaign.

BUSH'S STRATEGY: THE IRAQ WAR AS AN INDICATION OF LEADERSHIP STRENGTH

Bush's campaign manager, Ken Mehlman, articulated his campaign strategy by explaining that "elections are usually about attributes, not issues."[3] And, consistent with the book's theory, Mehlman therefore argued that "issues are lenses through which voters look and make a judgment about an individual candidate."[4] Mehlman further explained how the Bush campaign believed that "the president's attribute that would be most important and relevant to voters was the fact that he was a strong leader, particularly a strong leader at a time when the country faced a war."[5] Mehlman thus designed Bush's strategy for reelection around the premise that "the election was going to fundamentally be about leadership and national security."[6] "What was always important to us," Mehlman explained, "was that we always won on the strong leadership question."[7] Bush's chief campaign strategist, Matthew Dowd, described a similar belief that voters "were very reluctant to make that jump between 'I may not like all his policies' to 'I want to replace him.'"[8]

It would be one thing to argue that the Bush campaign believed their candidate's reputation for strong leadership helped to deflect criticism for how he had handled Iraq. In that case, voters' attitudes toward Bush's Iraq policy and his personal traits might be independent factors that just so happened to push voters in opposite directions. But the Bush campaign believed they could burnish Bush's reputation for strong leadership *as a result* of his Iraq policies and not just in spite of the way he had handled the war. Stated in terms of the book's theoretical framework, Bush's campaign viewed the politics of the Iraq War as an issue-image trade-off.

In particular, Bush's advisers believed that his commitment to the war in Iraq demonstrated a willingness to "stick to his guns" in the face of public criticism. Bush's communications director, Nicolle Devenish, argued that the campaign's most important message was that "you may not always agree with me, but you'll always know where I stand."[9] That was, in fact, the first argument that Bush invoked in his first presidential debate with John Kerry, when asked to explain why he would do a better job of protecting the country from terrorism. "I understand everybody in this country doesn't agree with the decisions I've made," Bush replied. "But people know where I stand. . . . The best way to defeat them [terrorists] is to never waver."[10]

Bush's campaign placed these claims front and center in its public messaging.[11] Bush's director of advertising, Mark McKinnon, argued that Bush's unwillingness to back down in the face of criticism was his primary political asset during the 2004 election. McKinnon thus recounts that the primary goal of Bush's campaign advertisements was "to articulate the idea that, even if you didn't like this guy, you knew where he stood, you knew what he believed, you knew where he was headed."[12] The slogan that the Bush campaign used most often to promote this message was "Steady Leadership in Times of Change." When asked to summarize the most important message that the campaign aimed to convey through those advertisements, Bush's media adviser Tucker Eskew simply replied, "strong leader."[13]

KERRY'S STRATEGY: THE IRAQ WAR AS AN INDICATION OF POOR JUDGMENT

Kerry drew no significant policy contrasts with Bush in terms of how he would manage the Iraq War moving forward. Though Kerry said he would try to withdraw all US combat troops from Iraq during his first term as president, this four-year time frame went beyond anything that the Bush administration had publicly suggested. At one point, Kerry even criticized Bush for attempting to withdraw US troops from Iraq too quickly.[14] Kerry's chief campaign strategist, Robert Shrum, later wrote that the principal difference between the two candidates' approaches to Iraq was that Kerry would rely more heavily on assistance from allies, but Shrum acknowledged that Kerry never explained what that meant.[15] Whatever role the Kerry campaign hoped the Iraq War to play in the 2004 presidential election, it could not have involved appealing to voters' policy preferences.

Kerry's advisers agreed with their opponents that voters' dissatisfaction with the Iraq War was less important than broader assessments of foreign policy competence. Kerry's campaign manager, Mary Beth Cahill, explained that "throughout this whole race, voters wanted a change in policy, and it was clear to us, not necessarily a change in leadership."[16] Shrum agreed that strong leadership was "what I think the campaign was ultimately about."[17] Kerry's communications adviser, Bill Knapp, argued that "they [voters] wanted the policies of this administration changed but the leadership was a different issue. . . . We had to constantly fight to reassure people that we were going to be good on that dimension." These quotes are all consistent with the book's argument that foreign policy debates are dominated by the politics of image-making rather than appealing to voters' policy preferences.

Kerry's main strategy for undermining perceptions of Bush's foreign policy competence was to argue that Bush's handling of the war reflected poor judgment. Kerry argued that the Bush administration had prematurely jumped to conclusions about Iraq's presumed weapons of mass destruction programs, and that the White House had rushed to war without securing support from key allies. Kerry's campaign channeled these arguments through advertisements in which he claimed that "to win the war on terror, we have to be tough and smart," while promising that Kerry would make the United States "stronger at home, respected in the world."[18] After Bush argued in a presidential debate that his Iraq policy revealed strong leadership, Kerry responded: "I believe in being strong and resolute and determined, and I will hunt down and kill the terrorists, wherever they are. But we also have to be smart." He continued by hammering home the importance of having a commander in chief who combined strong leadership with good judgment: "This president has made, I regret to say, a colossal error of judgment. And judgment is what we look for in the president of the United States of America."[19] These quotes are all consistent with the book's argument that hawkish foreign policies expose leaders to critiques for possessing poor judgment.

WHY BUSH'S STRATEGY WORKED: STRENGTH, JUDGMENT, AND EVALUABILITY

To summarize, the Bush and Kerry campaigns both believed that their candidates' positions on the Iraq War were less important than what those positions implied about the candidates' fitness to be commander in chief. Both campaigns saw Bush's reputation for leadership strength as his best political asset. Both campaigns believed that this reputation stemmed from Bush's hawkish foreign policy. And both campaigns designed their messages about Iraq to shape voters' perceptions of the candidates' personal traits, rather than to draw policy contrasts on how they would handle the Iraq War moving forward.

The firsthand accounts of Bush and Kerry's advisers are also consistent with my argument about why the commander-in-chief test favors leaders who use hawkish policies to craft impressions of leadership strength. Throughout this book, we have seen how it is much harder for leaders who criticize hawkish foreign policies to demonstrate that they possess good judgment. Kerry indeed struggled with this challenge throughout the 2004 presidential campaign.

Kerry's main obstacle on this front was that he had voted to authorize the invasion of Iraq in October 2002. Kerry claimed that he had only voted to authorize the war to enhance Bush's leverage for reaching a peaceful settlement with Saddam Hussein. Kerry also argued that, even if Congress had given Bush the legal authority to invade Iraq, that did not excuse mishandling intelligence or conducting the invasion without greater support from US allies. These arguments involved a level of nuance that the Bush campaign could easily portray as waffling or disingenuousness. And Bush's advisers recognized from the start of the campaign that this dynamic worked to their advantage. Shortly after Kerry secured the Democratic nomination, Bush's top aides gave on-the-record interviews explaining how they planned to portray Kerry as a "flip-flopper" for the way that he seemed to have shifted his stances on the war.[20]

The most concrete example of Kerry's alleged flip-flopping involved his decision to vote against an October 2003 bill that provided $87 billion in supplemental war funding. Kerry initially supported the bill, but he also criticized the bill's reliance on deficit financing. Kerry proposed a revenue-raising amendment to cover the $87 billion, he promised to oppose a bill that was not revenue neutral, and he kept that promise when his amendment was rejected. Since the funding bill passed the Senate by an overwhelming margin of 87–12, Kerry's vote was nothing more than a symbolic protest. This episode nevertheless handed the Bush campaign an opportunity to portray Kerry as being weak on national defense. The day after Kerry secured the Democratic nomination, the Bush campaign began to highlight Kerry's vote on the $87 billion in advertisements saying that he opposed funding that US soldiers needed for critical items such as body armor. Bush's attacks on this issue led Kerry to make a now-infamous statement that "I actually did vote for the $87 billion before I voted against it." As Bush's advertising chief Mark McKinnon put it at the time, "You don't get gifts like that very often."[21]

It is important to note that Kerry's positions on the Iraq War were, in fact, coherent and consistent throughout the 2004 presidential campaign. Congress' decision to authorize the war did not justify the White House's handling of intelligence, its poor prewar planning, its decision to invade Iraq without more support from allies, or its choice to finance the war with debt. Kerry's position on the $87 billion was defensible on its merits, especially since voters generally agree that the government should avoid raising the deficit. And protest votes are a standard legislative practice. The notion that Kerry's vote on the $87 billion reflected indecisive "flip-flopping" was largely a matter of optics—a product of the fact that Kerry's positions did not fit into crisp soundbites.[22] Kerry sought to trivialize this problem in a debate with Bush by saying, "When I talked about the $87 billion, I made a mistake in how I talk about the war. But the president made a mistake in invading Iraq. Which is worse?"[23]

Both campaigns agreed that Kerry's mistake was worse from a political standpoint. Bush's campaign manager, Ken Mehlman, explained that Kerry's comments about the $87 billion gave Bush a golden opportunity to frame the 2004 election as a contrast of "constancy versus inconstancy."[24] Kerry's campaign manager Mary Beth Cahill explained that Kerry's position was so hard to articulate that any attempt to defuse accusations of flip-flopping would only reinforce concerns that Kerry's positions were disingenuous.[25] Kerry's senior advisor Joe Lockhart similarly believed that the substance of Kerry's positions was less important than their lack of clarity. "My point to him," Lockhart recounted, "was, great, if we can sit every voter down and take the ten minutes that just took [to explain why Kerry's positions made sense], we're gonna be fine. Absent that, it was too easy to distort."[26]

These accounts are all consistent with my theory of how the politics of image-making generally favor foreign policy hawks. Kerry's argument about possessing better judgment than Bush depended on nuance, and nuance is inherently difficult to communicate. By contrast, Bush's argument about being a stronger leader than Kerry relied on the simple claim that he had "stuck to his guns" in the face of public criticism. The fact that Bush's message lacked nuance was exactly why it was effective. Both presidential campaigns believed that this advantage helped Bush to convince voters that he would be a more effective commander in chief.

BUSH'S AUGUST SURGE

In addition to agreeing on why Bush held a political advantage with respect to the politics of the Iraq War, both campaigns' strategists held similar views about when and how that advantage developed heading up to the 2004 election. In particular, both campaigns agree that a quirk in campaign finance laws gave Bush a special opportunity to craft his leadership message starting in August.

Bush and Kerry had both accepted public financing for their general election campaigns. This meant that neither campaign could spend more than $75 million once their candidate accepted his party's nomination. By tradition, the party that does not control the White House holds its convention first. In most election years, the gap between conventions is only one or two weeks. In 2004, however, the Republicans scheduled their nominating convention five weeks after the Democrats' (August 30 versus July 26). During this time, the Bush campaign could spend money that it had raised during the primaries without drawing down its $75 million war chest for the general election.[27]

This funding imbalance gave Bush a unique opportunity to dominate campaign messaging. Kerry's chief strategist, Robert Shrum, recounts the campaign's deliberations on this matter: "If we hoped to be competitive with Bush in the fall, then, we had agreed, August for us had to be the month without advertising money."[28] Kerry's media advisor Tad Devine later said "If there is one lesson to learn for Democrats [from the 2004 presidential campaign], it's not to let that happen again. Do not give an incumbent president an advantage of five weeks of a general election where you have to spend general election money and they spend primary money. That is too big of an advantage."[29]

August was also the month when a political action committee called Swift Boat Veterans for Truth began running advertisements that received widespread media attention. The "Swift Boat ads" alleged that Senator Kerry had misrepresented his military service in Vietnam and argued that Kerry had betrayed his fellow soldiers through his subsequent antiwar activism.

Though many of the Swift Boat ads' factual claims were false or exaggerated, they made it harder for Kerry to leverage his war record as a basis for appealing to voters. Kerry's advisers later said that it was a mistake not to respond to those attacks more forcefully, but that they felt they could not spare the resources to do so given their temporary financing disadvantage.[30] Thus, in addition to agreeing that voters prioritized personal images over policy issues in the 2004 presidential campaign, Bush's and Kerry's advisers offer a common narrative about how that trade-off broke in Bush's favor at a specific point in time, and for a specific reason: the Bush campaign dominated the national conversation in August, and they used that opportunity to undermine perceptions of Kerry's leadership strength.

To be clear, I am not arguing that Bush won the election by gaming campaign finance laws. My theory predicts that Bush's message of leadership strength was always bound to end up dominating Kerry's message about good judgment. The value of understanding Bush's August messaging advantage is to explain why this time period offers a unique opportunity to test whether Bush's political strategy worked. If that were the case, then we would expect to see Bush's advantage on perceptions of leadership strength surge in August, and we would expect this shift to primarily reflect voters losing faith in Kerry's capabilities. The firsthand accounts from Bush's and Kerry's advisers thus generate testable predictions about how voters' attitudes shifted in specific ways at specific times due to specific elements of campaign strategy.

USING FIRSTHAND ACCOUNTS TO GENERATE TESTABLE CLAIMS

This section used firsthand accounts from Bush and Kerry's campaign advisers to develop four testable claims. The first of these claims is that perceptions of leadership strength explain Bush's 2004 vote share better than perceptions of how Bush had handled the Iraq War. The idea that personal images matter more than foreign policy issues is consistent with the book's core argument about issue-image trade-offs.

Both sets of campaign advisers also believed that leadership strength was more closely associated with Bush's electoral success than any other personal attribute. Confirming this claim would help to show that leadership strength played a predominant role in the 2004 election, and that voters who saw Bush as a strong leader were not simply "saying nice things" about a candidate whom they supported for other reasons. If that were the case, then we would have no reason to expect that perceptions of Bush's leadership strength would be more correlated with his margin of victory than perceptions of other personal traits.

The third testable claim developed in this section is that Bush's advantage on leadership strength surged in August, during a period when Bush held a unique advantage for shaping national debates. Confirming this element of the campaign advisers' narrative would provide evidence that Bush's political strategy mattered.

Finally, we saw how both campaigns believed that Bush's August surge primarily reflected voters losing faith in Kerry's leadership strength. This presumed asymmetry—the notion that Kerry lost more ground after the start of August than Bush gained—provides an additional avenue for distinguishing this section's narrative from other factors. If voters' assessments of leadership strength simply reflected them justifying a preference for Bush that they held for other reasons, then we would expect voters to become more likely to express positive views toward Bush at least as much as they became less likely to hold positive views of Kerry. By contrast, if the data confirm that Bush's August surge primarily reflected voters losing faith in Kerry's leadership, then that would provide additional evidence of how voters responded to the specific message that the Bush campaign promoted at a specific time.

Evidence from the National Annenberg Election Survey

This section tests the four hypotheses that I developed from firsthand accounts of the 2004 presidential campaign by examining evidence drawn from the National Annenberg Election Survey. I begin by describing why the NAES data set is uniquely useful for this purpose. Next, I describe how I use a statistical concept called "level importance" to gauge the extent to which different political attitudes can explain the outcome of the 2004 presidential election. Consistent with expectations, these data show that leadership strength was more closely associated with Bush's margin of victory than his handling of the Iraq War or any other personal attribute. My analysis also confirms that Bush's perceived advantage as a strong leader developed in August, and that this surge primarily resulted from voters losing faith in Kerry's leadership. The chapter's qualitative and quantitative evidence thus reinforce a common narrative of how President Bush turned the Iraq War into an asset for the purposes of political image-making, despite the fact that voters generally disapproved of how he had handled that conflict.

HOW VOTERS PERCEIVED BUSH AND KERRY

The 2004 National Annenberg Election Survey is a collection of 81,422 telephone interviews. It was, by far, the largest academic public opinion survey ever administered during a presidential election.[31] An especially valuable feature of these data is that they capture voters' attitudes throughout the 2004 presidential campaign, whereas most academic public opinion surveys provide snapshots of single moments. This "rolling cross-section" research design makes it possible to examine how political attitudes change over time: a property that is crucial for evaluating the firsthand accounts provided

117

by Bush's and Kerry's campaign advisers. No other data set provides remotely comparable leverage for conducting such analysis.

Every NAES survey asked voters to say which presidential candidate they supported or which candidate they had already voted for. I use these data to code a variable called "Bush support." This variable takes a value of one if a respondent supported President Bush and zero if the respondent supported Senator Kerry. Following convention, I drop observations of respondents who supported third-party candidates, who did not register a candidate preference, or who said they did not vote.[32] Political scientists use the term "two-way vote share" to describe such data. According to that metric, 51.8 percent of NAES respondents supported Bush over Kerry on Election Day. This figure is very close to Bush's actual two-way vote share of 51.2 percent.

Most NAES surveys asked voters to say whether or not they approved of how President Bush had handled the Iraq War. I used this question to create an index of Iraq War approval. This data point takes a value of 1 if the respondent approved of Bush's handling of the war, 0 if the respondent disapproved of Bush's handling of the war, and 0.5 if voters had no opinion on the matter. This index has an average value of 0.43 across the NAES data set, confirming that voters generally disapproved of how Bush had handled the invasion of Iraq.

Most NAES surveys asked respondents to describe the extent to which they thought Bush and Kerry would be strong leaders. Respondents rated each candidate independently on scales ranging from zero ("not at all") to ten ("extremely"). I used these data to create a leadership strength index, which captures the difference between Bush's leadership rating and Kerry's leadership rating. Bush outperformed Kerry on this metric by 0.53 points across the NAES data.

Table 6.1 shows how NAES surveys asked voters to rate Bush and Kerry with respect to ten additional attributes, such as "trustworthy" or "knowledgeable."[33] I reverse-coded ratings for undesirable attributes, such that positive scores always reflect views that are more favorable to Bush. Table 6.1 reveals substantial variation in how respondents assessed the candidates' personal attributes. Five of the eleven attributes that the NAES studied favored Bush, five favored Kerry, and one was a statistical tie. This shows that NAES respondents were not simply saying nice things about their favored candidates. Instead, the data reveal voters drawing systematic distinctions among personal attributes that Bush and Kerry appeared to possess or to lack.

Table 6.1 also shows that the candidates' personal images were consistent with the firsthand accounts from Bush's and Kerry's advisers. Bush held his largest lead when it came to voters' perceptions of who would be a strong leader, and who would be less likely to "say one thing and do another." In the context of the 2004 campaign, the latter rating almost surely reflects the perception that Bush "stuck to his guns" whereas Kerry was a "flip-flopper." We have seen that this was Bush's core message regarding leadership

Table 6.1 NAES descriptive statistics

	Mean	95% confidence interval
Iraq War approval	0.43	[0.43, 0.44]
Says one thing, does another	0.66	[0.59, 0.72]
Strong leader	0.53	[0.46, 0.60]
Easy to like	0.32	[0.26, 0.39]
Trustworthy	0.08	[0.01, 0.15]
Inspiring	0.06	[0.00, 0.13]
Shares my values	0.04	[−0.03, 0.12]
Out of touch	−0.24	[−0.31, −0.18]
Cares about people like me	−0.39	[−0.46, −0.32]
Arrogant	−0.54	[−0.60, −0.48]
Knowledgeable	−0.74	[−0.80, −0.68]
Reckless	−0.85	[−0.91, −0.79]

"Iraq War approval" reflects the proportion of NAES respondents who approved of how Bush had handled the Iraq War. All other indices in table 6.1 present the average difference in how respondents rated Bush and Kerry on ten-point scales. I have oriented those scales such that positive values always reflect views more favorable to Bush.

strength. By contrast, Bush's least favorable attribute was recklessness, which is consistent with how Kerry criticized Bush's decision to invade Iraq as reflecting poor judgment.

LEVEL IMPORTANCE

The descriptive statistics in table 6.1 tell us that Bush and Kerry had distinct personal images. Yet, those statistics do not tell us how much those images affected the outcome of the 2004 presidential election. The natural tool to use for this purpose is the concept of "level importance."[34] Level importance is the product of two factors: a candidate's overall advantage on some index (like the ones shown in table 6.1) and the extent to which that index predicts vote choice. Multiplying these figures together allows us to attribute different fractions of a candidate's vote share to specific political attitudes.

Level importance provides information that we cannot glean directly from standard statistical analyses of political behavior. For example, one of the best predictors of how citizens vote tends to be whether or not they approve of how the incumbent president is handling the economy. But if voters are evenly split in assessing whether the president has done a good job of handling the economy, then this factor would not confer an electoral advantage to either candidate. By contrast, we might find that voters' attitudes toward something else—say, whether a candidate seems like a strong leader—explain relatively little variation in individual vote choice. But if one candidate seems like a much stronger leader than the other, then this could end up swinging a significant number of votes in their direction.

As with the book's previous analyses of observational data, we have to be careful about using level importance to draw causal inferences. Political scientists thus primarily rely on level importance as a tool for gauging the comparative salience of political attitudes. If nothing else, level importance allows researchers to identify which political attitudes bear a closer relationship than others to voters' collective behavior. For example, Adam Berinsky's book *In Time of War* uses level importance statistics to understand which armed conflicts have impacted presidential voting more than others.[35] Berinsky's analysis includes a discussion of how attitudes about the Iraq War predicted President Bush's vote share in 2004. This section extends Berinsky's work by comparing the level importance of the Iraq War approval index to the level importance of other political attitudes during the 2004 presidential campaign. The appendix provides a fuller description of this methodology for readers interested in the details.

ISSUES AND IMAGES IN THE 2004 PRESIDENTIAL ELECTION

Figure 6.1 presents level importance statistics for fifteen political attitudes during the 2004 presidential election. This analysis indicates that voters' general disapproval of the Iraq War can explain 0.64 percentage points of Kerry's overall vote share. Voters' perceptions of leadership strength appear to have been roughly twice as impactful, capturing 1.21 percentage points of Bush's vote share.[36] This comparison supports the narrative provided by Bush's and Kerry's campaign advisers, who argued that perceptions of leadership strength explained the outcome of the 2004 presidential race better than perceptions of how Bush had handled the Iraq War. Figure 6.1 also supports the campaign advisers' claims about how perceptions of leadership strength were more closely associated with Bush's vote share than those of any other personal attribute. In fact, we see that leadership strength explains more than twice the amount of Bush's vote share as his next most favorable attribute ("easy to like").[37]

None of the level importance estimates in figure 6.1 explains more than one or two percentage points of vote share, and that may not seem like much. Yet, a one- or two-percentage-point change in vote share can easily determine the balance of a presidential election. It is certainly the kind of advantage for which we would expect presidential candidates to fight. The firsthand narratives described earlier in this chapter confirm that these fights played a central role in both campaigns' political strategies.

BUSH'S AUGUST SURGE

So far, this section has confirmed that leadership strength was President Bush's most favorable attribute during the 2004 presidential campaign and

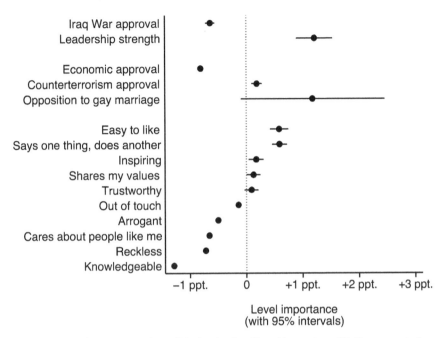

Figure 6.1. Level importance for political attitudes. "Level importance" is the amount of Bush's vote share that we can attribute to a given political attitude.

showed that this advantage substantially outweighed voters' disapproval of how Bush had handled the Iraq War. Yet, these patterns do not, by themselves, show that Bush's strategy worked. Voters might have entered the 2004 election season with predetermined views about how Bush was a strong leader. In that case, campaign debates about the Iraq War might have had no impact on the candidates' personal images.

This is why it is important to analyze dynamic changes in voters' political attitudes over time. The first half of the chapter developed two hypotheses on this front based on firsthand accounts from Bush's and Kerry's advisers. First, I explained how both campaigns believed that Bush gained a decisive advantage in August. Confirming this claim would refute the notion that voters' perceptions of the candidates' personal attributes were fixed in advance of the 2004 presidential campaign. Second, I explained how both campaigns believed that Bush's August advantage was particularly associated with Kerry seeming like a weak leader. This would show that voters were not simply praising their favored candidates and criticizing their opponents, but rather that voters reacted to the specific content of the Bush campaign's political message. The NAES data's rolling cross-section design is ideally suited for testing these predictions. I conducted these tests by

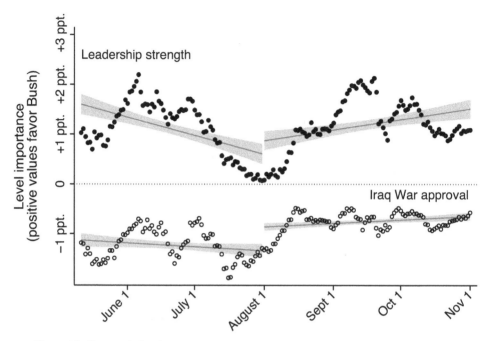

Figure 6.2. Changes in level importance over time.

analyzing every two-week window of data from May 2004 through Election Day.[38]

The results of this analysis are exactly what one would expect given the firsthand accounts from Bush's and Kerry's advisers. Figure 6.2 shows that Bush entered the campaign with an advantage in perceived leadership strength, but this advantage faded from May through July, during the period when Kerry was making headway in criticizing Bush's handling of the Iraq War. By July, Bush's advantage on leadership strength had dwindled to a level that was statistically indistinguishable from zero, and it was substantially outweighed by voters' disapproval of how Bush had handled the invasion of Iraq. On balance, we could say that this trade-off between issues and images favored Kerry in midsummer.

These dynamics shifted immediately at the start of August, just as Bush's and Kerry's advisers claimed. To show this shift, figure 6.2 compares linear trend lines in the data before and after August 1. The difference in these trend lines is substantively significant: it is equivalent to Bush expanding his national vote share by 0.6 percentage points per month, which amounted to a total gain of 1.8 percentage points by Election Day.[39] This shift in vote share was substantively significant: in fact, it accounts for nearly all of Bush's 2.4-percentage-point margin of victory in the popular vote.

The data show that voters' attitudes toward the Iraq War also shifted in Bush's favor at the start of August. But that shift was four times smaller than the corresponding trend break for leadership strength.[40] This comparison confirms the firsthand accounts from Bush's and Kerry's campaign advisers, who argued that Bush's August surge was particularly associated with perceptions of his leadership strength, which was exactly the message that his campaign was promoting at the time.

The data also reveal that Bush's advantage on leadership strength surged in August more than in any other month. To test that claim, I looked for trend breaks in the data at the start of July, September, and October. Once again, I compared trends before and after the start of each month, and I estimated the degree to which those trends differed. When examining leadership strength, I found that the trend break for August was nearly three hundred times larger than the trend break for any other month. (See the appendix for details.) These comparisons provide further evidence that the Bush campaign gained special momentum in August, when it was in a position to dominate national political discourse.

The data additionally confirm that Bush's August surge primarily reflected voters losing faith in Kerry's leadership. To demonstrate this point, figure 6.3 plots the moving average of each candidate's leadership ratings over time.[41] These data show that, by the end of July, voters saw Bush and Kerry as being virtually identical with respect to leadership strength. Kerry's leadership strength ratings then cratered at the start of August. From that point forward, Kerry lost an average of 0.22 points per month on the NAES leadership strength index.

By comparison, the trend lines in perceptions of Bush's leadership strength remained fairly consistent throughout the summer: the start of August corresponds to a small acceleration in Bush's gains on this rating scale, amounting to just 0.08 percentage points per month. Altogether, the shift against Kerry was thus nearly three times larger than the shift in favor of Bush.[42] Moreover, no other month reveals a trend break that is anything close to the degree to which Kerry's leadership ratings collapsed in August. (Again, see the appendix for details.) These findings provide additional evidence that perceptions of Bush and Kerry shifted at exactly the right time and in exactly the right manner that we would anticipate given firsthand accounts from the candidates' political advisers.

Reinterpreting the Politics of the Iraq War

Viewed in isolation, I do not believe that either the quantitative or the qualitative evidence presented in this chapter would confirm my argument about the relationship between issues and images in the 2004 presidential

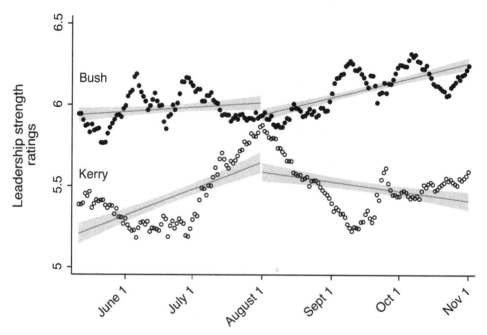

Figure 6.3. Changes in Bush's and Kerry's leadership ratings over time. Each data point represents a two-week moving average centered on a given date.

campaign. The judgment of campaign operatives can be fallible, and my discussion of their views relied primarily on after-the-fact explanations rather than the kinds of contemporaneous archival records that I examined in the book's previous chapters. And my analysis of observational survey data cannot, by itself, sustain causal claims. When combined, however, the chapter's qualitative and quantitative evidence help to cover each other's weaknesses. Together, they show that President Bush translated his unpopular handling of the Iraq War into favorable impressions of his leadership strength—thereby turning a foreign policy that voters opposed into a political asset that helped him to win reelection.

Several studies have already argued that perceptions of leadership strength played an important role in the 2004 presidential campaign.[43] This chapter's analysis adds to that scholarship in three principal ways. First, I described how political attitudes shifted over the course of the 2004 campaign, whereas most existing studies focus on survey data gathered near Election Day. To my knowledge, this chapter presents the first study that tracks changes in the electoral significance of issues and images over time.[44] I argued that these changes provide important analytic leverage for evaluating the effectiveness of Bush's campaign strategy.

Second, when other scholars analyze the roles that leadership strength and Iraq War approval played in shaping the 2004 presidential election, they often portray these topics as being independent of each other. These studies sometimes give the impression that Bush's image of leadership strength helped him to win reelection *despite* his generally unpopular handling of the Iraq War. By contrast, I have argued that Bush won reelection partly *because* debates about the Iraq War helped him to convince the public that his leadership qualities were superior to Kerry's.[45]

The work that most closely resembles this chapter's analysis comes from the book *The American Voter Revisited*, by Michael Lewis-Beck, William Jacoby, Helmut Norpoth, and Herbert Weisberg. These scholars argue that debates about the Iraq War shaped public perceptions that Bush was a strong leader while making Kerry seem like a flip-flopper.[46] "What is remarkable," they write, "is that while [voters'] policy responses on war and peace were mostly unfavorable to Bush, the personal responses were mostly favorable." In other words, *The American Voter Revisited* identifies the politics of the Iraq War during the 2004 presidential campaign as constituting what this book would call an issue-image trade-off. Yet, Lewis-Beck and his colleagues also say that it is unusual for voters' perceptions of issues and images to diverge, and they acknowledge that they cannot explain why this would be the case. These authors even speculate that their findings may be misleading, because their analysis of personal attributes involved open-ended survey data and their analysis of attitudes toward the Iraq War involved closed-ended survey data. These data are not directly comparable, because the kinds of people who take the time to answer open-ended survey questions may not be representative of voters writ large. Lewis-Beck and his colleagues thus caution readers not to draw too much from their analysis of issues and images in the 2004 presidential campaign.

My analysis goes beyond *The American Voter Revisited* in several ways. I explained why Bush was able to use an unpopular policy issue as a tool for crafting a favorable personal image. I showed that Bush's advisers deliberately pursued that strategy from the start of their campaign. I developed hypotheses for testing when and why Bush's strategy worked. I confirmed those hypotheses by analyzing a large-scale data set from which I only examined closed-ended survey questions. And, rather than portraying these political dynamics as an idiosyncratic feature of the 2004 presidential campaign, I explained how the relationship between Bush's handling of the Iraq War and perceptions of leadership strength is consistent with a broader theory of how public opinion shapes US foreign policy.

The chapter's final contribution thus involves placing the 2004 campaign into a broader theoretical and historical perspective. Most existing treatments of how the Iraq War shaped the 2004 election are highly context specific. For instance, Helmut Norpoth and Andrew Sidman have argued that the Iraq War helped to extend the "rally effect" that Bush enjoyed after the 9/11 terrorist attacks.[47] Jennifer Merolla and Elizabeth Zechmeister have made related claims about how the 9/11 attacks caused voters to attach special importance to leadership strength in the 2004 presidential election.[48] And, throughout this section, we have seen how many observers thought that Kerry's complex positioning on the Iraq War made him uniquely susceptible to charges of being indecisive.

Though I see no reason to doubt any of those claims, this chapter has also shown that debates about the Iraq War during the 2004 election fit broader patterns that generalize across the politics of US foreign policy. By now, I hope that readers will not be surprised to see that leaders do not always view unpopular foreign policies as political liabilities. The way that Bush used debates about the Iraq War as an indication of his leadership strength resembled the way that many other leaders used hawkish policy positions to cultivate favorable personal images. And Kerry's struggle to dent Bush's personal image was consistent with the book's argument about how it is inherently difficult for leaders to convey evaluable messages about good judgment. Seen in light of the book's broader argument, the 2004 campaign provides another example of how the politics of US foreign policy revolve around personal images and not just policy issues, and how those politics tend to favor foreign policy hawks. Chapter 7 shows how that same pattern holds across a wider range of US military interventions after the Cold War.

Image-Making in an Age of Endless Wars

The Politics of Military Intervention in Bosnia, Iraq, Afghanistan, and Libya

> They'd rather have someone who is strong and wrong rather than somebody who is weak and right.
>
> —President Bill Clinton

So far, this book has developed a new theory of how the politics of image-making shape US foreign policy. I tested that theory with sixty years of survey data, three preregistered survey experiments, and seven case studies. The book's analysis has focused on presidential elections in which foreign policy issues were highly salient, because elections provide the best opportunities to test my theory against other ideas for how public opinion shapes the politics of foreign policy. This chapter demonstrates that my argument applies to a broader set of contexts by explaining how the politics of image-making have shaped US military interventions after the Cold War.

To do that, I examine Bill Clinton's 1995 use of force in Bosnia, Congress' 2002 vote to authorize the Iraq War, Barack Obama's 2009 escalation of the war in Afghanistan, and Obama's 2011 choice to topple Muammar Qaddafi's regime in Libya. All of these events took place outside of presidential campaigns. Most of them occurred in environments where presidents were primarily focused on domestic programs, which helps to demonstrate that my argument does not solely apply to cases where foreign policy issues have high public salience. The chapter's discussion of the Iraq War also shows how the politics of image-making can influence congressional behavior, not just presidential decision making.

I will show that all of these cases fit a common pattern in which elected officials made choices designed to cultivate or maintain impressions of leadership strength, even when that required steering US foreign policy in a direction that was more hawkish than what voters wanted. To be clear, this chapter does not claim that the politics of image-making are the sole reason why the United States embarked on a series of controversial military interventions throughout the post–Cold War era. My goal is instead to push back against widespread notions of how the United States' recent string of "endless wars" have been undemocratic events that are largely disconnected from public opinion. Instead, I argue that this history provides further indication of how the relationship between public opinion and US foreign policy is more extensive—and more problematic—than the conventional wisdom assumes.

Bill Clinton and Bosnia

Bill Clinton was elected president in 1992, less than a year after the Soviet Union disbanded. Many foreign policy analysts believed that Clinton should have taken that opportunity to reap a "peace dividend" by reducing the country's overseas commitments.[1] Clinton nevertheless deployed US military power for humanitarian purposes in Haiti, Bosnia, and Kosovo. Clinton's decision to send twenty thousand ground troops to stop Bosnia's civil war was particularly significant, because it set a precedent for intervening in conflicts that had little direct relevance for US national security, and which would previously have been viewed as regional matters.[2] Clinton's national security advisor, Anthony Lake, later said that Bosnia occupied more of the administration's time and energy than any other foreign policy issue.[3]

Clinton's embrace of humanitarian intervention is frequently portrayed as a product of ideology and elite influence.[4] In these accounts, Washington's foreign policy establishment encouraged Clinton to aggressively promote liberal values, despite the fact that the public hoped to downsize its foreign policy commitments following the Soviet Union's collapse. This section offers a different narrative that places public opinion at the center of Clinton's decision making. I present this narrative in three parts.

First, I describe how Clinton took a hawkish stance on Bosnia during the 1992 presidential campaign. Though this stance was not particularly popular with voters, Clinton saw this issue as a vehicle for arguing that President George H. W. Bush had been overly complacent in managing international affairs. Next, I explain how Clinton attempted to delay intervening in Bosnia at the start of his presidency, and how that behavior amplified accusations that Clinton was incompetent at handling international affairs. Finally, I explain how Clinton came to believe that deploying military force to Bosnia would help to solve his perceived leadership crisis in advance of running for reelection in 1996.

BOSNIA AND THE 1992 PRESIDENTIAL CAMPAIGN

When Clinton ran for president in 1992, he faced widespread doubts about his fitness to be commander in chief. Clinton would be the first president since Calvin Coolidge who had no military experience, and Clinton's opponents accused him of having dodged the draft during the Vietnam War. By contrast, incumbent president George H. W. Bush had been a decorated bomber pilot in World War II, ambassador to the United Nations, envoy to China, director of the Central Intelligence Agency, and vice president of the United States. Bush's handling of the 1991 Gulf War had also been very popular. In the aftermath of that conflict, Bush's approval rating reached 89 percent, which was the highest level that Gallup had ever recorded.

Clinton's campaign determined that winning the presidency under these circumstances required focusing voters' attention on domestic policy and the economy. But Clinton and his advisers also believed they needed to identify a few foreign policy issues where they could claim that Bush had come up short. Their logic resembled the book's previous description of how John F. Kennedy exploited his stance on defense spending while running for president in 1960. In both cases, presidential challengers with limited foreign policy experience took hawkish foreign policy positions that allowed them to accuse incumbents of complacency, while implying that they could provide strong leadership in international affairs.[5] Clinton's top foreign policy adviser, Anthony Lake, later explained that logic as follows: "The point of it all . . . [was] that you weren't going to be able to politically deal with Bush on foreign policy issues if you didn't lay out your own views and in a way take it to him, get a jab in his face. Because otherwise, Clinton, like any candidate, would not pass what is, I think, the central test on foreign policy issues, and that is simply to demonstrate some level of competence."[6]

Bosnia was one of the issues that Clinton selected for this purpose. Clinton accused Bush of "remaining silent and paralyzed" in the face of the ethnic cleansing carried out by Serbian forces.[7] "It is time for real leadership," Clinton argued, "to stop the continuing tragedy in the former Yugoslav republics."[8] In order to provide that leadership, Clinton suggested that he would adopt a policy called "lift and strike." This policy involved removing the US embargo on arms transfers to Bosnia and then conducting airstrikes against Serbian positions.

Clinton's public statements reflected his advisers' encouragement to use Bosnia as a tool for shaping perceptions of the candidates' leadership qualities. For example, Richard Holbrooke argued that Bosnia presented a unique opportunity to portray Bush's leadership as being "weak and inadequate" and to show that Clinton would pursue "more vigorous" foreign policies that conveyed "real leadership."[9] Nancy Soderberg later explained the campaign's decision to take a hawkish stance on Bosnia by saying that "what you need to do in a foreign policy campaign—if you're not an incumbent president or vice president—is demonstrate that you can go to the mat with the incumbent on foreign policy and you're not afraid to challenge his views."[10] Sandy Berger similarly recounted how the campaign used Clinton's Bosnia policy as a tool for disarming criticisms that their candidate was not tough enough to be commander in chief. "In a sense," Berger explained, "we got to the right of Bush on Bosnia, and we were tougher on Bosnia than Bush was."[11]

Image-making considerations were certainly not the only reasons why Clinton took assertive positions on Bosnia. Several Clinton advisers believed the end of the Cold War presented new opportunities to promote liberal ideals. Lake, in particular, had argued for decades that US foreign policy should be guided by moral values and not just by traditional concerns about national security or economic interests.[12] Yet, the relevant question for this book's purposes is not whether decision makers believed their positions were justified on the merits, but why they thought those stances would be politically useful. During the 1992 presidential campaign, the political value of Clinton's positions on Bosnia revolved around conveying Clinton's leadership strength.[13]

It is also worth noting that Clinton's team found their position on Bosnia politically useful despite the fact that voters were largely apathetic about that issue. The most extensive analysis of public opinion on Bosnia, conducted by Richard Sobel, shows that a minority of Americans supported using force in that country.[14] Voters did not necessarily oppose intervening in Bosnia, either—rather, the mass public appeared essentially indifferent about how to handle this situation. Clinton's stance on Bosnia thus reflects the book's logic of how leaders can use foreign policy issues to bolster their personal images, even when voters do not agree with those policies on their merits.

CLINTON'S LEADERSHIP CRISIS

Clinton's need to demonstrate leadership strength grew throughout his first two years in office. Throughout this period, Clinton faced a raft of unfavorable media coverage about how he seemed uncomfortable interacting with the military and how he was uninterested in dealing with foreign policy issues.[15] Clinton made this problem worse by not implementing the lift-and-strike policy that he had originally proposed for Bosnia. The key obstacle to fulfilling this campaign promise came from European allies who had deployed soldiers to Bosnia to coordinate humanitarian relief. These soldiers were not prepared for intense combat, and their governments feared that Serbs would retaliate in the aftermath of any attempts to escalate NATO involvement in the conflict. European leaders therefore said that they would only accept lift and strike if the United States deployed its own troops to Bosnia. Unwilling to put boots on the ground or to provoke a crisis with his European partners, Clinton deferred making major decisions with respect to Bosnia for the first two years of his presidency.[16]

Clinton's job performance ratings suffered through these controversies. In February 1993, 65 percent of voters said they supported Clinton's handling of foreign policy. By June, that number was down to 38 percent.[17] Clinton's approval rating on foreign policy remained low for the next two years.[18] According to veteran journalist Elizabeth Drew, Clinton's pollsters told him that, even if foreign policy issues were not most voters' top priority, "the public did want a president to demonstrate competence in foreign policy," and that "the lack of public confidence in his management of foreign policy spilled over into a lack of confidence in his Presidency as a whole."[19]

MILITARY INTERVENTION IN BOSNIA

Clinton deployed US troops to Bosnia in August 1995. In the months leading up to this decision, internal debates about Bosnia were shaped by concerns about how the crisis was undermining the president's personal image. National Security Advisor Lake wrote a memorandum to the president arguing that the administration's "weak, muddle-through strategy in Bosnia was becoming a cancer on Clinton's entire foreign policy."[20] UN Ambassador Madeleine Albright circulated a similar assessment, claiming that the administration's Bosnia policy "makes the President appear weak" to an extent that was "destroying our foreign policy domestically and internationally."[21] Numerous other sources describe Clinton reacting to the politics of the Bosnia crisis by saying "we look weak," or "I don't look strong here," that "everything in foreign policy is seen through the prism of Bosnia," and that he was "getting creamed" on the issue.[22] It is worth repeating that voters did not actually support intervening in Bosnia at the time. Clinton's perception that he was "getting creamed" on Bosnia is thus consistent with the book's argument about how the politics of image-making do not simply track voters' policy preferences, and how leaders thus feel pressured to make foreign policy decisions that are more hawkish than what voters actually want.

Clinton believed that his apparent weakness in foreign policy was one of the main factors that could prevent his reelection in 1996.[23] Clinton's campaign manager, Dick Morris, shared that concern. In a memorandum that outlined key principles for securing a second term as president, Morris urged Clinton to "use foreign policy situations to demonstrate your strength and toughness to the American people."[24] Morris believed that taking decisive action in Bosnia was particularly important for "repairing the public's perception of the president's weakness."[25] According to Clinton's political advisor George Stephanopoulos, Morris made that argument repeatedly and explicitly, to the point of saying that Clinton should "bomb the sh[—] out of the Serbians to look strong."[26] Lake suspected that Clinton was open to this advice. As Lake later explained it, "Clearly the President was more and more concerned with what [Bosnia] was doing to the administration's political image on foreign policy issues. And I was saying to him this is a cancer on foreign policy. So he was very open to efforts to resolve it."[27]

Clinton's Republican opponents escalated political pressure for intervening in Bosnia by crafting a hawkish Bosnia policy of their own. In January 1995, Senate Majority Leader Bob Dole introduced a bill that would force Clinton to lift the embargo on arms transfers to Bosnia.[28] Dole was widely expected to be the Republican nominee for president the next year. Just as Clinton had originally recommended lifting the embargo in order to portray President Bush as being complacent in 1992, Dole framed his proposal as an attack on Clinton's leadership abilities. "The bottom line," Dole argued, "is that since the war in Bosnia began, America has been a follower, not a leader."[29] When Congress passed Dole's bill by large majorities in August, Democratic senator John Kerry called it "a significant repudiation of the president's policy and his lack of involvement."[30] Though Clinton vetoed the bill, his advisors warned that Congress would likely override that veto when it reconvened after Labor Day.

Most accounts of Clinton's decision making with respect to Bosnia agree that the looming confrontation with Congress pushed him to take decisive action on his own authority.[31] As Stephanopoulos recounts it, "Clinton could sustain a veto and avoid a political defeat only by forcing a peace in Bosnia now."[32] In order to secure European support for airstrikes in Bosnia, Clinton agreed to deploy US troops as part of a new peacekeeping force. NATO's bombing campaign commenced on August 30, less than a week before Congress resumed session.

INTERVENTION IN BOSNIA AS AN ISSUE-IMAGE TRADE-OFF

The politics of image-making were certainly not the only reason why Clinton decided to intervene in Bosnia. Clinton appears to have been genuinely horrified by Bosnia's ethnic violence, particularly after Serbs killed eight thousand civilians in Srebrenica in July 1995. Croatia's successful offensive against Serbian forces in early August also enabled US intervention by making the Serbians more amenable to a negotiated settlement. And US intervention did, in fact, help bring Bosnia's civil war to a close with the signing of the November 1995 Dayton Accords. Today, the Dayton Accords are widely viewed as one of the most important foreign policy achievements of Clinton's presidency. It would be implausible to say that Clinton intervened in Bosnia simply so that he could craft an image of leadership strength.

The purpose of this discussion is instead to explain why Clinton believed that intervening in Bosnia would appeal to mass public opinion at all. Even though voters did not support conducting airstrikes or sending ground troops to Bosnia, it appears that Clinton expected that those actions would help to shake the idea that he was incompetent at managing US foreign policy. And this strategy appears to have worked as Clinton and his advisers had hoped.

According to the Roper Center's iPoll database, Clinton's foreign affairs approval rating was 39 percent over the three months prior to the announcement of US intervention in Bosnia in August 1995. That rating climbed to 47 percent in the three months following that decision, and 49 percent over the first six months of 1996.[33] Clinton's chief of staff, Mack McLarty, later explained how, even though the decision to use force in Bosnia went against the polls, it allowed Clinton to craft an image of competence. "Ultimately the people in the country want a winner in the sense of somebody who can get things done," McLarty argued. "In the end, that's probably where people cast their ballot."[34]

Clinton drew a similar conclusion from the experience. According to journalist Bob Woodward, "Clinton a number of times voiced fascination that while 60 percent of the public had opposed the deployment of US troops to Bosnia, public approval of his foreign policy went up, not down, after he ordered the deployment anyway." Woodward then described how Clinton explained that phenomenon in a manner that closely resembled the book's logic of issue-image trade-offs. "He saw," Woodward wrote, "that toughness and decisiveness were appreciated even if people disagreed."[35] In his own words, Clinton thus perceived the use of force in Bosnia as an issue-image trade-off.

Why Did Congress Authorize the Iraq War?

This section examines the politics behind Congress' decision to authorize the invasion of Iraq in October 2002. I begin by explaining how voters were receptive to the idea of toppling Saddam Hussein's regime, but how they also wanted President George W. Bush to secure support from allies before doing so. Then I describe how the Bush administration pushed back against demands for multilateralism by associating the invasion of Iraq with strong leadership in the aftermath of the 9/11 terrorist attacks. This argument was particularly relevant to congressional leaders who could have made the war's authorization contingent on gaining support from international allies, or who could have simply delayed authorizing the war until Bush had tried to build a broader coalition. Even though this position would have been consistent with voters' policy preferences, constraining the Bush administration's ability to invade Iraq would have made congressional leaders look weak on national security. As Bill Clinton later summarized it: "When people are feeling insecure, they'd rather have someone who is strong and wrong rather than somebody who is weak and right."[36]

This section does not argue that public opinion was the sole reason why the United States invaded Iraq. In particular, I do not argue that the book's theory explains why the Bush administration chose to topple Saddam Hussein's regime. This section instead focuses on the specific question of why Congress granted Bush the authority to invade Iraq on a unilateral basis in October 2002, even though that was not what voters wanted at the time. This case provides another example of how issue-image trade-offs influence US foreign policy, while also showing how the book's argument applies to congressional politics, and not just to the behavior of presidents and presidential candidates.

PUBLIC OPINION AND THE INVASION OF IRAQ

Congress authorized the invasion of Iraq on October 10, 2002. At the time, polls showed that 55 percent of Americans supported taking military action to remove Saddam Hussein from power. But most Americans were also skeptical of invading Iraq on a unilateral basis. The Roper Center's iPoll database contains fourteen surveys conducted in the year before the invasion of Iraq that asked voters to say whether they would support going to war without securing cooperation from allies, whether they would support going to war conditional on securing cooperation from allies, or whether they opposed going to war either way. On average, 36 percent of voters said that they would support going to war without cooperation from allies, 21 percent supported going to war with allied assistance, and 37 percent opposed invading Iraq under either condition. The iPoll database contains another eighteen surveys conducted in the year prior to the war that specifically asked about invading Iraq with or without approval from the United Nations. On average, just 34 percent of voters said they would support invading Iraq without UN approval. A related series of five polls taken in the two months prior to the war's authorization asked voters to say how important it was to gain UN approval before invading Iraq. An average of 57 percent of Americans said this was "very important." These patterns are consistent with decades of survey data showing that Americans generally oppose the unilateral use of military force.[37]

Yet, when the United States overthrew Saddam Hussein in March 2003, the United Kingdom was the only ally who provided significant material assistance to the war effort.[38] The Bush administration's decision to overrule voters' preferences for multilateralism proved to be quite costly: given how the war had such devastating consequences for the United States, Iraq, and the broader Middle East, it is reasonable to conclude that the United States would have been better off building a multilateral coalition before toppling Saddam Hussein's regime, or else avoiding the invasion entirely.

This view is not simply the product of hindsight. When the Bush administration asked Congress to authorize the invasion in October 2002, both parties' legislators were skeptical of going to war on a unilateral basis.[39] The Democratic chairman of the Senate Armed Services Committee, Carl Levin, drafted a resolution that would require President Bush to obtain UN approval before going to war. The chairman of the Senate Foreign Relations Committee, Joe Biden, drafted his own resolution that would require Bush to return to Congress to explain why war was necessary if the United Nations refused its endorsement. Two of Biden's Republican colleagues on the

Foreign Relations Committee, Richard Lugar and Chuck Hagel, cosponsored Biden's resolution. The *Washington Post* endorsed the Biden-Lugar-Hagel resolution.[40] If nothing else, Congress could simply have delayed voting to authorize the war until the Bush administration had made a greater effort to obtain multilateral support.[41]

Congress nevertheless voted in October 2002 to grant the Bush administration unconditional authority to invade Iraq. Even Senators Biden, Lugar, and Hagel ultimately voted for unconditional authorization. In order to understand the politics of invading Iraq, we thus need to know why Congress decided to overlook voters' preferences to build a multilateral coalition before attacking Saddam Hussein. The remainder of this section explains how that behavior is consistent with the book's theory of issue-image trade-offs.

THE CONGRESSIONAL POLITICS OF THE IRAQ WAR

During the summer and fall of 2002, the Bush administration engaged in an extensive public relations campaign designed to associate the invasion of Iraq with strong leadership in the global war on terrorism. In his public speeches, Bush argued that "we must take the battle to the enemy," and claimed that "failure to act would embolden other tyrants," potentially provoking new waves of state-sponsored terrorism.[42] Even though Iraq had no practical connection to Al Qaeda, the Bush administration's rhetoric convinced most Americans that those threats were somehow related, and that they deserved to be treated with similar urgency.[43]

Once the Bush administration had framed the Iraq War as an act of strong leadership in the global war on terrorism, it could portray opponents of the war as being weak on national security. Ronald Krebs and Jennifer Lobasz have explained how leaders who sought to restrain the Bush administration's authority to go to war exposed themselves to charges of tolerating terrorism—or even of tolerating evil itself.[44] Jane Kellett Cramer offers a similar analysis of how the Bush administration portrayed any effort to constrain its ability to invade Iraq as being unpatriotic.[45] It is important to note that these dynamics are distinct from arguing that the Bush administration convinced the US public to support the war on its merits. Krebs's, Lobasz's, and Cramer's arguments are important because they explain how the Bush administration framed the war in a manner that pressured congressional leaders to give the Bush administration the authority to conduct the invasion on a largely unilateral basis, even if that is not what voters wanted at the time.

These dynamics were especially painful for congressional Democrats heading into the 2002 midterm elections.[46] Voters generally saw the Republican party as being stronger than the Democratic party on national security issues. With 9/11 at the forefront of voters' minds, congressional Democrats feared giving Republicans any additional leverage to claim that they were weak on national security. These arguments would be especially damaging to

Democrats who planned to run for president in the near future, including Joe Biden, Hillary Clinton, and John Kerry. If these Democrats opposed a war that ultimately went well for the United States, then that would hand Republican opponents an opportunity to argue that they would be too reluctant to use military force if elected as commander in chief.

This concern was not hypothetical—in fact, it was a widely accepted political lesson of the 1991 Gulf War, which most congressional Democrats had opposed. When the United States subsequently won the Gulf War in decisive fashion, Republicans argued that Democrats' reluctance to support the conflict revealed that they were weak on national security. Democratic senator Sam Nunn was particularly candid about how he believed his "no" vote on the Gulf War cost him a chance to run for president. "I knew perfectly well," Nunn later explained, "that the position I had taken on the war in the next election would become the major debating point."[47]

By contrast, if congressional Democrats voted to authorize a war that went poorly, they could always blame the Bush administration for misusing its authority. John Kerry later claimed that he thought the Iraq war resolution would improve Bush's leverage at the United Nations (and thus that voting to unconditionally authorize the war would make it easier to build a multilateral coalition).[48] Joe Biden later argued that he thought the Iraq war resolution would indicate the United States' resolve to Saddam Hussein (thereby potentially lowering the chances that the United States would end up going to war at all).[49] Hillary Clinton later said that she would not have voted for the war if she had known that the Bush administration would invade before UN weapons inspections were complete.[50] While all three of these senators later said that they regretted their vote, they also argued that the Bush White House bore primary responsibility for the war because it had misled the public about intelligence on Saddam Hussein's weapons of mass destruction programs and because Bush had not exhausted diplomatic options before invading Iraq.

The politics of Congress' Iraq War vote thus reflect the book's argument about why the dynamics of image-making favor foreign policy hawks. Voting to authorize the war allowed members of Congress to send a clear and immediate indication that they were strong on national security.[51] And the open-ended nature of the Iraq War authorization gave those leaders an opportunity to deflect future accusations that they lacked good judgment. These incentives made it politically appealing for Congress to grant the Bush administration the authority to invade Iraq on a unilateral basis, even if that is not what voters wanted at the time.

IRAQ WAR AUTHORIZATION AS AN ISSUE-IMAGE TRADE-OFF

Were congressional Democrats simply convinced that invading Iraq was the right thing to do? If so, then one would not need to invoke the politics of image-making to understand why Congress authorized the war in October 2002. The main reason to be skeptical of this argument is that Congress held an unusually perfunctory debate about whether to invade Iraq. Congress received the crucial National Intelligence Estimate (NIE) documenting Iraq's presumed weapons of mass destruction programs just three days before opening debate on the Iraq war resolution. Only 6 out of the 535 members of Congress read the NIE.[52] Congress then debated the Iraq war resolution for six days. For comparison, the same Congress had spent eighteen days debating a farm bill, nineteen days debating a trade bill, twenty-one days debating education reform, and twenty-three days debating energy policy.[53]

This behavior is not consistent with the notion that congressional leaders carefully deliberated the merits of backing the Levin or Biden-Lugar-Hagel resolutions over White House opposition and ended up deciding to support a controversial position on its merits. Instead, Congress' attempt to minimize debate over the Iraq war resolution is exactly what one would expect to see if congressional leaders were aiming to shield themselves from charges of being weak on national security while avoiding public statements that could later be used to question their judgment. This behavior resembled the way that Lyndon Johnson rushed an open-ended authorization to use force in Vietnam through Congress while running for president in 1964. As one Senate Foreign Relations Committee staffer explained it, "We had an election coming up. The Democrats were afraid of being seen as soft on Saddam or on terrorism. The whole notion was, 'Let's get the war out of the way as fast as possible.'"[54]

Another plausible critique of this section's argument is that it might not have mattered a great deal if Congress had forced the Bush administration to make greater efforts to build a multilateral coalition before authorizing the war. Yet, it is almost certainly the case that deferring this vote until spring 2003 would have made it easier for Congress to oppose the invasion. Between November 2002 and March 2003, international inspectors conducted nearly one thousand visits to more than five hundred sites that were reportedly involved in producing weapons of mass destruction. Since Iraq was not producing weapons of mass destruction, these inspections found no evidence to support the Bush administration's stated justification for going to war. Meanwhile, several pieces of intelligence that the Bush administration used to make its public case for war were debunked, such as the claim that Saddam Hussein had acquired uranium from Niger or that he was preparing to use remotely piloted vehicles to conduct terrorist attacks in the United States. It was also clear by the spring of 2003 that the Bush administration had conducted negligible planning for postinvasion operations and that it had developed only cursory estimates of the war's prospective time and cost.

If Congress had deferred war authorization for just a few months, then it could have held this debate without the political constraints imposed by a looming election. That would have mitigated the pressure congressional

Democrats felt to convey strong leadership just a few weeks before voters went to the polls. Delaying the war vote would also presumably have reduced congressional leaders' ability to use a vague resolution as a tool for deflecting concerns about their judgment. If the Bush administration had returned to Congress after failing to assemble a multilateral coalition, then congressional leaders could not have justified their votes by claiming that they expected the United States' allies to support the invasion of Iraq. The Bush administration appears to have recognized these dynamics, which is one reason why the White House pressured Congress to conclude its debate before the 2002 midterms.[55]

Congress' decision to grant unconditional authorization for war in October 2002 thus represented a significant turning point in the war's politics. If Congress had instead adopted the Levin or Biden-Lugar-Hagel resolutions, that would not only have been consistent with public preferences for multilateralism, but it would have given Congress a subsequent opportunity to challenge arguments for war that grew increasingly tenuous over time. If Congress had simply decided to delay voting on the Iraq war resolution until after the 2002 midterms, that alone would have strengthened the leverage of the war's opponents while reducing political pressure to take military action. This political pressure was consistent with the dynamics of issue-image trade-offs that we have seen throughout the book.[56]

Barack Obama and the "Washington Playbook"

When Barack Obama ran for president in 2008, he promised to end the Iraq War and to reduce the degree to which US foreign policy revolved around the use of military force. Yet, by the time Obama left office in 2017, many observers were disappointed that he had not made deeper changes to the United States' global role. For example, even though President Obama withdrew US forces from Iraq, he did so on the timetable that had previously been established by President George W. Bush.[57] Meanwhile, Obama escalated the war in Afghanistan and overthrew Libya's government. According to Charles Kupchan, Obama's tenure as commander in chief thus demonstrated to many voters that the era of "sustained strategic overreach" would not end with the Bush administration.[58] Andrew Bacevich similarly argues that "it was during [Obama's] presidency that the very idea of war termination vanished from national security circles. The concept of 'forever wars' took hold."[59]

This section shows that the politics of image-making encouraged President Obama to implement the Afghan Surge and to intervene in Libya. In both cases, we will see that decisions about the use of force became litmus tests for gauging Obama's leadership strength, and that this link between issues and images encouraged Obama to take foreign policy positions that were more hawkish than what voters wanted.

In December 2009, President Obama announced that he had decided to "surge" US forces to Afghanistan. This involved deploying an additional thirty thousand soldiers as well as shifting US strategy from a relatively limited focus on counterterrorism toward a long-term, resource-intensive counterinsurgency campaign.[60] The Afghan Surge was a key turning point in the conflict, escalating US involvement in a losing cause that would ultimately become the longest-running war in US history.

The Afghan Surge proposal originated with the commander of international forces in Afghanistan, General Stanley McChrystal. Contemporary reporting and participant memoirs agree that Obama was initially skeptical of McChrystal's surge strategy, instead preferring a proposal from Vice President Joe Biden to keep US involvement in Afghanistan limited to a narrower counterterrorism mission.[61] Nearly all accounts of the Afghan Surge decision stress that Obama then faced significant political pressure to approve McChrystal's plan.

This pressure became particularly acute after McChrystal's troop request leaked to the *Washington Post*.[62] This leak was widely viewed as an attempt to force Obama to accept McChrystal's proposal, by making it clear that the military supported a significant escalation of US involvement in Afghanistan.[63] McChrystal amplified this pressure by publicly comparing Biden's counterterrorism proposal to fighting a fire "by letting half the building burn down," and by declaring that he would not support a presidential decision to implement Biden's idea.[64] Meanwhile, Chairman of the Joint Chiefs of Staff Michael Mullen and head of Central Command David Petraeus publicly endorsed the Afghan Surge.[65] Secretary of Defense Robert Gates later wrote that "virtually everybody in the Obama White House saw this as blatant lobbying designed to force the president to approve more troops."[66] In Obama's telling, "[White House Chief of Staff] Rahm [Emanuel] remarked that in all his years in Washington, he'd never seen such an orchestrated, public campaign by the Pentagon to box in a president. Biden was more succinct: 'It's f[—]ing outrageous.' I agreed."[67]

In a 2016 interview, Obama explained how the military's efforts to "jam" him into approving the Surge were aided by the foreign policy establishment's broader tendency to support militarized responses to foreign policy challenges. According to Obama, "There's a playbook in Washington that presidents are supposed to follow. It's a playbook that comes out of the foreign-policy establishment. And the playbook prescribes responses to different events, and these responses tend to be militarized responses. . . . [Y]ou get judged harshly if you don't follow the playbook, even if there are good reasons why it does not apply."[68]

On its face, Obama's description of the "Washington Playbook" resembles standard theories of elite influence: when seemingly credible experts support a foreign policy decision, then that creates public pressure for presidents to follow suit. Yet, despite military leaders going public with their support for the Afghan Surge, voters did not support the idea. According to seventeen polls in the Roper Center's iPoll database that were administered in the two months prior to Obama's announcement of the Afghan Surge, voters leaned against sending additional forces to Afghanistan by an average margin of 52 to 42 percent. If the foreign policy establishment wielded public pressure to support the Afghan Surge, then that pressure must have involved a channel besides shaping voters' policy preferences. The book's theoretical framework suggests that this pressure involved linking debates about the Afghan Surge to broader questions about President Obama's leadership qualities.

Consistent with this claim, critics portrayed Obama's skepticism toward the Afghan Surge as an indication that he was a weak commander in chief. These criticisms revolved around the idea that Obama was "dithering" and "indecisive" because he held nine meetings over three months before deciding to approve the Afghan Surge.[69] McChrystal amplified those critiques by giving a *60 Minutes* interview in which he claimed that President Obama had only spoken to him once since he took command.[70] These remarks contributed to perceptions at the White House that the military was trying to portray Obama as being out of his depth in dealing with national security. As then CIA director (and subsequent secretary of defense) Leon Panetta later described it, "Obama was a new president, a Democrat without military experience. For him to defy his military advisers on a matter so central to the success of his foreign policy would have represented an almost impossible risk."[71]

A prominent example of this image-oriented pressure campaign comes from an October 2009 *New York Times* essay written by David Brooks.[72] In that essay, Brooks described interviewing several military experts about the Afghan Surge. Brooks reported that these experts were "largely uninterested" in debating the Afghan Surge on its merits. "They are not worried about [Obama's] policy choices," Brooks wrote. "Their concerns are more fundamental. They are worried about his determination." Brooks continued:

> Their first concerns are with Obama the man. They know he is intellectually sophisticated. They know he is capable of processing complicated arguments and weighing nuanced evidence. But they do not know if he possesses the trait that is more important than intellectual sophistication and, in fact, stands in tension with it. They do not know if he possesses tenacity, the ability to fixate on a simple conviction and grip it, viscerally, and unflinchingly, through complexity and confusion. They do not know if he possesses the obstinacy that guided Lincoln and Churchill, and which must guide all war presidents to some degree. . . . The experts I spoke with describe a vacuum at the heart of the war effort—a determination vacuum.

Brooks's essay vividly captures the book's core argument. As Brooks described it, foreign policy experts placed a lower priority on debating the merits of policy issues than on assessing President Obama's leadership strength. And he argued that Obama could not allay doubts about his leadership strength unless he shifted US foreign policy in a direction that was more hawkish than what voters wanted.

One might be inclined to dismiss such examples as small parts of a broader public discourse. Yet, President Obama also described the politics surrounding the Afghan Surge as placing concerns about his leadership strength over substantive policy debate. According to Deputy National Security Advisor Ben Rhodes, Obama asked his advisers, "Why is this whole thing being framed around whether I have any balls?"[73] Assistant Secretary of Defense Derek Chollet similarly recounts Obama's view that many "politicians and pundits proclaimed the need to be 'strong' and 'decisive' seemingly just for the sake of doing so, with little regard for what that actually meant in practice. . . . He believed that too often [in Washington], strength is explained as bold action with military might, and acting in the name of being 'tough.'"[74] When Obama discussed this episode in his memoir, he did not write about how he felt pressured to support the Afghan Surge in order to accommodate voters' policy preferences. Instead, he described how "columnists accused me of 'dithering' and questioned whether I had the intestinal fortitude to lead a nation during wartime."[75]

Of course, saying that the Obama administration felt political pressure to approve the Afghan Surge is not the same as demonstrating that such pressure played a decisive role in their decision making. Obama later claimed that he came around to the view that it was necessary to augment US forces in Afghanistan. But Obama also wrote that no one ever provided a convincing explanation for why the Afghan Surge required so many troops. Instead, Obama described those troop levels as being primarily driven by "ideological and institutional concerns rather than by the objectives we'd set."[76] Why would Obama approve a risky counterinsurgency strategy that he saw as placing ideological and institutional concerns over substantive considerations? The evidence suggests that Obama felt that he could not push back more forcefully against these arguments without exposing himself to charges of being a weak leader.

The main purpose of this section, however, is not to estimate how much public opinion contributed to the Afghan Surge decision. Instead, I have advanced three claims. The first of these claims is that Obama's White House believed that political pressure pushed in the direction of sending more forces to Afghanistan. Second, I have shown that this political pressure did not reflect voters' policy preferences. Instead, I argued that political pressure to support the Afghan Surge stemmed primarily from the way that military officials and foreign policy elites connected policy disputes to broader concerns about President Obama's leadership qualities. The Afghan

Surge debate is thus consistent with the book's broader argument about how the politics of image-making pushes US foreign policy in a direction that is more hawkish than what voters want.

MILITARY INTERVENTION IN LIBYA

A year and a half after escalating a war that he inherited in Afghanistan, President Obama launched a new military intervention in Libya. This intervention was a response to Libya's civil war, which began in February 2011. On March 18, Obama ordered airstrikes against Libya's armed forces. These strikes helped Libya's rebels to unseat the country's long-standing dictator, Muammar Qaddafi. When the rebels then proved unable to consolidate their hold on power, Libya descended into protracted fighting that enabled the expansion of the Islamic State, al-Qaeda, and other terrorist groups.[77] Obama later said that his worst mistake as president was using force in Libya without having a clear conception of how the rebels would create a new government.[78] This mistake was ironic given how Obama had campaigned for the presidency by criticizing the way that George W. Bush had toppled a Middle Eastern government without planning for what came next. How did Obama end up doing the same thing?

The Libya intervention cannot be attributed to voters' policy preferences. When a March Pew survey asked Americans to say whether they thought the United States had a responsibility to stop the fighting in Libya, 63 percent said "no" and just 27 percent said "yes."[79] A FoxNews poll similarly showed that 65 percent of voters opposed US military involvement in Libya, with just 25 percent supporting such action.[80] Other surveys found that voters supported limited military intervention to create a "no-fly zone" in Libya.[81] But the no-fly zone idea was a nonstarter, because Qaddafi's army was primarily attacking the rebels with ground forces who would not be impeded by a lack of air cover.[82]

Most of Obama's national security team was similarly skeptical of using military force against Qaddafi. UN Ambassador Susan Rice was the only national security principal who supported intervening in Libya from the start. Secretary of State Hillary Clinton originally opposed intervention, but later switched her view. Opponents of the Libya intervention included Vice President Joe Biden, Secretary of Defense Robert Gates, Chairman of the Joint Chiefs of Staff Michael Mullen, National Security Advisor Tom Donilon, and White House Chief of Staff Bill Daley. Thus, the Libya intervention was clearly not the product of a herd mentality within the United States' foreign policy establishment.[83]

President Obama was initially inclined to stay out of Libya's civil war. Obama later recalled how "I found the idea of waging a new war in a distant country with no strategic importance to the United States to be less than prudent."[84] Nor did Obama believe that intervention was necessary on humanitarian grounds. Though aides warned that Qaddafi might massacre civilians in the rebel stronghold of Benghazi, that risk was speculative and it hardly reflected a unique humanitarian emergency.[85] As Obama noted in his memoirs, civil war in the Democratic Republic of the Congo had already claimed millions of civilian lives, and few administration officials were calling for the United States to intervene there.[86] Thus, while Obama issued a statement on February 25 that called for Qaddafi to leave power, he deliberately avoided saying how the United States would make that happen.

Most accounts of the Libya intervention agree that the key turning point in US decision making occurred when Britain and France declared they would seek UN Security Council authorization for a no-fly zone. Since the United States would have to vote on the no-fly zone proposal, it was now impossible for President Obama to refrain from taking a public stance on whether or not to support the use of military force in Libya.[87] Given that the no-fly zone would not meaningfully constrain Qaddafi's army—and since Britain and France lacked the ability to project power into Libya on their own—Obama and his advisers saw the British-French proposal as an attempt to force their hand. UN Ambassador Susan Rice thus reportedly accused her French counterpart of trying "to drag us into your sh[—]ty little war."[88] Obama later recounted how "I was irritated that [French President Nicolas] Sarkozy and [British Prime Minister David] Cameron had jammed me on the issue."[89]

Obama's fears about getting "jammed" with respect to the use of force in Libya resembled the way he described debates about the Afghan Surge. In both cases, there was no evidence that voters supported taking hawkish military actions. Instead, political pressures largely revolved around fending off criticisms that Obama was a weak leader. The British-French intervention proposal amplified those pressures. As Deputy National Security Advisor Ben Rhodes put it during a crucial March 15 meeting: "We'd have to explain to the American people and the world why we're choosing not to join the international community in doing something."[90] Secretary of State Clinton similarly argued that, if the president was in doubt about the merits of the issue, then it was better to "get caught trying"—in other words, that the risk of criticism for being overly aggressive was less than the risk of criticism for seeming to exercise weak leadership.[91] Derek Chollet recounts how Obama endorsed that reasoning, explaining to his national security team that "I'm as worried as anyone about getting sucked into another war. But if Benghazi falls, we'll get blamed. We can't underestimate the impact on our leadership."[92]

Consistent with these claims, public debates over the Libya intervention revolved to a large degree around assessments of President Obama's leadership strength.[93] The *Economist* ran an essay on the Libya debate, titled "The Courage Factor," which criticized Obama for not taking more aggressive actions in the Middle East since the start of the Arab Spring and asked readers to consider: "Has Barack Obama ever been brave?"[94] Obama's own former State Department director of policy planning, Anne-Marie Slaughter, wrote a *New York Times* op-ed whose title accused Obama of "Fiddling While Libya Burns."[95] Michael Hastings's account of Obama's decision to intervene in Libya described how that choice took place in the context of a "national narrative" about how Obama "has repeatedly failed to provide the kind of tough, uncompromising leadership needed to move the country forward on almost every front."[96] These claims are all consistent with Obama's description of how elites pressure presidents to taking military action by translating foreign policy debates into litmus tests of their leadership qualities.

The way that Obama publicly justified the invasion also reveals an attempt to use military intervention as an indication of strong leadership. In a March address announcing his decision to use force in Libya, Obama argued that "to brush aside America's responsibility as a leader . . . would have been a betrayal of who we are. . . . [A]s president, I refused to wait for the images of slaughter and mass graves before taking action."[97] Similarly, in a 2012 presidential debate against Mitt Romney, Obama argued that "I and Americans took leadership in organizing an international coalition. . . . This is an example of how we make choices."[98]

Nearly every account of the Libya intervention stresses that this choice was a close call, with Obama himself calling it as "a 51–49 decision."[99] Since this debate involved a broad range of strategic and humanitarian considerations, it would be inappropriate to say that US intervention in Libya was dictated by political considerations alone. Yet, when faced with a tough decision, Obama and his advisers saw their political incentives as pushing in the direction of armed conflict, even though voters did not support that choice on its merits. The Obama administration's decision to intervene in Libya is thus consistent with the book's argument about how the politics of image-making can tip the balance of foreign policy debates in a hawkish direction.

WHAT ABOUT OBAMA'S WITHDRAWAL FROM IRAQ?

Of course, Obama's foreign policy was still less hawkish than George W. Bush's. And, given how Obama fulfilled his 2008 campaign promise to withdraw US forces from Iraq, one might even say that he retrenched US military commitments on the whole.[100] Yet, there are two reasons why Obama's withdrawal from Iraq does not contradict this section's argument.

First, voters supported withdrawing from Iraq.[101] The Iraq case thus shows that the politics of image-making do not always cause leaders to make foreign policy decisions that are more hawkish than what the public wants. But that is not what the book argues. Instead, I have argued that the politics of image-making generally steer US foreign policy in a hawkish direction. Refuting this argument would require identifying cases in which presidents pursued unpopular, dovish policies in order to burnish their personal images. The 2011 withdrawal from Iraq does not constitute such a case.

Second, and as mentioned at the top of this section, Obama withdrew from Iraq on a timetable that had already been established by the Bush administration. In order to keep US forces in Iraq after 2011, Obama would have had to negotiate a new Status of Forces Agreement with Iraq's government. Some scholars have criticized Obama for not trying harder to do so, but the point is that Obama did not really decide to withdraw US forces from Iraq in 2011—that was the default option given the policies that Obama inherited. By contrast, Obama's Afghan Surge and his intervention in Libya added new liabilities to the United States' strategic balance sheet. This behavior surprised many observers, and it flew in the face of growing public frustration with so-called forever wars. This section nevertheless explained how Obama's behavior was consistent with the book's theory of how public opinion shapes US foreign policy.

BROADER IMPLICATIONS OF OBAMA'S PRESIDENCY

The Obama presidency has important implications for understanding the nature of elite influence in US foreign policy. Elites played a role in generating political pressure to escalate the war in Afghanistan and to intervene in Libya. Yet, in both the Afghan and Libyan cases, we saw that foreign policy elites could not convince voters to support hawkish policies on their merits. The Afghanistan and Libya cases are thus inconsistent with standard ideas of how elites gain influence through their capacity to shape voters' policy preferences. Instead, I argued that elites' influence over debates about Afghanistan and Libya largely flowed from their ability to shape Obama's personal image by turning his reluctance to use military force into an indication of weak leadership.

Obama's tenure as commander in chief also demonstrates the difficulty of bringing structural change to US foreign policy. This section began by describing how many of President Obama's supporters were ultimately discouraged by the fact that he did not do more to reduce the United States' security commitments or to end the country's involvement in so-called forever wars. Obama's decisions to approve the Afghan Surge and to intervene in Libya show that the political obstacles to conducting a restrained foreign policy run much deeper than designing policies that voters support on their merits. The Obama presidency demonstrates that leaders who wish to reduce the degree of militarism in US foreign policy must find other ways of cultivating perceptions of strong leadership. The conclusion to this book explores what these strategies might look like and develops several other extensions of the book's argument.

Conclusion

Rethinking the Relationship between Public Opinion and Foreign Policy

This book's analysis supports three principal conclusions. First, I have argued that the relationship between public opinion and US foreign policy revolves around personal images and not just policy preferences. This argument departs from conventional notions of democratic politics, which assume that voters evaluate leaders' policy positions and support public officials whose views resemble their own. This idea is not just an academic convention. Polls that elicit voters' policy preferences are the standard tool that journalists and pundits use to understand what citizens want. I have argued that this information provides an incomplete—and often misleading—way to analyze the relationship between public opinion and US foreign policy.

The book's second principal conclusion is that public opinion plays an underestimated role in shaping US foreign policy. Scholars typically evaluate democratic responsiveness by assessing the extent to which leaders' decisions correlate with voters' policy preferences. By contrast, this book has explained how leaders often use unpopular foreign policies to craft favorable impressions of their foreign policy competence. I used this idea of issue-image trade-offs to explain political behavior on issues that scholars normally portray as being disconnected from public opinion: rising defense budgets, open-ended military interventions, and unilateralism. I have thus argued that democratic responsiveness in US foreign policy is more extensive—and also more problematic—than the conventional wisdom expects.

The book's third principal conclusion is that the politics of image-making steer US foreign policy in a direction that is more hawkish than what voters want. This is not an iron law that holds in every case. Chapter 5, for example, showed how Hubert Humphrey advocated a bombing pause in Vietnam in order to demonstrate his political independence. But we have nevertheless seen how leaders generally believe that hawkish foreign policy decisions provide the best tools for cultivating impressions of leadership strength. The book deployed a combination of surveys, experiments, and archival evidence to confirm that foreign policy hawks do, in fact, possess consistent advantages in the politics of image-making.

Chapter 1 developed the theoretical implications of my argument in detail. Rather than rehashing that material, this conclusion tackles four new topics. First, I explain how the book's theory provides a novel lens for understanding the politics of US foreign policy under Donald Trump. Next, I discuss how leaders can avoid having to make issue-image trade-offs. The conclusion's third section suggests directions for future research. It closes by offering an overall assessment of the extent to which the commander-in-chief test ultimately distorts US foreign policy.

Issue-Image Trade-offs and Donald Trump's "America First" Foreign Policy

Arguably the most distinctive element of Donald Trump's approach to global affairs was the unusually abrasive posture he adopted toward allies and international institutions. For example, President Trump withdrew the United States from several multilateral compacts, such as the Iran nuclear deal, the Transpacific Partnership, and the Paris Climate Agreement; he withheld US support from several international organizations, such as the UN Human Rights Commission and the World Health Organization; and he repeatedly criticized allies in NATO and East Asia for not paying their fair share of costs to maintain collective security. Trump is thus widely characterized as the first modern president who was actively hostile toward the liberal international order, representing a sharp unilateral turn in US foreign policy.[1]

Trump's unilateralist impulses were all the more notable because they appeared to contradict Americans' policy preferences. For instance, voters generally opposed withdrawing from the Iranian nuclear deal, the Transpacific Partnership, and the Paris Climate Agreement. Most Americans retained favorable opinions of both the United Nations and NATO throughout Trump's presidency. Sixty-four percent of Americans said that the United States should work more closely with the United Nations, even if that requires making policy compromises. Seventy-five percent of Americans supported maintaining or increasing America's commitment to NATO. Eighty-eight percent of voters thought that it was important to be publicly supportive of allies.[2] On their face, these data appear to reinforce the perception that Trump's foreign policy was a political anomaly: a pattern of behavior that was largely divorced from historical precedent or mass public opinion, and that is best explained by Trump's personal idiosyncrasies, or by his attempts to energize his political base.

Yet, we have seen that presidents frequently use controversial foreign policy stances as vehicles for crafting their personal images. And that is exactly how Trump portrayed his posture toward allies and international

147

institutions. One of Trump's core foreign policy messages while campaigning for president in 2016 was that prior administrations had made a series of poorly negotiated deals that were unfair to the United States.[3] As Hal Brands puts it, Trump portrayed the United States' tradition of multilateral diplomacy as "a naïve giveaway that enriched an ungrateful world at America's expense."[4]

This rhetoric laid the foundation for another of Trump's core messages: that he was a hard-nosed bargainer who could negotiate better deals on the United States' behalf. Thus, when Trump announced the launch of his presidential campaign in June 2015, he argued that "this is going to be an election that's based on competence, because people are tired of these nice people and they're tired of being ripped off by everybody in the world."[5] In his own words, Trump's political strategy revolved around showing that he would be a strong leader who would stick up for the United States in international negotiations. Trump's 2016 deputy campaign manager, Michael Glassner, later argued that this image was crucial to Trump's political success. Glassner argued:

> That was one of the bases of his candidacy and of his rhetoric—his ability or his promise to make better deals that would improve jobs and the economy, better trade deals that would have an immediate impact on the economy and help create more jobs at a local level. That even extended to foreign policy. The Iran deal was going on throughout the pre-primary period, and that was one of his favorite talking points about how the politicians in Washington are making bad deals, and I think everybody understood that.[6]

Trump's hostility toward allies and international institutions can thus be viewed as an issue-image trade-off: a series of hawkish foreign policy positions that voters did not support on the merits but that nevertheless allowed Trump to craft an image of fighting hard to prevent other countries from exploiting the United States. And there are many reasons to think that voters were receptive to Trump's message. For example, a 2017 Program for Public Consultation survey found that 55 percent of Americans think that the United States generally does "more than its fair share" in solving world problems, that 79 percent of Americans think that allies rely too much on the United States for their own protection, and that 83 percent of Americans want allies to take additional responsibilities so that the United States can reduce its presence abroad.[7] A 2019 Center for American Progress study found that 79 percent of voters think that other countries should "pay more for their own security," while 65 percent of Americans agree that "for too long, the US has let other nations take advantage of us in terms of global trade and economic policies."[8]

International negotiations are also a domain in which hawkish foreign policies may be particularly useful in the politics of image-making. Agreements such as the Transpacific Partnership and the Iran nuclear deal are exceedingly complicated. International relations experts frequently struggle to determine the extent to which these agreements serve US interests. It is implausible to expect that most voters will find it easy to evaluate whether any particular stance on these matters reflects good judgment. By contrast, Trump's public friction with allies and international institutions sent an unmistakable message that he was willing to confront other countries in a manner that his predecessors had not. In that sense, the unprecedented nature of Trump's hostility toward allies was exactly what made that behavior useful from the standpoint of signaling strong leadership. Treating Trump's unilateralism as another example of how presidents use hawkish policy positions to convey leadership strength suggests that his behavior was not as idiosyncratic as it has often been portrayed.

Can Leaders Avoid Making Issue-Image Trade-offs?

This book has shown that leaders have political incentives to adopt foreign policies that are more militaristic and less cooperative than what voters actually want. In the short run, these policies help leaders to craft impressions of leadership strength. In the long run, however, these policies do not always work to leaders' political advantage. For example, Lyndon Johnson's decision to pursue open-ended authorization for the use of force in Vietnam helped him win the 1964 election in a landslide, but the Vietnam War turned out so poorly that Johnson did not even bother to run for reelection in 1968. George W. Bush's willingness to "stick to his guns" in Iraq helped him hold on to the White House in 2004, but it exacerbated a war that ultimately made Bush one of the least popular presidents in US history. Barack Obama's decisions to approve the Afghan Surge and to intervene in Libya's civil war may have staved off short-term criticisms of his leadership strength, but these choices also contributed to the impression that Obama was simply extending the United States' "forever wars."

These cases all reflect the book's argument that voters value good judgment in foreign policy, but that good judgment is hard to evaluate quickly. Voters did not turn against the Vietnam War until 1968, violence in Iraq did not spike until 2006, and Libya's civil war did not relapse until 2014. Yet, by backing hawkish policies in these cases, Johnson, Bush, and Obama sent immediate signals of leadership strength. The role that hawkish foreign policies play in the politics of image-making is thus akin to consuming sugar-laden energy drinks: both provide short-term boosts while risking long-term crashes. Since presidents and presidential candidates face continual incentives to maximize their short-term popularity, the politics of image-making can thus encourage leaders to make decisions that are not necessarily in their own long-run interests, let alone in the interests of the country as a whole.

How can leaders avoid having to make these trade-offs? One approach to this challenge is what we might call "rhetorical pugilism." This strategy involves framing dovish foreign policies with aggressive rhetoric that by itself appears to suggest leadership strength. Today, this strategy is particularly common on the progressive left, where leaders often frame their antimilitaristic agenda with muscular language about promoting "big structural change" and combating the pernicious influence of foreign policy elites.[9] This strategy is certainly novel: until recently, it was virtually unheard of for presidents and presidential candidates to attack the US foreign policy establishment directly. Yet, it remains unclear how effective this strategy will be in allowing progressives to reorient the United States' foreign policy agenda. This approach essentially assumes that voters will equate talking tough with being tough, and that foreign policy doves somehow enjoy a natural advantage in deploying those rhetorical tools. That is fairly hard to imagine. Hawks can use feisty language too, and this book has shown that the substance of their foreign policy positions more naturally lends itself to crafting an image of being a competent commander in chief.

Another model for framing dovish foreign policies as indications of leadership strength ironically comes from George W. Bush's 2000 presidential campaign. Bush's main critique of Bill Clinton's foreign policy was that it was undisciplined. Bush argued that President Clinton had erred by dragging the US military into humanitarian interventions and nation-building rather than preparing for conventional military threats such as the rise of China. "If we don't stop extending our troops all around the world," Bush argued in the first presidential debate, "then we're going to have a serious problem coming down the road."[10] Bush's top foreign policy adviser, Condoleezza Rice, amplified that theme in a *Foreign Affairs* article that described Bush's foreign policy vision.[11] A key section of that essay, titled "Setting Priorities," explained that Bush's opposition to nation-building would put the United States in a better position to protect its core interests from conventional military threats.

This emphasis on discipline in foreign policy decision making could provide a viable path for framing dovish policies in terms of leadership strength. In this view, successful presidents need to possess the vision to set clear priorities, and then they need to be relentless in sticking to those priorities. Presidents who get sidetracked by secondary issues and crises are thus weak leaders who lack the foresight and willpower to keep their eye on the ball of protecting the country's core interests. Of course, Bush's actual behavior as president was largely defined by the way that he scrapped his initial foreign policy agenda after the crisis of the September 11 terrorist attacks, and so we are once again left to speculate about whether a president could successfully employ the rhetoric of discipline to justify dovish foreign policy behavior. But the rhetoric Bush initially used to critique wars of choice is at least worth considering as a tool that leaders could use to break the association between dovishness and weakness.

Scholars who advocate a grand strategy of restraint have special incentives to study these issues. Proponents of restraint advocate cutting the US defense budget, retrenching the United States' security commitments, and avoiding military interventions unless core national interests are at stake.[12] The book has shown that leaders who back these policies generally expose themselves to charges of being weak and complacent. The very word "restraint" connotes pulling back and doing less, which is exactly the opposite of the image that presidents and presidential candidates generally try to cultivate. Proponents of restraint thus face political disadvantages that have relatively little to do with what voters think of the restraint agenda's substance.

I am not aware of any existing research that directly examines how such rhetoric shapes perceptions of foreign policy leadership, but that is the point: if scholars and practitioners want to understand the political viability of new ideas, then they should not simply examine the degree to which those ideas align with voters' policy preferences. It is also necessary to understand how those policies shape the personal images of leaders who support them. Just as policymakers devote substantial emphasis to figuring out how to frame their proposals in a manner that maximizes their substantive appeal, researchers can direct similar efforts to determining how leaders can articulate sensible foreign policies in a manner that minimizes issue-image trade-offs.

Directions for Future Research

There are many ways that scholars could extend this book's analysis of the politics of image-making. For example, future research could examine the extent to which issue-image trade-offs shape foreign policy debates outside national security. This conclusion's discussion of Donald Trump has already suggested these dynamics may be just as prevalent in trade policy and other kind of international negotiations. My argument may also help to explain why elected officials have found it so difficult to implement immigration reform. Though most Americans agree on core elements of what these reforms should entail—such as offering a pathway to citizenship for undocumented migrants who currently live in the United States[13]—any leader who supports those measures runs the risk of being seen as "soft" on immigration. Lawmakers' desire to avoid those charges likely reduces the political viability of reforms that voters support on the merits.

A second topic for future research is how foreign policy positions shape perceptions of personal traits besides strong leadership and good judgment. Though these attributes were the main focus of my argument, the book's case studies also revealed leaders using foreign policy to shape other aspects of their personal images. For example, the book's discussion of the politics of Vietnam explained how Barry Goldwater sought to portray Lyndon Johnson as deceiving the public about foreign policy crises and how Hubert

Humphrey had to navigate questions about his loyalty when designing his policy positions on the war. Chapter 4 similarly explained how Ronald Reagan believed that directly criticizing President Jimmy Carter's handling of the Iranian hostage crisis would make it look like he was politicizing foreign policy. That was part of why Reagan devoted so much emphasis to his position on defense spending: this issue allowed him to portray Carter as being weak and complacent without making it seem as though Reagan was exploiting a national security crisis for political gain. If anything, these examples suggest that the book's theory and evidence understate the role that image-making plays in the politics of US foreign policy.

Future research could examine the role that journalists, government officials, and other foreign policy elites play in brokering issue-image trade-offs. A vivid example of this phenomenon is how President Barack Obama received sharp criticism for saying that the first principle of his foreign policy was "don't do stupid stuff." Of course, no one supports deliberately doing stupid things. Yet many foreign policy elites—including Obama's own secretary of state, Hillary Clinton—argued that Obama's emphasis on avoiding mistakes reflected his inability to develop a substantive and proactive foreign policy doctrine. Elites thus translated a statement that should have had unanimous public support into a negative message about the president's foreign policy competence.[14] Elites' ability to link foreign policy issues to leaders' personal images is a potentially significant source of political power that differs from standard theories of how elites provide cues that shape voters' policy preferences.[15] The book's theory and evidence suggest that elites do not need to convince voters to support a policy in order to build political pressure for that policy's adoption. This may be at least part of the reason why US foreign policy consistently reflects the views of elites rather than those of the general public.[16]

The book developed and tested a theory for explaining how leaders' foreign policy positions affect perceptions of competence. But it would be useful to study how other factors, such as race and gender, shape the outcome of the commander-in-chief test. If women and nonwhite leaders face unique hurdles in conveying foreign policy competence, then they might have even greater incentives to behave in the manner that my theory predicts. Yet, it is also possible that women and nonwhite leaders could face unique constraints that my theory does not anticipate. For example, there is substantial evidence that assertive women are seen as dislikable when compared to assertive men.[17] That could be one reason why, even though voters tended to rate 2016 Democratic presidential nominee Hillary Clinton quite highly on traits related to leadership strength, Clinton also scored poorly on traits related to warmth and compassion.[18] If attempting to convey leadership strength only undermines other aspects of a candidate's image, then we might expect women and nonwhite leaders to have *less* incentive to behave in a manner consistent with my theory. Resolving this ambiguity is important for predicting how increasing diversity in the United States' national leadership could reshape the politics of the commander-in-chief test.

The book's case studies focused on general presidential elections, but my argument might be even more relevant to the politics of presidential primaries, because primaries are more likely than general elections to feature candidates with questionable claims to foreign policy competence. These candidates should have particularly strong incentives to exploit issue-image trade-offs in order to establish their credibility. That may, in turn, pressure more mainstream candidates to hedge their own positions in order to avoid criticism. Presidential nominees may thus arrive in general elections having already incorporated issue-image trade-offs into their foreign policy platforms. This is yet another way in which the book's analysis has likely understated the role that image-making plays in the politics of US foreign policy.

Though this book focused on US foreign policy, there are many plausible examples of how issue-image trade-offs might surround the politics of foreign policy outside the United States. France, for example, has experienced a series of jihadist terrorist attacks since 2015. In response to those attacks, France declared a state of emergency that drew widespread criticism for undermining civil liberties. In 2017, French president Emmanuel Macron enacted an antiterrorism law that permanently expanded his government's authority to search private property, to conduct electronic surveillance, and to close mosques. While French voters have supported some of these efforts, the book's theoretical framework suggests that French leaders have incentives to push the boundaries of public preferences in order to indicate how seriously they are taking the threat of terrorism.

Brexit provides another example of how the book's theoretical framework can potentially shed light on foreign policy decisions outside the United States. The margin of support for Brexit among the British public was quite narrow; subsequent polls then showed that many British voters changed their minds about the issue. This is not the kind of policy issue on which we normally expect elected officials to stake their political fortunes. Yet, former British prime minister Boris Johnson made Brexit the main focus of his 2019 election campaign and used that position to win more votes for the Conservatives than any other British political party had received in forty years. The political upside that Johnson reaped from supporting Brexit thus appears to have gone well beyond that policy's relatively narrow margin of public support. The book's argument suggests that this extra upside involved the way that Johnson used Brexit as a tool to craft an image for being a leader who "put Britain first" and who would conduct international negotiations more aggressively than his predecessors had.

Finally, the book's theoretical framework may provide insight about domestic politics. Potential examples include leaders who support abortion restrictions to convey their commitment to traditional values, leaders who advocate defunding the police to indicate their commitment to protecting marginalized groups, leaders who oppose gun control to demonstrate their commitment to civil liberties, or leaders who support Medicare for All to communicate their concern for the well-being of working-class Americans. Since each of these policy positions is unpopular (at least in some formulations), they are usually seen as tools that leaders use to court extreme segments of the electorate. Yet, each of these policies can also plausibly serve to craft political images that resonate with a broader swathe of the general public.

Parting Thoughts on the Commander-in-Chief Test

This book began by describing how voters have legitimate reasons to care about a president's foreign policy competence. And a wide range of rigorous research shows that presidents' personal attributes shape the ways that they make high-stakes foreign policy decisions. It thus makes sense for voters to ask whether presidents and presidential candidates possess the "right stuff" to manage international affairs. In principle, it is clear why we want to have a commander-in-chief test.

Yet, in practice, I doubt that these judgments play a positive role in the United States' political discourse. Throughout the book, we have seen how debates about foreign policy competence often have little or nothing to do with job performance. In 1968, the politics of image-making focused debates over Vietnam around a strategically insignificant bombing pause rather than substantive questions about how Hubert Humphrey or Richard Nixon planned to handle the war. In 1976, Gerald Ford seemed ignorant because he made a subtle semantic error in articulating his policy toward Eastern Europe. In 1988, Michael Dukakis came across as a weak leader because he smiled while riding in a tank. The 2004 presidential election placed more emphasis on a symbolic vote that John Kerry had taken on a defense spending bill rather than on how he or George W. Bush planned to stabilize Iraq. In 2009, Barack Obama was accused of "dithering" over the Afghan Surge because he held some meetings on the subject.

The most generous interpretation of this history is that the ability to appear competent reflects some kind of cognitive capacity. If leaders cannot put on a good show when appearing in public, how can we trust their ability to handle matters behind the scenes? Yet, it seems just as plausible that passing the commander-in-chief test simply reflects the extent to which leaders are willing to invest energy in managing political optics for their own sake. The 1964 election provides a good example of that. Lyndon Johnson was far more careful than Barry Goldwater when discussing foreign policy issues in public. This discretion—some might call it deception—allowed Johnson to run for president as a peace candidate while secretly preparing to go to war in Vietnam. The country would almost surely have been better off if it had ignored the optics of Johnson's and Goldwater's statements and figured out what these men actually intended to do with the powers of the presidency.

Though the book's analysis sometimes portrays the politics of US foreign policy in a cynical light, it also supports an optimistic message about the capacities of voters themselves. As I conducted my research for this book, I was surprised at how sensible voters' foreign policy preferences often seemed. Consider for a moment what the history of US foreign policy might look like if leaders had no incentives to craft their political images, and instead pursued policies backed by a clear majority of voters.

If US foreign policy followed voters' preferences, then John F. Kennedy would not have launched a military buildup to close a missile gap that did not exist. Ronald Reagan would have expanded the defense budget in 1980 and 1981, but only in those two years, and no other president would have increased military expenditures since World War II. Accounting for inflation that would make today's defense budget no more than $500 billion, saving roughly one quarter of a trillion dollars annually. If the US government used that money to expand every one of its nondefense discretionary programs by 25 percent—public education, job training, environmental protection, law enforcement, and so on—it would still have enough funds left over to give taxpayers a rebate.

If US foreign policy followed voters' preferences, then Lyndon Johnson would not have gone to war in Vietnam in 1965 and Richard Nixon would have concluded that war prior to 1973. George W. Bush would not have overthrown Saddam Hussein without securing a multilateral coalition, which almost certainly means that the United States would not have invaded Iraq at all. Barack Obama would not have implemented the Afghan Surge, nor would he have pursued regime change in Libya. Donald Trump would not have promoted an "America first" agenda that alienated many long-standing allies.

Reasonable people can disagree about the merits of these choices. Yet, I suspect that few people could read the last two paragraphs without concluding that the country would have been better off if leaders had followed voters' policy preferences in at least some of those cases.

Throughout the book, I have argued that voters' policy preferences do not drive the politics of US foreign policy. Though most theories of democracy assume that leaders should try to adopt popular policy platforms, that does not provide a good descriptive model of either voter behavior or foreign policy decision making. But perhaps these ideas should still serve as our normative guide for how we *want* voters to evaluate the quality of foreign policy leadership. Ordinary citizens may not be experts on international affairs, and it is easy to see why they would care about whether their presidents are fit to be commander in chief. One might intuitively think that voters could do a better job of sizing up their leaders on a personal basis rather than grappling with complex foreign policy issues on their merits. Yet, the research presented in this book suggests that the opposite is true. When we debate foreign policy, we are better off sticking to the substance, and we should encourage our leaders to do the same.

Note: All data and code used in this book are stored in the Harvard Dataverse, https://dataverse.harvard.edu/.

Appendix to Chapter 1

PUBLIC DISCOURSE ON THE COMMANDER-IN-CHIEF TEST

In order to assess how well the book's concepts of strong leadership and good judgment map onto public debates about the "commander-in-chief test," I asked a group of research assistants to search the Lexis-Nexis database for news articles and political commentary during presidential election years from 2000 to 2020 that contained the phrase "commander-in-chief test" or else used the terms "fit" or "unfit" within ten words of the phrase "commander-in-chief." Then we identified the personal attributes that these sources associated with a competent commander-in-chief.

For example, after an October 2012 presidential debate between Barack Obama and Mitt Romney, a CNN roundtable discussed how the candidates fared on the "commander-in-chief test." Democratic strategist David Axelrod said that "the whole night was a case of a president [Obama] who's a strong, decisive commander-in-chief."[1] We coded this statement as defining the commander-in-chief test with respect to the attributes of "strong leadership" and "decisiveness."

Or, a July 2016 *Politico* article, titled "Why Trump Fails—and Clinton Passes—the Commander-in-Chief Test," argued that "we need an experienced and steady hand to guide use through the current challenges to American leadership and world order."[2] We coded this statement as defining the commander-in-chief test with respect to the attributes of "experience" and "steadiness."

Or, a February 2020 *Huffington Post* article, titled "How Elizabeth Warren Built a Foreign Policy That Passes the Commander-in-Chief Test," praised Warren's foreign policy agenda as "projecting responsibility, not revolution," but also noted doubts that Warren "hasn't learned enough to challenge national security establishment logic."[3] We coded these statements as defining the commander-in-chief test with respect to the attributes of "responsibility" and "knowledgeability."

This search process yielded twenty-seven attributes that the research team identified in at least three independent sources. Table A.1 lists these criteria and categorizes them according to how they fit with the book's concepts of strong leadership and good judgment.

It is important to point out that any exercise like this one is unavoidably subjective. (For example, we determined that "toughness" and "tenacity" are different traits, whereas "stability" and "steadiness" were essentially the same thing.) It is also worth noting that elite discourse does not necessarily mirror voters' ideas of foreign policy competence. This analysis nevertheless provides some empirical foundations for understanding the content of public debate about what it takes to be a competent commander in chief.

The first ten attributes in table A.1 are all related to the book's concept of strong leadership, which I defined as vigorously promoting US national interests and not backing down when challenged by the country's adversaries. These attributes include confidence, decisiveness, energy, strength, tenacity, toughness, and vigilance.

The first column of table A.1 also includes the attributes of patriotism, "having a clear vision for US foreign policy," and trustworthiness. Patriotism falls within my definition of strong leadership because leaders who are more patriotic would presumably be more committed to promoting US interests. "Having a clear vision for US foreign policy" similarly suggests the

Table A.1 A classification of traits that political pundits associate with a competent commander in chief

Strong leadership	Good judgment	Both	Neither
• Confident • Decisive • Energetic • Has a clear vision for US foreign policy • Patriotic • Strong leader • Tenacious • Tough • Trustworthy • Vigilant	• Common sense/sensible • Good judgment • Intelligent • Steady • Responsible • Thinks carefully before making decisions	• Knowledgeable about US foreign policy/the military • Learns quickly • Ready to lead on day one • Understands complex issues • Understands the threats facing the United States • Works well under pressure	• Dignified • Reassuring • Respects the military

"Strong leadership" is defined as vigorously promoting US interests and not backing down when challenged by US adversaries. "Good judgment" is defined as avoiding unnecessary risks and major foreign policy mistakes.

ability and willingness to exert vigorous leadership in international affairs. (For example, President Bill Clinton was frequently criticized for lacking a foreign policy vision. Chapter 7 explains how Clinton viewed these criticisms as a significant political threat.) The concept of "trustworthiness" falls within the book's definition of strong leadership because leaders who are not trustworthy would be more likely to "sell out" US foreign policy for personal or political gain.[4]

The second column in table A.1 contains six criteria that are consistent with the book's concept of good judgment, which I defined as the ability to avoid unnecessary risks and major foreign policy mistakes. These criteria are common sense, good judgment, intelligence, steadiness, responsibility, and "thinks carefully before making decisions."

The next six criteria in table A.1 are plausibly relevant to strong leadership and good judgment as I defined those terms. One of these criteria is how well a leader can handle pressure. A leader who cannot handle pressure might be more willing to back down in the face of aggression (weak leadership) or to make avoidable errors (poor judgment). The other items in this column are "knowledgeable about US foreign policy/the military," "learns quickly," "ready to lead on day one," "understands complex issues," and "understands the threats facing the United States." Leaders who lack these attributes would presumably struggle to devise effective strategies for promoting US interests and they would also likely find it harder to avoid taking unnecessary risks in foreign policy decision making.

In studying political discourse on the commander-in-chief test, my research team and I identified three attributes that are relevant to foreign policy competence and that do not map onto the book's constructs of strong leadership or good judgment. These involved pundits arguing that a commander in chief should be "dignified," "reassuring," and someone who "respects the military."[5]

In addition to the items listed in table A.1, the research team identified numerous instances where pundits argue that a commander in chief should possess prior military or diplomatic experience. Several sources also praised presidential candidates for possessing "close relationships with allies," which reflects their prior experience on the world stage. Political pundits generally use experience as a proxy for competence. In much the same way that a college degree in the liberal arts indicates a wide-ranging education, leaders who have more foreign policy experience have presumably absorbed a broad skill set that can help them to make high-stakes decisions. Since experience serves as a proxy for competence rather than reflecting specific personal traits, I consider experience to be distinct from my analysis of the attributes that a commander in chief would ideally possess. For example, the survey experiments that I present in chapter 2 will randomize leaders' background experience independently from descriptions of their other personal qualities.

Appendix to Chapter 2

FULL RESULTS FOR ANALYSIS OF PREFERENCE ALIGNMENT
AND LEADERSHIP STRENGTH

Table A.2 provides full results for chapter 2's analysis of preference alignment and leadership strength.

METHODOLOGY FOR FIGURE 2.2

I began this analysis by examining whether Democrats and Republicans tended to hold different preferences on each foreign policy issue. I conducted this analysis using univariate ordinary least squares regressions, with $p < 0.05$ thresholds for statistical significance, applied to every survey wave in which the ANES administered a particular question.

If a foreign policy issue displayed a partisan orientation in some years but not others, I dropped the latter observations from my analysis. There were two questions in the data set (regarding US strategy in Korea in 1952 and "how willing should the United States be to use military force to solve international problems" in 1992–1996) where foreign policy preferences did not display a statistically significant partisan orientation, and so I dropped those questions from my analysis. I found four cases where an issue's partisan orientation changed across presidential elections.[6] When an issue's partisan orientation changed across surveys, I treated those data as though they reflected different topics. I made each of the choices described in this paragraph on the grounds that they should amplify the correlation between foreign policy preferences and presidential voting. That, in turn, should make it harder to

Table A.2 Issues and images in presidential voting

	Model 1	Model 2	Model 3	Model 4
Defense spending	0.66 (0.09)***			
US-Soviet relations		0.78 (0.13)***		
Central America			0.58 (0.09)**	
Use of force				0.86 (0.27)**
Leadership strength	1.50 (0.10)***	1.45 (0.13)***	1.35 (0.21)***	1.39 (0.32)***
Partisanship	1.22 (0.07)***	1.19 (0.11)***	1.18 (0.18)***	1.18 (0.31)***
Ideology	0.57 (0.07)***	0.41 (0.11)***	0.61 (0.15)***	0.81 (0.27)**
Female (0,1)	0.41 (0.12)***	0.38 (0.18)*	0.50 (0.28)	0.43 (0.45)
Black (0,1)	−1.45 (0.38)***	−1.15 (0.48)*	−0.86 (0.64)	−1.97 (1.00)*
Domestic issues	1.16 (0.12)***	1.45 (0.21)***	1.53 (0.35)***	1.16 (0.38)**
Constant	−0.22 (0.09)**	0.15 (0.12)	0.14 (0.19)	−0.37 (0.29)
Years	1980–2008	1980–1988	1984	2004
N	4514	1945	756	534
AUC	0.97	0.97	0.96	0.99

* $p < 0.05$; ** $p < 0.01$; *** $p < 0.001$

confirm the claim that foreign policy preferences are less important than candidate images when it comes to explaining presidential vote choice.

INTERRATER RELIABILITY FOR CLASSIFYING OPEN-ENDED DATA

Table A.3 presents data on interrater reliability for chapter 2's analysis of open-ended data from American National Election Studies (ANES) and Cooperative Election Survey (CES) surveys. The "% agree" statistic measures the proportion of the time that randomly selected pairs of coding choices matched each other. Cohen's kappa is a more sophisticated measure of interrater agreement that describes the extent to which coding decisions agreed more than random chance. Cohen's kappa values over 0.60 are generally interpreted as reflecting a "substantial" level of agreement.

Table A.3 shows that interrater agreement was lowest when it came to judging which open-ended assessments belonged in the competence category. This was expected, given the inherent challenge of determining which personal attributes reflect the ability to govern as opposed to broader likability. Ironically, lower levels of agreement when classifying assessments of competence make the analysis in this section more robust. Measurement error generally reduces the statistical and substantive significance of statistical relationships. To the extent that assessments of competence are unusually ambiguous, that should make it harder to demonstrate that competence considerations

Table A.3 Interrater agreement for classifying open-ended responses

	Interrater reliability					
	6–0	5–1	4–2	3–3	% agree	Cohen's κ
ANES data						
All data	0.63	0.20	0.12	0.05	0.84	0.60
Competence	0.46	0.26	0.19	0.09	0.76	0.29
Issues	0.59	0.23	0.13	0.05	0.82	0.64
Likability	0.61	0.21	0.14	0.05	0.83	0.60
Experience	0.54	0.28	0.12	0.05	0.81	0.34
Foreign policy	0.89	0.07	0.02	0.01	0.96	0.86
Domestic policy	0.61	0.18	0.16	0.05	0.83	0.63
General policy	0.37	0.34	0.21	0.08	0.72	0.43
CES data						
All data	0.64	0.17	0.14	0.06	0.84	0.62
Competence	0.36	0.28	0.25	0.11	0.71	0.39
Issues	0.57	0.19	0.16	0.08	0.80	0.48
Experience	0.67	0.21	0.14	0.05	0.83	0.60
Party ownership	0.96	0.02	0.01	0.01	0.98	0.35

The columns of table A.3 reflect the balance of consensus among research team members when categorizing ANES and CES data. A "6–0" designation indicates that all six members agreed about whether or not a master code belonged within a given category. A "5–1" designation indicates that one rater disagreed with the majority view, and so on.

play a larger role than other factors when it comes to explaining vote choice. And, even here, raters agreed with each other's classifications 76 percent of the time.

POLITICAL KNOWLEDGE BATTERY

I employ three questions to test respondents' political knowledge in chapter 2's survey experiments, chapter 2's analysis of CES data, and chapter 3's survey experiment. The three questions are:

1. Which of the following countries are permanent members of the United Nations Security Council? You can select multiple options or none at all.

   a. France
   b. Sweden
   c. China
   d. Brazil
   e. Don't Know

2. Which of the following people served as US Secretary of State during the Trump administration? You can select multiple options or none at all.

   a. Boris Johnson
   b. Mike Pompeo
   c. Rex Tillerson
   d. Colin Powell
   e. Don't Know

3. In which of the following countries does the United States currently deploy more than 3,000 troops? You can select multiple options or none at all.

   a. Libya
   b. Afghanistan
   c. German
   d. Japan
   e. Don't Know

Response items were randomly ordered. Respondents received one point for each correct response (which included not selecting incorrect responses). Overall scores thus ranged from zero to twelve. Summary statistics across the three surveys were:

- YouGov (experiments A and B, chapter 2): Mean 8.1, Standard deviation 1.9.

- CES (chapter 2): Mean 5.8, Standard deviation, 1.3.

- Qualtrics (chapter 3): Mean 4.7, Standard deviation, 3.3.

LIST OF PERSONAL TRAITS AND POLICY POSITIONS
IN EXPERIMENT B

Competence: to be a strong leader; to be knowledgeable about foreign policy; to have good judgment; to work well under pressure; to be confident; to be decisive; to have a clear vision for US foreign policy; to have a close relationship with US allies; to be patriotic; to understand complex issues; to learn quickly; to be ready to lead on day one; to be reassuring; to respect the military; to be responsible; to be sensible; to be intelligent; to be steady; to be tenacious; to think carefully before making decisions; to be tough; to be trustworthy; to understand the threats facing the United States; to be vigilant; to be energetic.

Likability: to be charismatic; to be good looking; to be dignified; to be scholarly; to have a good sense of humor; to be likeable; to be articulate; to have a good family life; to be enthusiastic; to be comfortable on television.

Policy positions:

o {Would increase US military spending, Would decrease US military spending, Would keep US military spending about the same}

o {Would increase US cooperation with allies, Would decrease US cooperation with allies, Would keep US cooperation with allies about the same}

o {Would increase US troop levels in Afghanistan, Would decrease US troop levels in Afghanistan, Would keep US troop levels in Afghanistan about the same}

o {Would withdraw US troops from Syria, Would not withdraw US troops from Syria}

o {Supports a US policy of trying to remove Venezuelan president Nicolas Maduro from power, Opposes a US policy of trying to remove Venezuelan president Nicolas Maduro from power}

o {Would take military action to stop Iran from developing nuclear weapons, Would not take military action to stop Iran from developing nuclear weapons}

o {Would rejoin the Iran nuclear deal, Would not rejoin the Iran nuclear deal}

- {Would rejoin the Paris Climate Accords, Would not rejoin the Paris Climate Accords}

- {Would allow openly transgender soldiers to serve in the military, Would not allow openly transgender soldiers to serve in the military}

- {Would expand the US military presence in space, Would not expand the US military presence in space}

- {Would send US troops to defend Taiwan if China tried to invade, Would not send US troops to defend Taiwan if China tried to invade}

- {Would increase US efforts to contain China's influence in Asia, Would decrease US efforts to contain China's influence in Asia}

- {Says the US should work with dictators and authoritarian governments when it sees a chance to negotiate, Says the US should avoid working with dictators and authoritarian governments altogether}

- {Says the US does too much to help solve world problems, Says the US does too little to help solve world problems}

- {Thinks the president should always consult with Congress before conducting military strikes, Does not think the president should always consult with Congress before conducting military strikes}

- {Says diplomacy and sanctions are the best way to stop North Korea from continuing work on nuclear weapons and missiles, Says threatening military action is the best way to stop North Korea from continuing work on nuclear weapons and missiles}

- {Would increase economic sanctions on Russia, Would decrease economic sanctions on Russia}

- {Would send US troops to defend Ukraine if Russia invades the rest of that country, Would not send US troops to defend Ukraine if Russia invades the rest of that country}

- {Would increase foreign aid, Would decrease foreign aid}

- {Would prioritize promoting human rights in other countries, Would not prioritize promoting human rights in other countries}

- {Would prioritize promoting democracy in other countries, Would not prioritize promoting democracy in other countries}

- {Says that free trade agreements are generally in America's interest, Says that free trade agreements are not generally in America's interest}

- {Supports establishing an independent Palestinian state, Opposes establishing an independent Palestinian state}

- {Says the US should increase the number of refugees it accepts each year, Says the US should decrease the number of refugees it accepts each year}

- {Would increase the resources that the US devotes to fighting terrorism, Would decrease the resources that the US devotes to fighting terrorism}

Appendix to Chapter 3

LIST OF POLICY POSITIONS IN CHAPTER 3'S
SURVEY EXPERIMENT

These positions are grouped by number and letter, where *h* indicates the more hawkish position and *d* indicates the more dovish position. Candidates' policy positions were randomized such that they could only take one position on a policy issue.

1h. "opposes withdrawing US troops from Afghanistan"
1d. "supports withdrawing US troops from Afghanistan"
2h. "opposes withdrawing US troops currently fighting ISIS in Syria and Iraq"
2d. "supports withdrawing US troops currently fighting ISIS in Syria and Iraq"
3h. "thinks the United States should maintain its ground troops in South Korea"
3d. "thinks the United States should reduce its ground troops in South Korea"
4h. "would use US troops to defend Taiwan from a Chinese attack"
4d. "would not use US troops to defend Taiwan from a Chinese attack"
5h. "would use US troops to stop Russia from invading NATO allies such as Latvia, Lithuania, and Estonia"
5d. "would not use US troops to stop Russia from invading NATO allies such as Latvia, Lithuania, and Estonia"
6h. "would use US troops if Pakistan requested assistance in suppressing a radical Islamic insurgency"
6d. "would not use US troops if Pakistan requested assistance in suppressing a radical Islamic insurgency"
7h. "supports maintaining long-term military bases in the Middle East"
7d. "opposes maintaining long-term military bases in the Middle East"
8h. "would increase the frequency of drone strikes targeting suspected terrorists overseas"
8d. "would reduce the frequency of drone strikes targeting suspected terrorists overseas"

9h. "thinks it is generally justifiable to use military force against countries that pose a serious threat to US national security, even if those countries have not attacked us first"

9d. "thinks it is not generally justifiable to use military force against countries that have not attacked us first, even if those countries pose a serious threat to US national security"

10h. "supports a policy of trying to remove Venezuelan president Nicolas Maduro from power"

10d. "opposes a policy of trying to remove Venezuelan president Nicolas Maduro from power"

11h. "would raise overall levels of military spending"

11d. "would not raise overall levels of military spending"

12h. "thinks the United States should devote more resources to global counterterrorism"

12d. "thinks the United States should devote fewer resources to global counterterrorism"

13h. "would expand existing efforts to modernize America's nuclear arsenal"

13d. "would scale back existing efforts to modernize America's nuclear arsenal"

14h. "thinks it is important for America to remain the world's sole military superpower"

14d. "does not think it is important for America to remain the world's sole military superpower"

15h. "supports expanding the US military presence in space"

15d. "opposes expanding the US military presence in space"

16h. "thinks we should publicly criticize European allies who do not meet their obligations to support collective defense"

16d. "thinks we should avoid publicly criticizing European allies, even if they do not meet their obligations to support collective defense"

17h. "thinks the United States should actively work to limit China's rising power, even if that runs the risk of starting a military conflict"

17d. "does not think the United States should actively work to limit China's rising power if that runs the risk of starting a military conflict"

18h. "thinks threatening military action is the best way to prevent Iran from developing nuclear weapons"

18d. "thinks diplomacy and sanctions are the best way to prevent Iran from developing nuclear weapons"

19h. "thinks negotiating with North Korea would only reward that country's bad behavior"

19d. "thinks negotiating with North Korea would raise the chances of convincing that country to give up its nuclear weapons"

20h. "thinks the United States should not cooperate more closely with allies if that requires going along with policies that we would not otherwise support"

20d. "thinks the United States should cooperate more closely with allies, even if that requires going along with policies that we would not otherwise support"

21h. "thinks the United States should generally avoid working with the United Nations to solve global problems in cases where going it alone would allow us to do things faster and more effectively"

21d. "thinks the United States should generally work with the United Nations to solve global problems, even in cases where going it alone would allow us to do things faster and more effectively"

22h. "would increase economic sanctions on Russia"

22d. "would not increase economic sanctions on Russia"

23h. "opposes establishing a closer political and economic relationship with Cuba"

23d. "supports establishing a closer political and economic relationship with Cuba"

24h. "thinks the United States should expand its capabilities to conduct cyberattacks against other countries"

24d. "does not think the United States should expand its capabilities to conduct cyberattacks against other countries"

25h. "thinks there are circumstances under which it is acceptable to torture captured terrorists"

25d. "thinks there are no circumstances under which it is acceptable to torture captured terrorists"

26h. "thinks that military strength is a better way to ensure peace in comparison to diplomacy"

26d. "thinks that diplomacy is a better way to ensure peace in comparison to military strength"

Appendix to Chapter 4

TREND ANALYSIS OF KENNEDY'S VOTE SHARE ACROSS ISSUE AREAS

Each row in Table A.4 analyzes one of the eight core issue areas that Harris surveyed. Model 1 presents a simple linear regression measuring the extent to which Kennedy's vote share among voters who expressed concern with a given issue area grew over time. Model 2 then reestimates time trends while controlling for the overall proportion of voters who said they planned to vote for Kennedy in each Harris poll.

Table A.4 Changes in JFK's vote share over time

Issue area	Model 1	Model 2	
	Weekly increase in JFK vote share	Weekly increase in JFK vote share	Correlation between margin of support and JFK vote share
Ageing	0.81 (0.43)^	0.27 (0.46)	1.21 (0.48)*
Civil rights	0.92 (0.58)	−0.05 (0.58)	2.12 (0.47)***
Economics	0.94 (0.25)***	0.47 (0.27)^	1.05 (0.34)**
Education	1.27 (0.50)*	0.67 (0.50)	1.32 (0.27)***
Farming	0.94 (0.83)	0.95 (0.85)	−0.03 (0.74)
States' rights	0.84 (1.15)	0.80 (1.18)	0.09 (0.83)
Taxes	−0.00 (0.34)	−0.29 (0.33)	0.65 (0.22)**
War and peace	0.70 (0.24)**	0.54 (0.26)*	0.35 (0.25)

^ $p < 0.10$; * $p < 0.05$; ** $p < 0.01$; *** $p < 0.001$

Each row presents two statistical models. Model 1 is an ordinary least squares regression predicting change in Kennedy's vote share as a function of time among voters concerned with different issue areas. Model 2 controls for the proportion of respondents in each poll who said they planned to vote for Kennedy. Both models are weighted proportionally to states' electoral vote share. Standard errors in parentheses.

The last row of table A.4 shows that Kennedy's improved standing on foreign affairs cannot be attributed to a general rise in his popularity. Even when controlling for Kennedy's overall levels of support, his vote share on war and peace issues still increased throughout the presidential campaign in a manner that was statistically significant ($p < 0.05$). The same cannot be said for any of the other seven issue areas that Harris tracked. In each of these areas, Kennedy either failed to record statistically significant gains over the course of the campaign, or those gains fell outside the $p < 0.05$ boundary for statistical significance when accounting for Kennedy's overall approval.

DOCUMENTATION OF DEFENSE SPENDING DATA

The data presented at the end of this chapter draw on 439 surveys stored by the Roper Center's iPoll database. Those data include all polling questions that the Roper Center coded as corresponding to the topic of "Defense Spending",[7] that were conducted after January 1, 1946, and posted to iPoll before November 18, 2022; and that met the following criteria:

- Defense spending was the question's main focus. This excluded questions that asked respondents to consider their preferences on defense spending as an input to other fiscal objectives. For example: "To control inflation, would you be willing or not willing to . . . reduce government spending on military programs?" (USCBSNYT.011580.R18D) or "Do you think the federal government must have a more balanced budget even if that means spending less money on defense, or don't you think so?" (USCBSNYT.000686.R32).

- Respondents stated their preferences for defense spending writ large, and not their preferences for funding a specific program like antiballistic missiles (USHARRIS.70AUG.R05A) or military aid to Israel (USORC.07114A. R27). Even if respondents support increasing or decreasing this specific funding, that might not reflect their preferences for defense spending as a whole.

- The question was not premised on a hypothetical scenario that may not have reflected respondents' actual preferences for defense spending at the time. For example: "If there is a SALT (Strategic Arms Limitation) treaty with the Soviet Union, do you think the United States should or should not cut defense spending?" (USCBSNYT.061279.R32) or "If relations between the United States and the Soviet Union continue to improve, how much money do you think the United States will be able to save by reducing defense spending—a lot of money, some, not very much, or none at all?" (USCBSNYT.012490.R29).

- The question did not explicitly tie preferences on defense spending to other fiscal choices. For example: "If cutbacks in the federal budget are needed to reduce the deficit, would you prefer that cutbacks be made in spending for defense or domestic programs?" (USMARIST.90YEAR.R07) or "If government spending had to be cut in order to balance the budget, would it be acceptable or not acceptable to you to . . . reduce defense spending?" (USCBSNYT.052690.R32A).

- The survey was based on a nationally representative sample of adults, likely voters, registered voters, or exit polls.

- The survey gave respondents the opportunity to express a preference for increasing *or* decreasing defense spending. Thus, polling questions that adopt a referendum format (e.g., supporting or opposing a specific policy proposal) were excluded from the data.[8]

The Roper Center's broader polling library includes six General Electric polls (1965, 1966, 1967, 1968, 1969, 1971) that are stored in column binary format, and thus cannot be accessed digitally. Topline results from the 1965–1968 polls were recorded by Thomas Hartley and Bruce Russett, "Public Opinion and the Common Defense," *American Political Science Review* 86, no. 4 (December 1992): 905–15. Carl W. Brown at the Roper Center kindly hand-coded the 1969 and 1971 GE polls for the purposes of this study.

The resulting data set lacked information for 1955, 1958, 1959, 1963, and 1964. Estimated levels of public support for defense spending in those years can be found in Richard C. Eichenberg and Richard Stoll, "Representing Defense," *Journal of Conflict Resolution* 47, no. 4 (August 2003): 399–422. These data points appear in figure 4.3, but they are not included in the overall count of 439 surveys.

Appendix to Chapter 6

METHOD FOR ESTIMATING LEVEL IMPORTANCE

In order to estimate level importance, we need to know how well a given perception predicts presidential vote choice. I conducted this analysis using logit models. Every model included NAES measures of Iraq War approval and leadership strength along with standard control variables for respondents' party, ideology, gender, and race.

Most statistical analyses of the 2004 presidential vote control for several additional factors.[9] The first of these factors is whether voters approved of how Bush was handling the economy, as economic approval tends to be one of the best predictors of a president's prospects for reelection. The NAES elicits this attitude with a variable (economic approval) that I code as "1" if the respondent approved of how Bush was handling the economy, as "0" if respondents disapproved of how Bush was handling the economy, and as "0.5" if the respondent had no opinion on the matter. Most studies of the 2004 presidential vote also control for approval of Bush's counterterrorism policies, since this issue was at the top of voters' minds in the first presidential election following 9/11. I used the NAES survey data to code a counterterrorism approval variable along the same lines as the Economic Approval measure.

Studies of voting in the 2004 presidential election typically control for opposition to gay marriage and frequency of religious attendance (religiosity). These variables are relevant to the 2004 election, when Bush supported a constitutional ban on same-sex marriage as a way to build support among culturally conservative voters. The NAES measures opposition to gay marriage and religiosity on separate, five-point scales.[10]

Figure A.1 shows the extent to which the ten variables described in this section predict the likelihood of NAES respondents supporting President Bush.[11] I express these results as predictive margins that describe the extent to which we would expect a voter's probability of supporting Bush to increase if we changed each independent variable by one unit. As expected, figure A.1 shows that NAES respondents were more likely to support Bush when they approved of Bush's handling of the Iraq War or when they saw Bush as being a stronger leader than Kerry. Figure A.1 also shows that NAES respondents were more likely to support Bush when they approved of his counterterrorism or economic policies, and when they identified as Republicans or ideological conservatives. Black respondents were more likely to vote for Kerry. Women and voters with higher levels of religious attendance were more likely to vote for Bush.

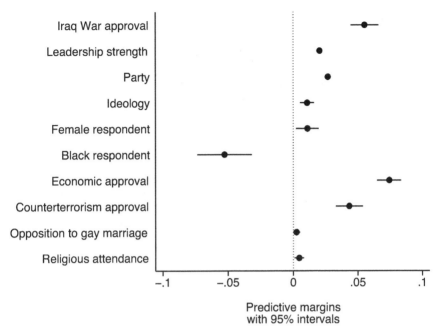

Figure A.1. Predictive margins used to generate estimates of level importance. This figure shows the expected change in probability of supporting Bush associated with increasing each independent variable by one unit. The dependent variable is vote intention, N = 14,207.

Table A.5 Trend breaks in voter perceptions

	July	August	September	October
Leadership strength (Level importance)	−0.002*** [−0.002, −0.001]	0.578*** [0.412, 0.743]	0.002*** [0.002, 0.003]	−0.000 [−0.000, 0.001]
Iraq War approval (Level importance)	−0.052 [−0.211, −0.106]	0.146*** [−0.056, 0.237]	−0.130* [−0.255, −0.005]	−0.245 [−0.564, 0.074]
Bush leadership strength (Avg. rating)	−2.46 e^{-4}*** [3.36 e^{-4}, −1.56e^{-4}]	0.076*** [0.043, 0.109]	−3.83 e^{-4}*** [3.00 e^{-4}, 4.66 e^{-4}]	8.55 e^{-5} [−1.43 e^{-5}, 1.85 e^{-4}]
Kerry leadership strength (Avg. rating)	0.001*** [0.001, 0.001]	−0.220*** [−0.270, −0.170]	−0.001*** [−0.001, −0.000]	−1.53 e^{-4} [−3.23 e^{-4}, −1.76 e^{-5}]

* $p < 0.05$; ** $p < 0.01$; *** $p < 0.001$

Ninety-five-percent intervals in brackets.

Voters who opposed same-sex marriage were also more likely to vote for Bush ($p = 0.06$).

I estimate level importance by multiplying the predictive margins shown in figure A.1 with Bush's average advantage or disadvantage on these measures, which I showed in table 6.1. The data that I used to generate estimates in figure A.1 and table 6.1 are identical.

TREND BREAKS IN LEVEL IMPORTANCE

Each cell in table A.5 represents a trend break, measured as the difference in slopes of linear regressions fit to data before and after the start of a calendar month. Estimates are scaled to represent monthly rates of change. Thus, table A.5 shows that trends in the level importance of leadership strength shifted in August in a manner that corresponds to Bush gaining 0.578 percentage points per month in aggregate vote share.

Notes

Abbreviations

Archives and works frequently cited have been identified by the following abbreviations.

ANES   American National Election Studies (1952–2020)

BG   Barry Goldwater Papers, Hayden Library, Arizona State University, Tempe, AZ

CES   Cooperative Election Study (2020)

FRUS   *Foreign Relations of the United States*, U.S. Department of State, Office of the Historian

HL-W   Hoover Library, Richard Wirthlin Papers, Stanford, CA

iPoll   Roper Center, iPoll database

JCL   Jimmy Carter Presidential Library, Atlanta, GA

JFKL   John F. Kennedy Presidential Library, Boston, MA

LBJL   LBJ Presidential Library, Austin, TX

MHS   Minnesota Historical Society, St. Paul, MN

NAES   National Annenberg Election Survey

RRL   Ronald Reagan Presidential Library, Simi Valley, CA

WHT   White House Tapes (Nixon administration)

Introduction

1. For example, Gaubatz 1999; Aldrich et al. 2006; Tomz, Weeks, and Yarhi-Milo 2020.
2. For example, Page and Bouton 2006; Jacobs and Page 2005; Walt 2018; Wertheim 2020.
3. Betts 2000.
4. Renshon and Larson, 2003.
5. Peter G. Peterson Foundation, "US Defense Spending Compared to Other Countries," May 11, 2022, https://www.pgpf.org/chart-archive/0053_defense-comparison.
6. Bond, Jr. and DePaulo 2006; Dana, Dawes, and Peterson 2013; Kleinberg et al. 2018.
7. Campbell et al. 1960; Lewis-Beck et al. 2008; Achen and Bartels 2016.

8. I chose to begin the book's historical analysis in 1960, because the United States only committed itself to playing a consistent global leadership role after the start of the Korean War. The next two presidential elections were then won by a five-star general, Dwight Eisenhower, whose military record dwarfed that of any other presidential nominee since Ulysses Grant. While Eisenhower's electoral success surely reflected voters' appreciation for his foreign policy competence, he did not need to take special measures in order to convey this credential to the public. The 1960 presidential election was thus the first modern contest in which we should expect the commander-in-chief test to be a central concern for voters, and where it was reasonable to ask which candidate had better qualifications for that role. I would not be surprised if the book's argument held in cases before 1960, but my argument does not depend on confirming that assumption.

9. Heffington, Park, and Williams 2019. Those data do not include information on the 2016 and 2020 elections. I filled in those dates by averaging together responses from the Roper Center's iPoll database, following the procedure that Heffington, Park, and Williams use in constructing their data set.

10. For example, Payne 2021; Thomson et al. 2017; Heffington 2018.

1. What Is the Commander-in-Chief Test and Why Does It Matter?

1. Popkin 1994, 61. See also Kinder 1986; Mondak 1995; Funk 1999; Fridkin and Kenney 2011.

2. Schelling 1960.

3. Jervis 1997; Powell 1999.

4. Fearon 1995.

5. For example, McDermott 2008; Saunders 2011; Kertzer 2016; Yarhi-Milo 2018; Rathbun 2019; Johnson 2020.

6. Delli Carpini and Keeter 1996; Kleinberg and Fordham 2018; Gries 2014, 227.

7. Schwartz and Blair 2020; Todorov et al. 2005; Klofstad, Anderson, and Peters 2012; Lawson et al. 2010.

8. Page 1978; Fenno 1978.

9. For example, Wattenberg 1991, 66–91; Merolla and Zechmeister 2009, 112–20; Berinsky 2009, 193–96; Cohen 2015, 63–106.

10. Hermann et al. 2001.

11. Kinder et al. 1980.

12. Rathbun 2019.

13. Kissinger 2022, xxii–xv.

14. Margaret Garrard Warner, "Bush Battles the 'Wimp Factor,'" *Newsweek*, October 19, 1987.

15. The three attributes that did *not* plausibly relate to strong leadership and good judgment were whether leaders would comport themselves with dignity on the world stage, whether they could be reassuring to Americans in the aftermath of a crisis, and whether they respected the military.

16. These definitions reflect the research of Eugene Wittkopf. To use Wittkopf's terminology, I consider foreign policies to be more "hawkish" when they are higher on the dimension of "military internationalism" and lower on the dimension of "cooperative internationalism." I use the word "hawkish" the way that Wittkopf used the word "hard-line" and I use the word "dovish" in the way that Wittkopf used the word "accommodationist." My departure from Wittkopf's terminology is purely semantic, though I believe that the words "hawkish" and "dovish" will be more intuitive for most readers. Wittkopf 1990.

17. Mann 2011.

18. For overviews of this scholarship, see Hsee et al. 1999; Hsee and Zhang 2010.

19. Betts 2000; Renshon and Larson 2003.

20. Jervis 1978; Glaser 2010.

21. See, for example, Susan E. Rice, "The Dire Consequences of Trump's Suleimani Decision," *New York Times*, January 4, 2020; Katie Glueck and Shane Goldmacher, "Joe Biden, Seeking Commander-in-Chief Moment, Denounces Trump's Iran Escalation," *New York Times*, January 7, 2020.

22. See, for example, Michael E. O'Hanlon, "Qassem Soleimani and Beyond," Brookings Institution, January 3, 2020; Michael Crowley, "For Some Never Trumpers, Killing of Suleimani Was Finally Something to Like," *New York Times*, January 6, 2020.

23. Max Greenwood, "Biden Says He Would Not Have Ordered Strike on Iranian General," *The Hill*, February 7, 2020.

24. See, for example, Catherine Lucey, "Trump Touts US Iran Strike at Ohio Campaign Rally," *Wall Street Journal*, January 9, 2020, and Trump's August 28, 2020, address accepting the Republican presidential nomination.

25. Michael Shear and David Sanger, "Biden Stands behind Afghan Withdrawal," *New York Times*, August 17, 2021, A1.

26. Shapiro 2001, 269 shows that public support for the Marshall Plan averaged about 70 percent while the program was operating. An August 1979 Harris poll found that at least 60 percent of voters agreed with each significant provision of the Camp David Accords (Roper Center, iPoll database, questions USABCHS.082779.R1A-E).

27. Similarly, the theory does not imply that literally every issue-image trade-off will favor foreign policy hawks. My argument is that, all else being equal, issue-image trade-offs will steer US foreign policy in a direction that is more hawkish than what voters actually want.

28. For example, Kertzer, Brooks, and Brooks 2021; Craig and Logevall 2009.

29. Gelpi and Grieco 2015.

30. Yarhi-Milo 2018.

31. Downs 1957; Aldrich, Sullivan, and Borgida 1989; Gaubatz 1999; Aldrich et al. 2006; Tomz, Weeks, and Yarhi-Milo 2020.

32. Kahneman and Renshon 2007; Mueller 2006; Kertzer et al. 2022.

33. Adams 1982; Ledbetter 2011; Thorpe 2014.

34. Walt 2018; Porter 2018; Mearsheimer 2018; Wertheim 2020b.

35. A related literature argues that elites influence foreign policy by sending messages (or "cues") that shape voters' policy preferences. But that would not explain why leaders frequently pursue foreign policies that voters say they do not support. See Kreps, Saunders, and Schultz 2018; Mattes and Weeks 2019; Saunders 2023.

36. Fiorina 1981; Healy and Malhotra 2013; Gelpi, Reifler, and Feaver 2007; Karol and Miguel 2007.

37. Smith 1998; Levendusky and Horowitz 2012; Nomikos and Sambanis 2019.

38. Richards et al. 1993; Smith 1996.

39. Jacobs and Shapiro 1994; Druckman, Jacobs, and Ostermeier 2004.

40. On how leaders' use of polling data can undermine democratic responsiveness, see Jacobs and Shapiro 2000; Manza, Cook, and Page 2002.

41. Petrocik 1996; Egan 2013; Gadarian 2010.

42. The book's argument also differs from the notion that candidates sometimes adapt their policy positions in response to disparities in perceived competence, as in Groseclose 2001; Stone and Simas 2010.

43. Shepsle 1972; Carson 2018; Payne 2023.

2. Personal Images, Policy Preferences, and Presidential Voting

1. See https://electionstudies.org/.

2. Formally, I define preference alignment as the absolute value of the difference between the voter's preference and her perception of the Republican candidate's position, minus the absolute value of the difference between the voter's preference and her perception of the Democratic candidate's position. Each measure of preference alignment has a mean that ranges from -0.55 to 0.05, with standard deviations ranging from 2.24 to 2.78.

3. From 2012 on, the ANES elicited these judgments with a different, five-point scale. Rather than merging different measures together, I report the larger body of pre-2012 data, but all of this chapter's findings hold using data from 2012 on.

4. All analyses of vote choice in this chapter are logit regressions. I employ ANES probability weights, adjusted so that each election year exerts equal impact on my analysis. Following standard practice in this literature, I only examine data for ANES respondents who reported voting for either the Democratic or the Republican presidential candidate. I analyze each foreign policy issue separately, because the ANES elicited these preferences in different survey waves.

5. All results presented in this section hold when any combination of these control variables is excluded from the analysis. See the appendix for full results. The coefficient for leadership strength is significantly greater than the coefficients for preference alignment on defense spending ($p < 0.001$), US-Soviet relations ($p < 0.001$), and intervention in Central America ($p < 0.05$). The contrast between leadership strength and preference alignment on willingness to use military force is less strong ($p = 0.25$), but that is almost certainly because this model contains the smallest number of observations. The coefficient on leadership strength in this model is still roughly twice as large as the coefficient on preference alignment (1.39 versus 0.86). In ordinary least squares regression where the dependent variable is the gap in feeling thermometer ratings between candidates—and where it is thus possible to include additional observations of voters who did not vote for one of the two major-party candidates—the difference between the leadership strength and preference alignment coefficients is statistically significant at the $p < 0.001$ level for all four models.

6. Aldrich, Sullivan, and Borgida 1989; Gadarian 2010; Anand and Krosnick 2003.

7. It is impossible to combine these variables into a single model because they involve questions asked in different ANES survey years. An alternative approach would be to analyze a series of statistical models that contain voters' foreign policy preferences on a given issue, along with leadership strength ratings, provided that ANES surveys gathered both kinds of data in overlapping years. It is possible to run these head-to-head comparisons for twenty-three foreign policy issues. In all cases but one, voters' foreign policy preferences predict less variation in presidential vote choice than their assessments of leadership strength (all comparisons $p < 0.05$). The only exception, involving perceptions of whether "the Iraq War was worth the cost" (2004), still reveals that policy preferences explain less variation in vote choice than perceptions of leadership strength, but this finding is only statistically significant at the $p < 0.10$ level.

8. As with all analyses of vote choice in this chapter, these models are logit regressions with ANES-provided probability weights that are adjusted to reflect unbalanced sample sizes across survey years.

9. Where statistical significance is defined as meeting the standard $p < 0.05$ threshold.

10. See, for example, Page 1994; Lodge and Taber 2013.

11. Zaller 1992.

12. There are technically more than three thousand master codes in the ANES data set, but they contain many duplications. For example, if the respondent's judgment mentioned the fact that a presidential candidate planned to raise defense spending, it could receive a different code depending on whether that judgment was made (a) in a positive or negative manner, (b) when assessing a Democrat or a Republican, or (c) before or after 1972, when the ANES implemented a new list of master codes.

13. Starting in 2008, the ANES began releasing open-ended responses without master codes. But the ANES does not make the original open-ended responses available before 2008. This makes it impossible to analyze data from both periods using identical procedures. I therefore focused my analysis on ANES mentions data spanning 1952 to 2004.

14. The ANES divides its master codes into different categories that are not useful for this chapter's purposes. For example, the ANES assigns several master codes to a category called "Stands on Foreign Affairs." This category contains assessments of issues (e.g., "will raise defense spending"), competence (e.g., "knows how to handle world affairs"), and experience (e.g., "has experience with foreign affairs").

15. The research team agreed on 84 percent of their classification choices. The appendix provides more detail on interrater reliability.

16. Technically, this process involved two separate bootstrapping processes. The first stage randomly sampled coding decisions from the research team, in order to incorporate uncertainty related to categorizing open-ended data. Then I drew another bootstrapped sample of

ANES respondents (stratified by year) in order to account for uncertainty related to ANES sampling. The book's replication materials contain code for this bootstrapping algorithm along with a full log of raters' coding choices.

17. This difference is statistically significant at the $p < 0.001$ level.

18. Similar patterns hold when separately analyzing assessments of Democratic versus Republican candidates, or when separately analyzing positive versus negative judgments.

19. Each index reflects the difference between (i) the sum of positive statements about the Republican candidate and negative statements about the Democratic candidate and (ii) the sum of positive statements about the Democratic candidate and negative statements about the Republican candidate. These indices follow Kelley's computation of "net scores"; see Kelley 1983, 24–25.

20. All findings hold when measuring model fit using AUC scores. As with all analyses of vote choice in this chapter, these models are logit regressions with ANES-provided probability weights that are adjusted to reflect unbalanced sample sizes across survey years.

21. This comparison is statistically significant at the $p < 0.001$ level.

22. This contrast is again statistically significant at the $p < 0.001$ level. Results hold if we add voter ideology to the data, though that requires restricting analysis to ANES surveys from 1972 onward.

23. The two experiments appeared in random order. All results hold when analyzing the first experiment that subjects completed. The survey was fielded from September 1 to 9, 2020. Participants were 54 percent female, 65 percent white, 15 percent Hispanic, and 12 percent Black. Thirty-one percent had a college degree. Thirty-seven percent said they were Democrats and 26 percent said they were Republicans. Median reported family income was between $50,000 and $60,000. Experimental designs and preanalysis plans were preregistered prior to data collection at Evidence in Governance and Politics, Study #20200807AA. The experiments were approved by the Dartmouth College Committee for the Protection of Human Subjects, Study #31634.

24. Barabas and Jerit 2010.

25. I based this experimental framework on Tomz, Weeks, and Yarhi-Milo 2020.

26. The choice of background characteristics, along with the choice to examine three foreign policy issues, follow Tomz, Weeks, and Yarhi-Milo 2020.

27. Standard errors clustered by respondent. All findings hold if we examine the first candidate comparison that respondents evaluated.

28. This difference is statistically significant at the $p < 0.001$ level.

29. Candidates' race and gender had no direct effect on perceptions of foreign policy competence. Republicans were generally seen as being more competent than Democrats on foreign policy, but that difference was small (two percentage points) and not statistically significant. Respondents were eighteen percentage points more likely to support candidates who shared their partisan affiliation. Candidates with extensive prior service in government or the military were roughly ten percentage points more likely to be selected as candidates who lacked prior experience in those areas.

30. Candidates' background information was identical to that in experiment A.

31. I sampled these issues from questions in the Roper Center's iPoll database of US public opinion surveys. Policy positions were included in this experiment if they were posed to a national audience from 2018 to 2020 and tagged by the Roper Center with the topics "defense," "diplomacy," or "war." This sampling strategy covered a variety of topics that polling organizations consider to be important for understanding Americans' foreign policy attitudes. Each profile contained anywhere from zero to five policy positions. The number of policy positions described in each profile was unrelated ($p = 0.60$ in ordinary least squares regression) to candidate ratings.

32. Asking respondents to state their policy preferences after voting for candidates could encourage some respondents to say that they support policies backed by their favored candidates. This posttreatment bias should make it harder to confirm the chapter's thesis, because we would expect this bias to increase the observed correlation between respondents' policy preferences and their simulated voting behavior.

33. There are many other ways to analyze those data: for example, recording the number of highly popular or highly unpopular positions that each candidate took rather than taking

a simple average of the platform's overall popularity. But those analyses did not generate any findings that were meaningfully different than what we get when analyzing aggregate popularity.

34. I took these traits from the ANES open-ended data described earlier in this chapter, selecting characteristics that my research team unanimously determined to be unrelated to political competence.

35. Unless otherwise described, all findings in this section are statistically significant at the $p < 0.001$ level. As with experiment A, all findings described in this section hold regardless of respondents' gender, race, party, education, and performance on a battery of questions that capture knowledge of foreign policy issues.

36. On average, adding a positive nonperformance trait to a candidate profile was associated with an 0.37-point reduction in a candidate's overall rating ($p = 0.56$). Adding a disputed nonperformance trait to a candidate's profile was associated with a 1.0-point reduction in the candidate's overall rating ($p = 0.18$).

37. Candidates' overall ratings were again statistically unrelated to their race and gender. Moving from zero to thirty years of political/military experience increased a candidates' rating by five percentage points, on average. Copartisan candidates were rated twelve percentage points higher, on average, than outparty candidates.

38. Fifty-eight percent of respondents were female, 71 percent were White, 11 percent were Black or African American, and 8 percent were Hispanic. Thirty-nine percent of respondents identified as Democrats and 24 percent identified as Republicans. All analyses in this section employ YouGov population weights, but all findings are robust across party, gender, race, education, and political knowledge.

39. I conducted this survey as part of the 2020 Cooperative Election Study (CES). The 2020 CES surveyed sixty-one thousand voters. The preelection portion of the survey took place between September 29 and November 2, and the postelection portion of the survey took place between November 8 and December 14. My survey was part of Dartmouth College's "team module," which was administered to one thousand of those voters. The survey was approved by the Dartmouth College Committee for the Protection of Human Subjects (Study #32157).

40. All of these questions appeared in the CES's preelection wave.

41. These questions appeared in random order.

42. These candidate ratings independently predicted respondents' vote choice ($p < 0.001$), even when controlling for partisanship, ideology, gender, and race. However, these ratings were also highly correlated with each other ($r = 0.95$). Just twenty-two out of one thousand respondents said that different candidates would do a better job of handling different policy domains. This means that the data are not well suited for explaining variation in respondent vote choice: to the extent that their expectations of performance in the domestic and foreign policy domains were so similar, we have little statistical basis for knowing which attitude was more important than the other.

43. "Why, in particular, do you think that [Biden/Trump] would do a better job when it comes to handling [foreign policy and national security / domestic policy and the economy]?" This question was excluded for any domain in which respondents saw no difference in the candidates' expected performance. The average respondent explained his or her views in seventeen words (standard deviation twelve). For comparison, the average length of open-ended mentions data in the 2016 ANES survey was ten words (standard deviation fourteen). The responses that I collected are thus at least as detailed as the most widely used data set of open-ended candidate evaluations in all of political science. To my knowledge, these data present the most direct evidence to date about what voters have on their minds when they evaluate presidential candidates' fitness to be commander in chief.

44. The fourth category in my earlier analysis was likability, which captured ANES responses that were unrelated to job performance (such as "He has a nice face"). Since my survey explicitly asked voters to assess candidates' job performance, it was no longer necessary to partition likability from the rest of the data. I also asked each member of the research team to note responses that they considered to be unintelligible, which meant that it was impossi-

ble to interpret the content of a respondent's statement. Though we were initially concerned that this could comprise a substantial fraction of data gathered via an online survey, we found that just 4 percent of voters' responses were unintelligible.

45. "Among the options listed below, which comes closest to the main reason why you think that [Donald Trump/Joe Biden] would do a better job than [Joe Biden/Donald Trump] when it comes to handling [foreign policy and national security/domestic policy and the economy]?" This question was again excluded for any domain in which respondents saw no difference in the candidates' expected performance.

46. These response options were randomly ordered.

47. Results for the open-ended data reflect the same bootstrapping procedure that I developed for analyzing ANES mentions data. Summary statistics for both open- and closed-ended data are weighted using YouGov population weights. All findings in table 2.3 hold regardless of respondents' party, gender, race, education, or political knowledge.

48. As with all analyses of the open-ended data, this process is based on a bootstrapped process that randomly samples researchers' codings.

49. The only significant change is an increase in the proportion of responses associated with party ownership. This is consistent with the idea that some voters used the open-ended responses to express partisan animosity. In the closed-ended format, these voters may have simply acknowledged that partisanship was the root of their reasoning.

3. The Hawk's Advantage

1. For example, Kreps, Saunders, and Schultz 2018; Mattes and Weeks 2019.

2. As in chapter 2, I weight ANES responses throughout this section so that each election wave comprises a nationally representative sample that exerts equal impact on my findings.

3. ANES respondents even draw sensible distinctions between the same presidential candidate's positions on defense spending across election years. Thus, voters understood that George W. Bush was less hawkish on defense spending in 2000 than when he ran for reelection during the Iraq War in 2004, and that Bill Clinton was less supportive of cutting the defense budget in 1996, as by that time he had already implemented the "bottom-up review" of military expenditures that he promised when running for president in 1992.

4. Because voters' assessments of two presidential candidates are not independent observations, it is standard practice to treat these assessments as a single observation, though we will see that the section's results do not rely on shaping the data in this manner.

5. Eighty-five percent of ANES respondents perceived at least some difference between presidential candidates' positions on defense spending. This variable takes an average value of 2.3 across the ANES data set (standard deviation, 1.6).

6. As noted in chapter 2, the ANES then switched to a different, five-point scale for measuring perceptions of leadership strength. All of this section's findings hold when analyzing these data, too.

7. ANES surveys do not define leadership strength in a manner that pertains specifically to a candidate's ability to handle foreign policy issues. As a result, some of the variation in these ratings may capture perceptions of leaders' expected performance outside the foreign policy domain. This should, if anything, make it harder to confirm the hypothesis that voters associate hawkish foreign policy positions with leadership strength. The survey experiment presented later in this chapter will also analyze a measure of leadership strength that is specifically oriented around handling foreign policy issues.

8. This finding is statistically significant at the $p < 0.001$ level.

9. For a formal specification of this model, see Friedman 2023. However, this detail is not crucial to understanding my analysis, because all of my statistical findings hold when omitting these variables.

10. I omitted "inspiring" from this list, because scholars generally see this attribute as being nearly indistinguishable from "strong leadership." These attributes indeed have a higher correlation ($r = 0.72$) than any other pair of traits in the ANES data.

11. When data from 2004 are removed from the analysis, the association between defense spending and morality falls short of statistical significance ($p = 0.14$), but the association between defense spending and leadership strength remains highly robust ($p < 0.001$).

12. This comparison is statistically significant at the $p < 0.05$ level.

13. When analyzing post-2008 data on candidate traits, which the ANES collected using different measures, some other personal traits—honesty, knowledgeability, and "cares about people like me"—show positive defense spending coefficients. This could be a product of small sample size. In any event, all of those coefficients remain smaller than the correlation between defense spending and leadership strength, and all of those comparisons remain statistically significant at the $p < 0.05$ level or better.

14. The model is estimated via logit. Following conventional practice, this analysis excludes observations for respondents who did not vote, or who voted for third-party candidates. This pattern is statistically significant at the $p < 0.001$ level. Again, see Friedman 2023 for full results.

15. Imai et al. 2010.

16. This follows the procedure developed by Aldrich, Sullivan, and Borgida 1989.

17. On average, voters preferred moderate positions across these foreign policy issues. The overall mean for voters' foreign policy preferences in this index is 4.2. Thus, once again, voters show no clear tendency to support hawkish foreign policy positions on their merits.

18. Page 1994; Lodge and Taber 2013.

19. For example, Gadarian 2010, 1051; Eichenberg and Stoll 2017.

20. Qualtrics distributed the survey to eligible voters between March 31 and April 7, 2021. Respondents matched national proportions with respect to gender (51% female), race (65% white, 13% Black, 14% Hispanic), age (median respondent between 45 and 54 years), household income (median $60,000–$69,999), and census region. Respondents were more educated than the US population (50% had a college degree versus 35% of national adults). Forty-five percent of respondents identified as Democrats and 27 percent identified as Republicans, compared to national proportions of 33 and 29 percent, respectively. The results presented in this section employ survey weights based on gender, race, age, education, and partisanship, but all findings hold using unweighted data. The experiment was approved by Dartmouth's Committee for the Protection of Human Subjects (Study # 32268) and preregistered prior to data collection at Evidence in Governance and Politics (Study #20210331AA). All findings hold if I examine the first candidate that each respondent rated.

21. This survey design was adapted from Gooch, Gerber, and Huber 2021, 1–10. These authors present a survey experiment showing that congressional candidates who take policy positions that break party norms are more likely to be viewed as ineffective legislators. They explain, "These results are, to our knowledge, the first to show that citizens alter their views of candidates' non-policy characteristics in response to their policy positions." In addition to extending this kind of analysis to the foreign policy domain, my theory differs from Gooch, Gerber, and Huber's in explaining how the link between issues and images can incentivize leaders to depart from voters' policy preferences, whereas Gooch, Gerber, and Huber are mainly interested in explaining adherence to party norms.

22. The content of candidates' background information was based on Tomz, Weeks, and Yarhi-Milo 2020.

23. This review included all surveys in the Roper Center's iPoll database that were fielded from 2017 to 2020 and tagged with the topics "Defense," "Diplomacy," or "War." I supplemented this search by examining surveys from the Chicago Council on Global Affairs, Gallup, and Pew. This is essentially an expanded list of policy positions from chapter 2's experiment B.

24. Another criterion for including foreign policy issues in the experiment is that one could clearly distinguish between hawkish and dovish positions. Following the definition of hawkishness developed in chapter 1, this means that candidates' positions on foreign policy issues differed with respect to reliance on military force or their willingness to pursue unilateral diplomacy. An example of a policy debate that does not reflect those criteria is the question of whether the United States should place a greater priority on protecting human rights. Without saying more about how the candidate plans to protect human rights—for instance, by multilateral sanctions versus military coercion—it is difficult to connect this issue to the book's

concept of hawkishness or dovishness. By contrast, when candidates take positions on removing troops from Afghanistan, building a closer political relationship with Cuba, or tightening economic sanctions on Russia, these stances all have obvious implications for the candidates' hawkishness as I defined that term.

25. Respondents received these questions in random order. These question phrasings generally reflected prompts from Gooch, Gerber, and Huber 2021.

26. The average preference alignment score was 4.3, standard deviation 1.9. I chose to measure preference alignment with a single scale, rather than asking voters to rate every one of a candidate's policy positions individually, because this allowed respondents to assign more weight to policy positions that they cared about most.

27. Mean 3.0, standard deviation 0.9.

28. Mean 2.4, standard deviation 1.0 (reverse-coded).

29. This procedure follows Gooch, Gerber, and Huber's method of eliciting candidate images by averaging together multiple, related questions.

30. Mean 2.8, standard deviation 1.0.

31. Mean 2.0, standard deviation 0.9 (reverse-coded).

32. Estimates with a univariate ordinary least squares (OLS) regression with standard errors clustered by respondent. The pattern is highly statistically significant ($p < 0.001$). This coefficient remains unchanged if I control for preference alignment or for any of the randomized attributes that appeared in each presidential candidate's profile.

33. Figure 3.5a also shows that this effect follows a smooth, linear trend. The smoothness of this trend suggests that respondents generally found the combination of policies in these profiles to be plausible. If we instead saw that respondents primarily reacted to profiles that were entirely hawkish or entirely dovish, then that would suggest they essentially ignored profiles that included a mix of hawkish and dovish policies. Instead, we see that respondents drew relatively fine-grained distinctions between candidates' policy positions, and that those distinctions shaped the candidates' personal images in the manner that my theory predicts.

34. In a univariate OLS regression with standard errors clustered by respondent, the estimated relationship between hawkishness and preference alignment is 0.01 ($p = 0.81$).

35. It is also statistically significant at the $p < 0.001$ level.

36. All findings are estimated using univariate OLS regressions with standard errors clustered by respondent.

37. The correlation between those factors is not remotely statistically significant ($p = 0.65$).

38. The exceptions are deploying US troops to stop Russia from invading NATO allies and deploying US troops to help Pakistan stop an Islamist insurgency.

39. The exceptions are maintaining/removing bases from the Middle East, developing a closer relationship to Cuba, and a candidate's overall preference for military strength versus diplomacy.

40. The only survey demographic for whom this section's findings do not hold are respondents who identified as Black or African American. These respondents did not consistently associate hawkish foreign policies with leadership strength ($p = 0.59$). This could reflect Black respondents comprising just 13 percent of the sample. An alternative hypothesis is that Black Americans are more skeptical of hawkish foreign policies, and thus less prone to view hawkish leaders as possessing favorable personal attributes. However, candidate hawkishness was statistically unrelated to Black respondents' assessments of preference alignment ($p = 0.15$). And, even if my argument somehow did not pertain to Black Americans, this would not undermine the conclusion that the logic of issue-image trade-offs generalizes widely across the politics of foreign policy.

41. Ford headed into the debate expecting to receive a question about whether or not the United States accepted a Soviet "sphere of influence" in Eastern Europe. This had been a subject of recent controversy following remarks by a Ford aide, Helmut Sonnenfeldt, which suggested that the Ford administration would tolerate such a sphere of influence. Ford had been heavily briefed on the importance of denying that he accepted a Soviet sphere of influence in Eastern Europe. This appears to have caused him some confusion when interpreting and answering a different question about whether the Soviet Union did, in fact, dominate Eastern Europe. Witcover 1977, 594–608.

4. Peace through Strength

1. See table I.1 for details.

2. Unless otherwise noted, all documents cited below are drawn from archives at the John F. Kennedy Presidential Library (JFKL), and all speeches cited below are drawn from the official record of Kennedy's campaign statements: US Senate Committee on Commerce, *Freedom of Communications: The Speeches, Remarks, Press Conferences, and Statements of Senator John F. Kennedy, August 1 through November 7, 1960* (Washington, DC: US Government Printing Office, 1961). The Harris polls are located in JFKL, Robert F. Kennedy Pre-Administration Political Papers, boxes 43–45, and JFKL, Lawrence O'Brien Personal Papers, boxes 11–17.

3. On how Kennedy relied on these data to inform his campaign strategy, see Jacobs and Shapiro 1994.

4. On the international context surrounding the 1960 presidential campaign, see Ellis 2017.

5. Theodore Sorensen, "Memorandum: Campaign Strategy 1960," JFKL, Sorensen Papers, box 22.

6. John K. Galbraith to Kennedy (July 29, 1960), JFKL, John K. Galbraith Papers, box 529. See also Galbraith, "The Issue of Experience in the 1960 Campaign" (undated, likely May 1960), JFKL, John K. Galbraith Papers, box 529; and Galbraith, "Memorandum: Campaign Strategy 1960" (undated), JFKL, John K. Galbraith Papers, box 530.

7. Ithiel de Sola Pool, "Simulmatics Report No. 4: Kennedy, Nixon, and Foreign Affairs" (August 25, 1960), JFKL, DNC Papers, box 212, 2.

8. I weighted these polls according to each state's electoral vote count.

9. The difference between these proportions is statistically significant at the $p < 0.001$ level.

10. Even with a relatively small sample of twenty-six surveys to draw on, Kennedy's deficit on war and peace was statistically significant at the $p < 0.10$ level.

11. George Belknap, "Public Opinion and the 1960 Elections" (June 20, 1960), JFKL, Myer Feldman Papers, box 4, IV-1 to IV-5.

12. Alexander Klein, "Memo. For Sen. Kennedy" (August 27, 1960), JFKL, Robert Kennedy Pre-Administration Political Files, box 33, 2.

13. Richard Goodwin, speech materials (undated), JFKL, Presidential Campaign Files, box 996.

14. Pool, "Kennedy, Nixon, and Foreign Affairs," 3, 28.

15. Ithiel de Sola Pool, "Simulmatics Report No. 3, "Nixon Before Labor Day" (August 25, 1960), JFKL, DNC Papers, box 212, 3, 13. Also see Pool's "Simulmatics Report No. 2: Kennedy Before Labor Day" (August 25, 1960), JFKL, DNC Papers, box 212, 2, 4: "The foreign affairs issue is his [Kennedy's] greatest weakness. . . . The feeling that Kennedy is less competent than Nixon to deal with Khrushchev and to keep the country out of war is pulling many Democrats away from the head of their party's ticket. This is Kennedy's major weakness."

16. These were common features of Kennedy's campaign rhetoric. The quotes are from speeches given in Alexandria, VA (August 24, 1960) and Detroit, MI (August 26, 1960). See also Albany, NY (September 29, 1960); St. Paul, MN (October 2, 1960); Anderson, IN (October 5, 1960); Crestwood, MO (October 22, 1960); Los Angeles, CA (November 1, 1960); Springfield, MA (November 7, 1960).

17. Friedberg 2000, 124–39.

18. Arthur Schlesinger, Jr., "The Shape of National Politics to Come" (May 12, 1959), JFKL, Sorensen Papers, box 22, 11, 16, 21–22.

19. Aldous 2017, 321.

20. Schlesinger, "Shape of National Politics to Come," 21–22.

21. Kennedy 1960, 226.

22. Walt W. Rostow, "Memorandum: A Democratic Strategy for 1960" (January 2, 1960), JFKL, John F. Kennedy 1960 Campaign Files, box 995, 1–2.

23. Kennedy 1960, 4; San Diego, CA (September 11, 1960).

24. Washington, DC (January 14, 1960).

25. Snead 1999.

26. Los Angeles, CA (November 1, 1960); Alexandria, VA (August 24, 1960); Washington, DC (August 30, 1960); Dayton, OH (October 17, 1960); Miami, FL (October 18, 1960).

27. Preble 2004.

28. Preble 2003.

29. Kennedy 1960, 40.

30. San Diego, CA (September 11, 1960).

31. Harris, "Analysis of the Third Kennedy-Nixon Debate" (October 19, 1960), JFKL, Richard M. Scammon Papers, box 8.

32. Rostow to Cox (October 10, 1960), JFKL Cox Files, box 202.

33. Rostow to Sorensen and Cox (July 26, 1960), JFKL, DNC Files, box 204

34. Rostow, "Democratic Strategy for 1960," 6.

35. Emphasis added.

36. White 2009, 180–208; Rorabaugh 2009, 111–12.

37. Schlesinger, "Shape of National Politics to Come," 22.

38. Sorensen 1965, 183–84.

39. That trend was statistically significant at the $p < 0.01$ level.

40. Ledbetter 2011.

41. See, for example, Aldrich et al. 1989; Bartels 1991.

42. "Reagan for President Campaign Plan" (June 29, 1980), Ronald Reagan Presidential Library (RRL), 1980 Presidential Campaign Papers, box 177, 79.

43. "Reagan for President Campaign Plan" (June 29, 1980), 36–37. Emphasis in original.

44. "Reagan for President Campaign Plan" (June 29, 1980), 79.

45. "Reagan for President Campaign Plan" (June 29, 1980), 83.

46. As Wirthlin explained it, the goal was to "focus campaign resources to reinforce the Governor's image strengths" (which he listed as "leadership, competence, strength, and decisiveness") while at the same time "we must minimize the perception that he is dangerous." Richard Wirthlin, "Seven Conditions of Victory" (October 9, 1980), reproduced in Wirthlin, Breglio, and Beal, 1981, 44. See also Wirthlin and Hall 2004, 49–50.

47. Richard Wirthlin, "Focused Impact Theme: Foreign Affairs" (August 9, 1980), cf. Wirthlin, "Status of the Campaign and Some Strategic Considerations" (October 9, 1980). These documents are reproduced in Drew 1981, 351–87.

48. Rafshoon to President Carter (May 20, 1979), Jimmy Carter Presidential Library (JCL), Rafshoon Papers, Container 11.

49. Patrick Caddell to President Carter (June 25, 1980), JCL, Chief of Staff Files, Container 77.

50. Caddell 1981, 270.

51. Patrick Caddell to President Carter (June 25, 1980). See also Patrick Caddell oral history, Miller Center of Public Affairs, April 2, 1982.

52. Patrick Caddell to President Carter (June 25, 1980). Carter's communications director, Jerry Rafshoon, similarly expressed the campaign's central question as being: "Can you imagine Ronald Reagan in this job?" Rafshoon oral history. See also Rafshoon to President Carter (July 3, 1980), JCL, Rafshoon Papers, Container 11.

53. New York, NY (August 14, 1980). Unless otherwise noted, all speeches cited in this section are archived by the American Presidency Project (https://www.presidency.ucsb.edu).

54. For a useful overview of both campaigns' strategies and perceptions, see Interview of Pat Caddell and Dick Wirthlin (December 2, 1980), Hoover Library, Richard Wirthlin Files (HL-W), box 241. See 107–9, in particular, on how Wirthlin felt that the "war and peace issue" was Reagan's primary vulnerability late in the campaign.

55. Decision/Making/Information, National Survey of Voter Attitudes (July 1980), HL-W, box 115.

56. Decision/Making/Information, National Tracking (October 14–November 2, 1980), HL-W, box 120. Of course, voters who were becoming more favorable toward Carter for other reasons might have become more likely to criticize Reagan's personality traits. In order to rule out that possibility, Wirthlin asked voters an open-ended question about what kinds of "bad

things" might happen if Reagan were elected president. The most common responses to this question always fell into a category that Wirthlin labeled "possibility of war." Voters' concerns on this front also grew over time. In June, 13 percent of voters said that the possibility of war was their main worry about Reagan as president, with another 4 percent giving answers that Wirthlin coded as relating to "poor foreign policy." By September, those proportions had doubled to 25 percent and 8 percent, respectively. Discussions of how the "warmonger issue" was the principal threat to Reagan's candidacy recur throughout the Reagan's campaign's discussion of public opinion data and communications strategy. See, for example, Robert Teeter to Ronald Reagan, "Debate Strategy" (September 12, 1980), RRL, 1980 Presidential Campaign Files, box 247; C. T. Clyne, "The Reagan Candidacy Advertising Strategy for 1980" (October 22, 1979), RRL, 1980 Presidential Campaign Files, box 232; and Steve Cohen, "Marketing Strategy" (July 9, 1980), RRL, 1980 Presidential Campaign Files, box 232.

57. Wirthlin, Broglio, and Beal 1981, 47.

58. Hedrick Smith, "Poll Shows President Has Pulled to Even Position with Reagan," *New York Times*, October 23, 1980, A1.

59. See Jim Baker to Stu Spencer (October 14, 1980), RRL, 1980 Presidential Campaign Files, box 140, along with several related memos in that same box. Carter's team understood that a debate would advantage Reagan for exactly that reason but believed that Carter could not back out of his previous demand to debate the former governor, which he had made when trailing badly in the race. See Patrick Caddell, "Debate Strategy" (October 21, 1980), JCL, Jack Watson White House Subject Files, container 110.

60. Richard Wirthlin and Richard Beal to Ronald Reagan, William Casey, and James Baker, "First Debate—Integrating Memorandum" (September 12, 1980), RRL, 1980 Presidential Campaign Files, box 247.

61. "Reagan for President Campaign Plan," 56.

62. "Reagan for President Campaign Plan," 9.

63. Detroit, MI (July 17, 1980).

64. Chicago, IL (August 18, 1980); Chicago, IL (March 17, 1980).

65. Available at https://www.presidency.ucsb.edu/documents/republican-party-platform-1980.

66. "Reagan for President Campaign Plan," 129.

67. Bill Casey to Ronald Reagan (October 26, 1980), RRL, 1980 Campaign Files, box 140. See also David Gergen, "Summary Defense Paper," Debate Book II (September 1980), RRL, 1980 Presidential Campaign Files, box 138.

68. Republican National Convention acceptance speech: Detroit, MI (July 17, 1980).

69. See, for instance, White House Office of Media Liaison, "National Defense—The Budget and the Record" (June 12, 1980), JCL, Jack Watson White House Subject Files, Container 106.

70. Rafshoon to President Carter (July 3, 1980), JCL, Rafshoon Papers, container 11.

71. The ANES measures defense spending preferences on a seven-point scale, where "four" entails holding the defense budget constant. In 1980, the median voter registered a preference of "five" on that scale, corresponding to a "slight increase."

72. Boston, Mass. (August 20, 1980). Recorded in Debate Issues Briefing Book (September 29, 1980), JCL, Powell Files, container 8.

73. Commission on Presidential Debates, https://www.debates.org/debate-history/1980-debates/#oct-28-1980.

74. See data in figure 4.3.

75. The survey showed 51 percent disapproval to 42 percent approval. Reagan/Bush Polling/Planning, "Reagan Foreign Policy Approval" (July 1984), RRL, James Baker Files, box 9.

76. Just 28 percent said they felt the world had become safer under Reagan's leadership. Richard Wirthlin, "Major Findings from the July National Survey" (July 16, 1984), RRL, Baker Files, box 9.

77. For comparison, the next most common category of negative responses was economic policies (29 percent) with increasing unemployment (15 percent) being the most common concern in that area. Richard Wirthlin, "1984 Presidential Vote" (September 2, 1983), RRL, Deaver Files, box 65.

78. Ryan 2017.
79. Wirthlin, "National Tracking" (September 27, 1984), RRL, Baker Files, box 10.
80. Wirthlin, "National Tracking."
81. See, for example, Richard Darman's description of these events in Moore 1986, 41–42, 110, 190. As one might expect, Darman denies that the Year of Peace was designed solely for political purposes, but he acknowledged that those actions had a politically favorable effect in reassuring voters about Reagan's judgment.
82. All of these comparisons are statistically significant at the $p < 0.001$ level.
83. See figure 4.3.
84. Wirthlin, "1984 Presidential Vote."
85. Jamieson 1992, 232–33.
86. Richard Wirthlin and John Moss to James Baker, "Some Suggested Debate Strategy for October 7th" (October 2, 1984), RRL, Deaver Files, box 67. For an earlier statement along similar lines, see Wirthlin, "Reagan-Bush '84 Campaign Decisions" (June 11, 1984), RRL, Baker Files, box 9.
87. Richard Darman, "Proposed Plan to Re-elect the President" (July 16, 1984), RRL, Deaver Files, box 67. See also Darman, "A Few Thoughts on Strategy" (June 1984), cited in Goldman and Fuller 1985, 413.
88. Michael Deaver, "Memorandum for Outreach Strategy Group" (June 6, 1983), RRL, Deaver Files, box 68.
89. Bill Galston to Walter Mondale, "Preparation for the Brinkley Show" (September 14, 1983), MHS, Mondale Files, box 146.L.9.1B.
90. Peter Hart to Jim Johnson, "Preparing for the Main Event" (December 16, 1983), MHS, Mondale Files, box 148.J.18.2F.
91. MRK Research, "Focus Group Research" (October 1, 1984), MHS, Mondale Files, box 148.J.18.1B.
92. For an internal memorandum documenting Mondale's extensive record of opposing defense programs in the Senate and noting this as a "point of vulnerability" in his campaign, see Joan Hartman, "Mr. Mondale's Senate Defense Record," MHS, Mondale Files, box 146.L.8.6F.
93. On how Reagan's campaign exploited this situation, see Jim Lake, "Talking Points: Fritz Flops on Defense" (October 10, 1984), RRL, Baker Files, box 10. On Mondale's attempt to appear moderate on the defense issue—rejecting Gary Hart's cuts but opposing Reagan's continued buildup—see Mondale's March 14, 1984, speech to the Chicago Council on Foreign Relations, Minnesota Historical Society (MHS), Mondale Files, box 146.L.8.6F, along with the Mondale campaign's May 1984 "Fact Sheet on Arms Control" (idem).
94. "Platform Briefing Materials: Defense Budget" (May 1984), MHS, Mondale Files, box 146.L.8.6F; "Fact Sheet on the Budget (January 1984), MHS, Mondale Files, box 153.J.1.9B.
95. Galston to Mondale, "Preparation for the Brinkley Show."
96. Peter Hart to Walter Mondale, "New York Times / CBS Poll Results" (January 27, 1984), MHS, Mondale Files, box 148.J.18.2F.
97. Peter D. Hart Research Associates, Inc., "A Survey of Voter Attitudes in the United States" (September 21, 1984), MHS, Mondale Files, box 148.J.18.2F.
98. See, for example, "Address to Chicago Council on Foreign Relations" (March 14, 1984), MHS, Mondale Files, box 146.L.8.6F.
99. "Talking Points on the Reagan Platform: Defense" and "Talking Points on the Reagan Platform: Defense and Social Spending Comparison," MHS, Mondale Files, box 146.L.8.6F; "Debate Preparation Materials: Foreign Policy Briefing Book: Defense Budget," MHS, Mondale Files, box 146.L.9.1B.
100. Peter D. Hart Research Associates Inc., "Options on the Nuclear Arms Control Issue" (September 1, 1984), MHS, Mondale Files, box 148.J.18.2F.
101. MRK Research, "Focus Group Research" (October 17, 1984), MHS, Mondale Files, box 148.J.18.1B. These arguments specifically pertained to the defense budget and arms control issues.
102. Goldman and Fuller 1985, 287.
103. The sole exception is George W. Bush, who dropped the slogan when running for re-election during the Iraq War in 2004, but who nevertheless had invoked it when seeking the presidency in 2000.

104. Jamieson 1992, 3–9.
105. This difference is statistically significant at the $p < 0.01$ level.
106. Ornstein and Schmitt 1989, 43.
107. These data are mostly drawn from the Roper Center's iPoll database; see the appendix for detail.
108. These trends do not reflect a broader aversion to raising federal expenditures. According to data from the American National Election Studies and the General Social Survey, majorities of voters consistently support raising government spending on a wide range of domestic programs.
109. For example, Thorpe 2014; Walt 2018; Ledbetter 2011.
110. For example, Hartley and Russett 1992; Eichenberg and Stoll 2005; Soroka and Wlezien 2010.

5. Campaigning in a Quagmire

1. See table I.1 for details.
2. Johnson 2009, 266–67. Johnson accomplished that goal, defeating Goldwater by nearly 16 million votes.
3. Johnson's primary political weakness overall was likely a series of corruption allegations that had emerged before the campaign, but that did not significantly influence Johnson's position taking.
4. Doyle Dane Bernbach, "Population, Voting Records, and Political Issues," June 1964, LBJ Presidential Library (LBJL) Aides Files: Moyers, box 21.
5. The next most unpopular issue that Doyle Dane Bernbach identified was urban renewal, listed as unfavorable to Johnson in twenty-two states, but favorable to Johnson in nine states.
6. The polls span February–October 1964. Quayle's methodology, which Louis Harris pioneered while working for John F. Kennedy's 1960 presidential campaign, asked voters to identify open-ended "issues of concern," and then to state whether they approved or disapproved of how Johnson was handling those issues. See LBJL Aides Files: Panzer, boxes 168–79; and LBJL Aides Files: Moyers, box 40.
7. The next most unpopular policy issues for Johnson were taxes and desegregation, which received disapproval ratings worse than the Vietnam War in just five states apiece.
8. LBJL, telephone conversation #3520 (May 27, 1964). Johnson offered a similar impression two weeks later, explaining to Russell that "we're doing just fine except for this damned Vietnam thing." LBJL, telephone conversation #3680 (June 11, 1964).
9. For example, Allcock 2017, 160; Johns 2010, 45.
10. Miller Center presidential recordings, May 27, 1964 (11:57 a.m.).
11. For representative statements of Goldwater's emphasis on "winning" in foreign policy, see Goldwater's January 3, 1964, speech announcing his presidential candidacy, in Arizona State University's Personal and Political Papers of Barry Goldwater (BG), box 120; Barry Goldwater, "My Proposals for a 'Can-Win' Foreign Policy," Life, January 17, 1964; and Goldwater's convention speech (BG box 120), delivered in Daly City, California (July 16, 1964).
12. For representative statements, see Goldwater's "Meet Barry Goldwater" television program (May 14, 1964), BG box 136; Goldwater's "Issues and Answers" interview (May 24, 1964), BG box 121; and speeches in Washington, DC (April 18, 1964), BG box 121, and Ventura, CA (May 17, 1964), BG box 121.
13. Goldwater's private polls showed that only 35 percent of voters supported escalating the war. Even Republicans opposed Goldwater's position. See, for example, Opinion Research Corporation, "Voters Appraise the Johnson Administration," BG box 122; Memorandum, "October 5 Campaign Survey" (October 1964), BG box 121.
14. For example, A. B. Hermann, "Summary of Confidential Questionnaires" (September 22, 1964), Arizona State University, Dean Burch Collection, box 11; RNC Research Division, "Some Indications of Public Opinion at the Close of 1963" (November 1963), BG box 121; Opinion Research Corporation, "Voters Appraise the Johnson Administration."

15. See, for example, Goldwater's speeches in Manchester, NH (March 5, 1964), BG box 121; Omaha, NE (May 11, 1964), BG box 121; and Houston, TX (October 15, 1964), BG box 136.

16. These statements were from March 6, and April 11, respectively (both BG box 121).

17. "A Conversation at Gettysburg" (September 22, 1964), BG box 122. Goldwater offered a more aggressive version of this statement in a February 19 speech in Newport, NH (BG box 121): "It is reckless to offer the American sugar candy promises when what we really need to do is to face facts. This isn't a sugar candy world! This is a tough world and we face tough enemies. Soft words and soft men will never turn back those enemies."

18. Moyers to Johnson (July 3, 1964), LBJL White House Central Files [WHCF], PL box 116.

19. Moyers, "The Politics of Peace: 1964" (February 12, 1964), LBJL Aides Files: Moyers, box 40.

20. Mann 2011.

21. "Memorandum on the Southeast Asia Situation" (June 12, 1964), LBJL, Vietnam Country File (VCF), box 76.

22. Thus, in a June 9 (6:20 p.m.) phone call with Secretary of Defense Robert McNamara, Johnson argued that "if you start doing it [debating escalation], they're going to be hollering, 'you're a warmonger. . . . I think that's the horn the Republicans would like to get us on." Miller Center presidential recordings. William Bundy made a similar argument in his June 12 "Memorandum on the Southeast Asia Situation."

23. Memorandum for discussion (June 10, 1964), LBJL, VCF, box 77.

24. Summary Record of the Meeting on Southeast Asia (June 10, 1964), LBJL, NSC Histories, box 38.

25. For extensive discussion of the May/June resolution debates, see William Bundy's unpublished manuscript on Vietnam War decision making at LBJL, W. Bundy Papers, box 1, chs. 12–14.

26. Moïse 1996.

27. The White House press release defending the Gulf of Tonkin Resolution was drawn nearly verbatim from a text drafted in June. Both documents are at LBJL, VCF, box 76.

28. Woods 1995, 353–55. For more on Fulbright's role, see Woods 1995, 344–48; Berman 1988, 15–32.

29. This figure reflects the difference in mean approval for Johnson's handling of Vietnam across Quayle's state polls conducted prior to the Gulf of Tonkin Resolution, versus polls conducted after the Gulf of Tonkin Resolution. This comparison is statistically significant at the $p < 0.05$ level, even when controlling for Johnson's overall favorability or his two-way vote share in each state poll.

30. Louis Harris, "Harris Survey" (August 10, 1964), LBJL, WHCF, ND box 214.

31. Louis Harris, "WH Poll per Fred Panzer" (August 10, 1964), LBJL, WHCF, ND box 214.

32. Allcock 2017.

33. Stewart Alsop, "Can Goldwater Win in '64?," *Saturday Evening Post* 237 (August 24, 1963): 21.

34. LaFeber 2005, 103–10.

35. Ambrose 1989, 139–50.

36. Whalen 1972, 137–38.

37. Daddis 2015.

38. Nelson 2018; Scanlon 2017.

39. Nelson 2014, 158.

40. Lawrence O'Brien, "Presidential Campaign Plan" (August 27, 1968), John F. Kennedy Presidential Library (JFKL), Lawrence O'Brien Papers, box 173.

41. Gerald Hursh, "The Humphrey Image" (September 24, 1968), Minnesota Historical Society (MHS), 1968 Campaign Files, box 150.F.15.7B. The original Quayle polls are located in the same folder. Humphrey's policy committee discussed this analysis on September 27 (see MHS, DNC/O'Brien Files, box 150.G.4F), explicitly connecting Humphrey's image problem with his stance—or lack thereof—on Vietnam and the bombing pause.

42. "Voter Opinion on Campaign Issues" (August 1968), MHS, Humphrey research files, box 147.D.4.10F.

43. Institute for Motivational Research, "The Undecided Voter" (September 1968), JFKL, O'Brien Papers, box 172.

44. Roper Center, iPoll questions USGALLUP.766.Q13, USGALLUP.68-767.R18A, USGALLUP.768.Q08, USGALLUP.769.Q10, and USGALLUP.770.Q14.

45. Huntington to Humphrey, "Vietnam in the Campaign" (September 11, 1968), MHS, Welsh Papers, box 3.

46. Gerald Hursh, "The Vice President, Riots, and Vietnam," September 27, 1968, MHS, DNC files, box 150.G.5.4F.

47. For polling data on this subject, see Page and Brody 1972.

48. Vietnam Task Force (July 25, 1968), MHS, Task Force files, box 148.B.14.4F.

49. This conversation is recounted in the September 27 diary entry of Humphrey aide Edgar Berman (MHS, Solberg Papers, box 1) and Ted Van Dyk's oral history (March 12, 1979, MHS, Solberg Papers, box 2).

50. Berman diary (August 9), MHS, Solberg chapter notes, box 4; Ted Van Dyk oral history.

51. This episode is extensively documented in two folders of archival material related to the Vietnam plank debate in MHS, 1968 Convention files, box 150.G.5.2F, as well as in oral histories by David Ginsburg (November 24, 1982) and Charles Murphy (September 14, 1981), both in MHS, Solberg Papers, box 1.

52. *New York Times*, August 28, 1968; *Washington Post*, August 30, 1968; *Washington Post*, September 2, 1968.

53. Van Dyk oral history.

54. William Connell oral history (November 15, 1980), MHS, Solberg Papers, box 1.

55. Rostow to LBJ (August 22, 1964), MHS, Solberg chapter notes, box 4.

56. Ginsburg oral history. The convention plank disagreement largely came down to a single word. Humphrey wanted the timing of the bombing pause to "take into account the security of our troops," while Johnson forced the plank to say that a bombing pause should only occur "*when* this action would not endanger the lives of our troops" (emphasis added).

57. Evron Kirkpatrick, "Vietnam: The Bombing Pause" (September 1968), MHS, Kampelman Papers, box 19.

58. "Voter Opinion on Campaign Issues" (August 1968), JFKL, O'Brien Papers, box 167.

59. Humphrey's Campaign Policy Committee Minutes from September 27, 1968, MHS, DNC files, box 150.G.5.4F, demonstrate that Humphrey's aides all understood this point immediately before writing the Salt Lake City speech.

60. Huntington, "Vietnam in the Campaign."

61. Campaign Policy Committee Minutes (September 27, 1968), MHS, DNC files, box 150.G.5.4F.

62. Institute for Motivational Research, "The Undecided Voter."

63. Lawrence O'Brien, "A Campaign Strategy" (September 13, 1968), JFKL, O'Brien Papers, box 172.

64. This trend shift is statistically significant at the $p < 0.01$ level. Connell recounts in his oral history: "Next day the End-the-War pickets were down. We never saw them again." On the positive effects of the Salt Lake City speech on Humphrey's campaign events, see Offner 2018, 318–35; Solberg 1984, 386–402.

65. Johns 2020, 129.

66. For examples of each of these arguments, applied specifically to debates about the Vietnam war in the 1968 presidential election, see Page and Brody 1972.

67. The Roper Center's iPoll database contains seventeen surveys that asked Americans to identify the most important problem facing the country during Nixon's first term as president. Vietnam was the most commonly selected answer in fourteen of those surveys. A fifteenth survey, from May 1970, listed "campus protests" as the country's most important problem. Since that result almost certainly reflected reactions to the Kent State shootings, it, too, reflected voters' concerns about Vietnam.

68. Kimball 2003; Hanhimäki 2003.

69. Asselin 2002, xi, 86; Kimball 1999, 240.

70. Nguyen and Schecter 1986, 123.

71. White House Tapes (WHT), Conversation 466–012 (March 11, 1971).

72. H. R. Haldeman Diaries, Nixon Presidential Library, July 27, 1971.

73. WHT, Oval Office Series, Conversation 527–016 (June 23, 1971).

74. WHT, Conversation 788–001 (September 29, 1972).

75. WHT, Conversation 474–008 (March 26, 1971).

76. WHT, Conversation 760–006 (August 3, 1972).

77. WHT, Conversation 793–006 (October 6, 1972).

78. Ehrlichman 1982, 316.

79. H. R. Haldeman Diaries, Nixon Presidential Library, December 21, 1970, and December 15, 1970.

80. WHT, Conversation 471–002 (March 19, 1971).

81. WHT, Conversation 527–016 (June 23, 1971).

82. Conversation with Kissinger; WHT, Conversation 700–002 (April 3, 1972).

83. Hughes 2015, 3–4.

84. Nguyen 2012, 228.

85. For more detail on McGovern's Vietnam policies—both prior to and during the 1972 campaign—see Miroff 2007 and Knock 2016.

86. Just 13 percent supported this proposal. Roper Center, iPoll question USHARRIS.061272.R2.

87. Just 23 percent of voters disagreed with that assessment. Roper Center, iPoll question USHARRIS.082872.R3A.

88. Roper Center, iPoll question USHARRIS.091172.R2.

89. Roper Center, iPoll question USHARRIS.110272.R4.

90. McGovern was one of the Senate's earliest and strongest critics of the war. In 1970, McGovern even refinanced his house to fund television advertisements that advocated withdrawal. Knock 2016, 315–46; Webb 1998.

91. Thus, in a September speech, McGovern said that "[Nixon's] secret plan will remain forever a secret in the hearts of 20,000 Americans who were alive at the time that plan was announced and who are no longer with us." McGovern 1974, 121. On McGovern's broader efforts to portray Nixon as a hypocrite, see Jamieson 1996, 314–18, 325.

92. Hughes 2015, 101–3.

93. Jamieson 1996, 310–25.

94. Asselin 2002, 81–85. Nixon and Kissinger furthermore negotiated a time frame for withdrawal of just sixty days—even faster than McGovern's ninety-day window.

95. Asselin 2002, 72, 120.

96. Transcript of a telephone conversation between Nixon and Kissinger (October 4, 1972), *FRUS, 1969–1976* VIII, doc. 279. On other occasions, Kissinger described the settlement as "so far better than anything we dreamt of"—a "smashing victory" that "far exceed[ed] the expectations of the American public." WHT, Conversation 366–006 (October 12, 1972); WHT, Conversation 149–014 (October 15, 1972); Kissinger to Haig (October 21, 1972), *FRUS, 1969–1976* IX, doc. 35.

97. WHT, Conversation 149–014 (October 15, 1972).

98. Nixon, *RN*, 700. See also Ehrlichman 1982, 312.

99. WHT, Conversation 759–005 (August 2, 1972).

100. WHT, Conversation 793–006 (October 6, 1972).

101. Telephone Conversation between Nixon and Haig (October 21, 1972), *FRUS, 1969–1976* IX, doc. 38. The next day, Nixon instructed Haig to "put the lid on this thing and hold it. . . . [T]here's no problem, but it must not be before the election." WHT, Conversation 151–011 (October 22, 1972).

102. "One possibility, if we're going to be cold-blooded about it, is to settle it with the North Vietnamese and hold it until after the election in return for their being quiet during this period." Transcript of a telephone conversation between Nixon and Kissinger (October 4, 1972), *FRUS, 1969–1976* VIII, doc. 279.

103. Transcript of a telephone conversation between Nixon and Kissinger (October 4, 1972), *FRUS, 1969–1976* VIII, doc. 279; WHT, Conversation 752–006 (July 25, 1972). Kissinger held out hope that Thieu and Nixon could be persuaded to accept the deal before Election Day but, as

these quotes show, he nevertheless supported Nixon's goal of concealing the terms of peace deal from the public until the last possible minute.

104. Transcript of a telephone conversation between Nixon and Kissinger (October 4, 1972), *FRUS, 1969–1976* VIII, doc. 279. Haig similarly claimed that "if this opportunity is not grabbed, the chances of the war being prolonged are serious." Transcript of a telephone conversation between Nixon and Haig (October 21, 1972), *FRUS, 1969–1976* IX, doc. 37.

105. Clodfelter 1989, 177–202.

106. Domestic criticisms of the Christmas bombings were unusually harsh, even by the standards of Vietnam War–era politics. The *Boston Globe*'s editorial board (December 20, 1972) described the Christmas bombings as "Stone Age level morality, humanity and savagery." The *Washington Post*'s editorial board (January 7, 1973) said the bombings were "so ruthless . . . as to cause millions of Americans to cringe in shame and to wonder at their President's very sanity."

107. The January peace accord involved minor adjustments from the October proposals, but few observers expected North Vietnam to respect those conditions. Kissinger biographer Barry Gewen, who offers a generally sympathetic portrait of the Nixon administration's decision making in Vietnam, argues that "there was no more cold-blooded decision taken during the entire Vietnam war than the one to use military force against North Vietnam at the end of 1972" rather than accepting the terms that Hanoi offered in October. Gewen 2020, 275. For similar assessments, see Brigham 2018, 235–38; Schwartz 2020, 202–7.

108. Kissinger 1979, 1477. The most famous assessment of this period arguably belongs to Kissinger's aide, John Negroponte, who quipped: "We bombed them into accepting our concessions." See Berman 2001, 240.

109. Roper Center, iPoll question USYANK.72VOT4.RQ11AE. An August survey put those margins at 68–16 percent (USYANK.72VOT1.Q11A12).

110. Roper Center, iPoll question USHARRIS.102372.R1A (October 1972). A contemporaneous Time/Yankelovich poll (USYANK.72VOT4.Q11AL) reported even larger margins on this question of 72–11 percent; and Roper Center, iPoll question USHARRIS.102372.R1B.

111. For example, McGovern dominated Nixon on questions about who would do a better job of closing tax loopholes (42–21 percent), who would do a better job of treating minorities fairly (45–28 percent), and who would "pay more attention to the needs of the little man." Meanwhile, polls showed that a substantial majority of voters praised McGovern's "courage to say what he thinks" (63–11 percent), a majority said that McGovern deserved credit for his early opposition to the Vietnam War (54–21 percent), and 56 percent of voters had a positive impression of McGovern overall. See iPoll questions USYANK.72VOT1.Q11A04, USYANK.72VOT1.Q11A01, USYANK.72VOT1.Q11A05, USHARRIS.060572.R1A, USHARRIS.060572.R1G, USGALLUP.859.Q010J.

112. Roper Center, iPoll question USYANK.72VOT4.Q06A1.

113. The Roper Center's iPoll database contains eight polls that asked this question to nationally-representative samples in October–November 1972. An average of 55 percent of voters (minimum 52 percent) said that they approved of how Nixon was handling the war, against an average of just 33 percent disapproval (maximum 35 percent).

114. Indeed, the iPoll database contains four October polls showing that voters were more likely to say that they believed that Nixon would bring US troops home sooner than McGovern (USHARRIS.210272.R2, USORC.1022272.R17D, USHARRIS.110272.R3, and USHARRIS.102372.R1D).

115. Harris Teeter to H. R. Haldeman, "Nixon/McGovern Strong/Weak Issues" (August 8, 1972): Gerald R. Ford Presidential Library, Teeter Papers, box 65.

6. Staying the Course

1. This difference is statistically significant at the $p < 0.001$ level. These data omit five surveys that allowed voters to express "mixed feelings," which typically absorbed 15–20 percent of responses.

2. This difference is also statistically significant at the $p < 0.001$ level. The iPoll database contains thirty-five such national polls administered from July to October 2004. On average,

51 percent of respondents said the war was not worth the cost, with 45 percent taking the opposite view. The former position received greater support in twenty-seven polls.

3. Mehlman, Southern Methodist University (SMU) oral history (http://cphcmp.smu.edu /2004election/), December 13, 2013.

4. Mehlman, SMU oral history.

5. Mehlman, SMU oral history. See also Mehlman interview in John F. Kennedy School of Government 2006, 36.

6. Mehlman, SMU oral history.

7. Mehlman interview in John F. Kennedy School of Government 2006, 114, 192.

8. Dowd interview in John F. Kennedy School of Government 2006, 169.

9. Devenish interview in John F. Kennedy School of Government 2006, 131.

10. First presidential debate, September 30, 2004.

11. Spielvogel 2005; E. J. Dionne, Jr., "Doing an Atwater on Kerry," *Washington Post,* July 16, 2004, A21; Dan Balz and Jim VandeHei, "Candidates Debut Closing Themes," *Washington Post,* October 15, 2004.

12. McKinnon interview in Jamieson 2006, 40.

13. Eskew interview in Jamieson 2006, 168.

14. John Kerry, Council on Foreign Relations address (New York, NY), December 3, 2003.

15. Shrum 2007, 467–68.

16. Cahill interview in Jamieson 2006, 32.

17. Shrum interview in John F. Kennedy School of Government 2006, 145.

18. These claims come from two of Kerry's most widely used television spots, titled "War on Terror" and "Wrong Choices." The Museum of the Moving Image provides videos of the ads cited in this chapter at http://www.livingroomcandidate.org/commercials/2004.

19. Commission on Presidential Debates (September 30, 2004). See also "Kerry, Bush Clash Over Iraq War," *BBC News,* September 6, 2004; Maria Newman, "Kerry Says Iraq War Raises Questions on Bush's Judgment," *New York Times,* September 20, 2004.

20. Adam Nagourney interview in John F. Kennedy School of Government 2006, 80–81.

21. On the origins and impact of the "flip-flopping" attacks, particularly with respect to Kerry's vote on the $87 billion in war funding, see interviews with Mehlman and Devenish in John F. Kennedy School of Government 2006, 110–11, and Rove 2010, 379, 384–85.

22. Kerry's logic in voting against the $87 billion almost certainly involved an attempt to court left-wing voters without coming out more forcefully against the war as a whole. His position could thus be criticized for being excessively political—but that is not the same thing as saying that Kerry was indecisive or that he had changed his stance on the war.

23. Commission on Presidential Debates (September 30, 2004).

24. Mehlman, SMU oral history.

25. Cahill interview, John F. Kennedy School of Government 2006, 87.

26. Lockhart interview in Jamieson 2006, 163.

27. Ken Mellman, SMU oral history; Joe Lockhart, SMU oral history, August 12, 2014; Shrum 2007, 456–59, 470–71; Kerry 2018, 277–79, 304.

28. Shrum 2007, 468.

29. Devine interview in John F. Kennedy School of Government 2006, 137.

30. Shrum 2007, 468–71.

31. Romer et al. 2006.

32. I only code this variable for questions that assumed Kerry would be the Democratic presidential nominee. Otherwise, it is not obvious whether voters who planned to support another Democratic candidate (say, John Edwards) would necessarily vote for Kerry, defect to Bush, or stay home in the general election.

33. These are all of the attributes for which the NAES provides consistent coverage from the time when Kerry secured the Democratic presidential nomination through Election Day.

34. Achen 1982, 71–73. Berinsky 2009, 182–83, uses level importance statistics to understand which armed conflicts have impacted presidential voting more than others.

35. See also Miller and Shanks 1996.

36. This difference is statistically significant at the $p < 0.001$ level.

37. This difference is statistically significant at the $p < 0.001$ level.

38. Thus, I would identify a day (say, July 10); I would collect all NAES data within a week of that date (July 3–July 17); I would estimate the level importance for different political attitudes within that window; and then I would shift the analysis forward by one day (centering the next batch of analyses on July 11). To my knowledge, this is the first study to measure dynamic changes in level importance over time.

39. The trend break is also statistically significant at the $p < 0.001$ level.

40. This difference in trend breaks is statistically significant at the $p < 0.001$ level.

41. As noted earlier, the NAES measures perceptions of candidates' leadership strength on separate, ten-point scales.

42. This difference in trend breaks is statistically significant at the $p < 0.001$ level.

43. See, for example, Campbell 2005; Merolla and Zechmeister 2009; Abramson et al. 2007.

44. Of course, many studies describe how political attitudes fluctuate over time—but that is not the same as tracking how much those attitudes *mattered* for explaining candidate preference.

45. Weisberg and Christenson 2007 present a related argument about how Bush used debates about the Iraq War to "prime" voters' concerns about counterterrorism. Since the public generally believed that Bush would do a better job of handling counterterrorism, Weisberg and Christenson say that this trade-off worked in Bush's favor. This chapter's argument goes beyond Weisberg and Christenson's analysis by showing how Bush used debates about the Iraq War to craft a broader image of strong leadership. Since my statistical models controlled for public approval of Bush's counterterrorism policies, it is both conceptually and empirically distinct from Weisberg and Christenson's analysis. (The results in figure 6.1 also show that perceptions of leadership strength explain the results of the 2004 vote nearly ten times better than attitudes toward Bush on counterterrorism.)

46. Lewis-Beck et al. 2008, 52–53.

47. Norpoth and Sidman 2007, 175–95.

48. Merolla and Zechmeister 2009, 99–120.

7. Image-Making in an Age of Endless Wars

1. Posen and Ross 1996; Gholz, Press, and Sapolsky 1997.

2. For comparison, Clinton could justify his intervention in Haiti as maintaining security in America's backyard, or as a way to staunch the flow of refugees onto American soil. Clinton's decision to intervene in Kosovo in 1998 then largely followed the precedent that Bosnia had set.

3. Lake, Miller Center oral history, 2002.

4. For example, Bacevich 2020, 105; Mearsheimer 2018, 176–79; Walt 2018, 62–68.

5. For accounts of Clinton's foreign policy positions and electoral strategy during the 1992 presidential campaign, see Dumbrell 2017, 317–35; Boys 2021, 80–94.

6. Lake, Miller Center oral history, 2002.

7. "Statement by Governor Bill Clinton in Killings in Serbian Camps," August 4, 1992.

8. "Statement by Governor Bill Clinton on the Crisis in Bosnia," July 26, 1992.

9. Holbrooke memo to Clinton (August 23, 1992), reprinted in Holbrooke 1998, 41–42.

10. Nancy Soderberg, Miller Center oral history, May 10, 2007, 3–4.

11. Sandy Berger, Miller Center oral history, March 24, 2005, 16–17, 22.

12. Boys 2015, 28; Chollet and Goldgeier 2008, 29–32, 41–43, 63–71.

13. For similar explanations of Clinton's position taking on Bosnia and democracy promotion, see Drew 1994, 138; Chollet and Goldgeier 2008, 32–43; Hames 1993, 315–30.

14. Sobel 2000, 111–31.

15. Dumbrell 2009, 63–71.

16. Chollet 2005, 7; Lake 2008, 144–45.

17. Soderberg 2005, 16.

18. For example, the Roper Center's iPoll database contains twenty surveys that measured approval of how Clinton was handling foreign policy throughout the first half of 1995—the period just before Clinton intervened in Bosnia. Across those surveys, Clinton's average favorability rating was 42 percent. Meanwhile, a January 1995 *Wall Street Journal* poll showed that just 31 percent of Americans saw Clinton as a "strong leader" and that just 34 percent of voters thought that Clinton was an effective commander-in-chief (Roper Center, iPoll survey USNBCWSJ1995-4056). A series of four CBS polls in 1994–1995 found that only 13 percent of Americans believed that Clinton had "a clear plan for his foreign policy" (USCBSNYT.042594.R13, USCBS.062494.R15, USCBSNYT.JUL94C.Q35, USCBS.060795.R03). All of those figures were noticeably lower than Clinton's overall job approval rating: averaging across seventy surveys from January to June 1995 in the Roper Center's iPoll database, Clinton's overall approval rating was 48 percent.

19. Drew 1994, 419.

20. As paraphrased in Woodward 1996, 253.

21. Albright, "Elements of a New Strategy," June 21, 1995, quoted in Chollet 2005, 20. See also Albright 2003, 186.

22. See, for instance, Stephanopoulos 1999, 383; Harris 2005, 117, 200; Halberstam 2001, 317; Chollet 2005, 20; Soderberg 2005, 76; Soderberg oral history, 58.

23. Branch 2009, 300.

24. Morris 1998, 38.

25. Morris 1998, 176.

26. Stephanopoulos 1999, 381–82.

27. Lake, Miller Center oral history, 2002.

28. Cassata 1995, 1653–54.

29. Bob Dole, "Let Bosnia Control Its Own Future," *Newsweek*, August 7, 1995, 23.

30. Elaine Sciolino, "House, Like Senate, Votes to Halt Bosnia Embargo," *New York Times*, August 2, 1995, A6; "Bosnian War Sparks Conflict at Home," *1995 Congressional Quarterly Almanac*, 10–12.

31. See, for example, Daalder 2000, 63, 166; Chollet 2005, 38.

32. Stephanopoulos 1999, 383.

33. Roper Center, iPoll database, sample sizes of ten, nine, and three surveys, respectively.

34. McLarty oral history, 77.

35. Woodward 1996, 368.

36. Adam Nagourney, "Clinton Says Party Failed Midterm Test Over Security Issue," *New York Times*, December 4, 2002, A1.

37. Klarevas 2002; Eichenberg 2005.

38. Kreps 2011.

39. Harvey 2011, 126–36.

40. "A Shallow Disagreement," *Washington Post*, October 2, 2002, A16.

41. Isikoff and Corn 2006, 127–28; Hess 2006, 112–15.

42. See, for example, Bush's West Point commencement address (West Point, NY, June 1, 2002) and his October 7, 2002, address in Cincinnati, Ohio. For a systematic assessment of such rhetoric, see Gershkoff and Kushner 2005.

43. Althaus and Largio 2004.

44. Krebs and Lobasz 2007, 409–51.

45. Cramer 2007, 489–524.

46. For related arguments, see Schuessler 2015, 100–102, 113–14; Western 2005, 128–32.

47. See Isikoff and Corn 2006, 128; Hess 2006; David Pace, "Nunn Regrets Vote on Gulf War," *Washington Post*, December 26, 1996.

48. Kerry 2018, 248.

49. Biden 2008, 339.

50. Clinton 2015, 134.

51. Or, at least, to avoid sending a clear indication that they were weak on national security.

52. Baker 2014, 223.

53. Cramer 2007, 509–11.

54. Isikoff and Corn 2006, 137–38.

55. Kreps 2011, 143; Western 2005; Woodward 2004, 168, 357.

56. Another potential critique of this section's argument is that it would have been inappropriate for Congress to constrain the Bush administration's ability to go to war. For example, Hillary Clinton later argued that making war authorization conditional on UN approval would effectively have "subordinated" US foreign policy to the United Nations. "I don't believe that is an appropriate policy for the United States," Clinton explained, "no matter who is our president" (Hillary Clinton, interview with Tim Russert on NBC News' *Meet the Press*, January 13, 2008). Yet, this argument does not explain why Congress needed to grant the Bush administration unconditional authority to go to war in October 2002, before Bush had tried to secure UN support. Clinton's appeal to the logic of appropriateness only makes sense if one believes that Congress can only grant authorization for war on an unconditional basis, and then only on a timetable dictated by the president. One can certainly see why it would have been politically difficult to slow momentum for war in October 2002. But that would be consistent with this section's argument, rather than with norms surrounding the use of force.

57. When George W. Bush left office, the United States and Iraq had signed a Status of Forces Agreement that required US forces to leave Iraq by the end of 2011.

58. Kupchan 2020, 323.

59. Bacevich 2020, 125.

60. McChrystal 2013, 316–33.

61. For an overview of divisions within Obama's administration, see Marsh 2014, 270–75; McHugh 2015, 11; Kaplan 2013, 297–310.

62. Bob Woodward, "McChrystal: More Forces or 'Mission Failure,'" *Washington Post*, September 21, 2009.

63. Rhodes 2018, 66; Chollet 2016, 81; Joe Klein, "The McChrystal Report," *Time*, September 21, 2009; Ben Smith, "A D.C. Whodunit: Who Leaked and Why?" *Politico*, September 22, 2009; Mann 2012, 135.

64. John F. Burns, "McChrystal Rejects Scaling Down Afghan Military Aims," *New York Times*, October 1, 2009; Alex Spillius, "White House Angry at General Stanley McChrystal Speech on Afghanistan," *Telegraph*, October 5, 2009.

65. Gordon Lubold, "Mullen Says US Needs More Troops in Afghanistan," *Christian Science Monitor*, September 15, 2009, 2; Michael Gerson, "In Afghanistan, No Choice But to Try," *Washington Post*, September 4, 2009.

66. Gates 2014, 367.

67. Obama 2020, 434.

68. Jeffrey Goldberg, "The Obama Doctrine," *The Atlantic* 317, no. 3 (2016): 76.

69. For example, Mark Memmott, "Obama is 'Dithering' on Afghanistan and 'Giving In' to Left, Cheney Says," *NPR.org*, October 22, 2009; Ewen MacAskill, "Barack Obama Accused of Dithering Over Troops in Afghanistan," *Guardian*, November 3, 2009, 17; Doyle McManus, "Obama Must Rethink Rethinking Afghanistan," *Los Angeles Times*, November 15, 2009, A36.

70. Hastings 2012, 130.

71. Panetta 2014, 255.

72. David Brooks, "The Tenacity Question," *New York Times*, October 30, 2009, A31.

73. Rhodes 2018, 76.

74. Chollet 2016, 43, 45.

75. Obama 2020, 434.

76. Obama 2020, 442.

77. Chivvis 2014.

78. Dominic Tierney, "The Legacy of Obama's 'Worst Mistake,'" *The Atlantic*, April 15, 2016.

79. iPoll: USPSRA.031411NII.R06B

80. iPoll: USASFOX.031811A.R21.

81. Averaging across five relevant polls in the iPoll database, 55 percent of voters supported using US airpower to establish a no-fly zone, to 38 percent opposed.

82. Rhodes 2018, 112; Power 2019, 302.

83. Gordon 2020, 173–82; Chivvis 2014, 43–53.
84. Obama 2020, 655.
85. For example, there was also no evidence that Qaddafi was systematically killing civilians in other cities that his forces had recaptured: see Kuperman 2013.
86. Obama 2020, 655.
87. Rice 2019, 281; Chivvis 2014, 34–37, 53–59.
88. Jo Becker and Scott Shane, "Hillary Clinton, 'Smart Power,' and a Dictator's Fall," *New York Times*, February 27, 2016.
89. Obama 2020, 658.
90. Rhodes 2018, 114.
91. Becker and Shane, "Hillary Clinton."
92. Chollet 2016, 98.
93. Mann 2012, 289.
94. "The Courage Factor," *The Economist*, March 19, 2011.
95. Anne-Marie Slaughter, "Fiddling While Libya Burns," *New York Times*, March 14, 2011, A25.
96. Michael Hastings, "Inside Obama's War Room: How He Decided to Intervene in Libya—and What It Says About His Evolution as Commander-in-Chief," *Rolling Stone*, October 13, 2011.
97. "Remarks by the President in Address to the Nation on Libya," March 28, 2011.
98. Third Presidential Debate, October 22, 2012.
99. Gates 2014, 519.
100. Though even this claim is contestable given how Obama later renewed US military involvement in Iraq due to the rise of ISIS (Islamic State of Iraq and Syria), which some analysts have attributed to Obama withdrawing from Iraq prematurely. See, for example, Brands and Feaver 2017, 7–54.
101. See, for example, Jeffrey M. Jones, "Three in Four Americans Back Obama on Iraq Withdrawal," *Gallup.com*, November 2, 2011.

Conclusion

1. For example, Ikenberry 2020, 2–3; Haass 2020, 24–34; and many of the essays in Jervis et al. 2018.
2. For these and other relevant data, see Friedman 2022.
3. Carnegie and Carson 2019, 742–43.
4. Brands 2018, 158.
5. Trump press conference (New York, NY), June 16, 2015.
6. John F. Kennedy School of Government 2017, 32. See 183–84 for similar assessments by Trump's subsequent campaign manager, Kellyanne Conway, and Trump pollster Tony Fabrizio. Mercieca 2020 documents Trump's systematic use of such rhetoric.
7. Steven Kull and Clay Ramsay, "Americans on US Role in the World," Program for Public Consultation, January 2017. For related discussion of how voters doubt that the liberal international order benefits ordinary citizens, see Colgan and Keohane 2017; Lacatus 2021; Adler-Nissen and Zarakol 2021.
8. Halpin et al. 2019.
9. See, for example, Wertheim 2020a; Warren 2019.
10. Boston, Mass. (October 4, 2000).
11. Rice 2000.
12. Posen 2014.
13. Krogstad 2020.
14. Jeffrey Goldberg, "The Obama Doctrine," *The Atlantic* 317, no. 3 (2016): 53; Rhodes 2018, 276–78.
15. Zaller 1992; Berinsky 2009; Saunders 2023.
16. Jacobs and Page 2005.

17. For example, Rudman 1998; Phelan and Rudman 2010.
18. Carroll 2009.

Appendixes

1. CNN transcript, October 22, 2012.
2. Michael Vickers, "Why Trump Fails—and Clinton Passes—the Commander-in-Chief Test," *Politico*, July 27, 2016.
3. Akbar Shahid Ahmed, "How Elizabeth Warren Built a Foreign Policy that Passes the Commander-in-Chief Test," *Huffington Post*, February 18, 2020.
4. This was the main thrust of critiques that Hillary Clinton and Donald Trump were not trustworthy enough to be commander in chief. See, for example, Ron Chusid, "Both Trump and Clinton Fail Commander-in-Chief Test," *Liberal Values*, September 9, 2016.
5. For example, Stephen Collinson, "Trump Looks to Pass Commander-in-Chief Test as Rivals See Weakness," *CNN.com*, April 3, 2016, praised Hillary Clinton for giving a speech that "was the kind of address a president might give in the aftermath of a terrorist attack, offering empathy, reassurance and concrete policy plans."
6. Approval for US counterterrorism policies (Republicans tended to support those policies in 2008 while they opposed them in 2012), support for import restrictions (which Republicans tended to support in 2016 but to oppose in prior elections), and two questions about US policy in Vietnam (which Republicans tended to oppose prior to 1968 but support afterwards).
7. See https://ropercenter-cornell-edu.dartmouth.idm.oclc.org/defense-spending-topics -glance/. The actual wording of these questions varies, referring to federal spending on: "arms and defense," "our armed forces," "the armed forces," "the army and navy," "the army, navy, and air force," "defense," "our defense forces," "the defense program," "defense purposes," "the military," "the military, armaments, and defense," "military defense," "the military and defense," "military and defense programs," "military and defense purposes," "military purposes," "national defense," and "national defense and military purposes."
8. See Stimson 2004, 10, on how "agree/disagree" questions are problematic for eliciting spending preferences. In particular, respondents have a tendency to agree with whatever proposition is offered to them.
9. I developed these control variables from reviewing prior studies explaining the 2004 presidential vote: Hillygus and Shields 2005; Klinkner 2006; Gelpi, Reifler, and Feaver 2007; Norpoth and Sidman 2007; Abramson et al. 2007; Weisberg and Christenson 2007.
10. The NAES measures religious attendance with a five-point scale ranging from no attendance to attendance more than once peer week over the past week. The NAES measures opposition to gay marriage by asking respondents to use a five-point scale indicating their levels of support/opposition to a constitutional amendment that would define marriage as being between one man and one woman.
11. Jointly estimated in a logit model that employs survey weights.

References

Primary Sources

American National Election Studies (1952–2020)
Barry Goldwater Papers, Hayden Library, Arizona State University
Congressional Election Study (2020)
Foreign Relations of the United States, U.S. Department of State, Office of the Historian
Hoover Library, Richard Wirthlin Papers
Jimmy Carter Presidential Library
John F. Kennedy Presidential Library
LBJ Presidential Library
Minnesota Historical Society
National Annenberg Election Survey
Ronald Reagan Presidential Library
Roper Center, iPoll database
White House Tapes (Nixon administration)

Secondary Sources

Abramson, Paul R., John H. Aldrich, Jill Rickershauser, and David W. Rohde. 2007. "Fear in the Voting Booth: The 2004 Presidential Election." *Political Behavior* 29 (2): 197–220. doi:10.1007/s11109-006-9018–1.
Achen, Christopher H. *Interpreting and Using Regression*. 1982. Beverly Hills, CA: Sage Publishing.
Achen, Christopher H., and Larry M. Bartels. 2016. *Democracy For Realists: Why Elections Do Not Produce Responsive Government*. Princeton, NJ: Princeton University Press.

Adams, Gordon. *Politics of Defense Contracting: The Iron Triangle.* 1982. New Brunswick, NJ: Transaction.

Adler-Nissen, Rebecca, and Ayşe Zarakol. 2021. "Struggles for Recognition: The Liberal International Order and the Merger of Its Discontents." *International Organization* 75 (2): 611–34. doi:10.1017/s0020818320000454.

Albright, Madeleine Korbel. 2003. *Madam Secretary.* New York: Miramax Books.

Aldous, Richard. 2017. *Schlesinger: The Imperial Historian.* New York: W.W. Norton & Company.

Aldrich, John H., Christopher Gelpi, Peter Feaver, Jason Reifler, and Kristin Thompson Sharp. 2006. "Foreign Policy and the Electoral Connection." *Annual Review of Political Science* 9 (1): 477–502. doi:10.1146/annurev.polisci.9.111605.105008.

Aldrich, John H., John L. Sullivan, and Eugene Borgida. 1989. "Foreign Affairs and Issue Voting: Do Presidential Candidates 'Waltz Before a Blind Audience?'" *American Political Science Review* 83 (1): 123–41. doi:10.2307/1956437.

Allcock, Thomas Tunstall. 2017. "The Virtues of Moderation: Foreign Policy and the 1964 Presidential Election." In *U.S. Presidential Elections in Foreign Policy,* edited by Andrew Johnstone and Andrew Priest, 154–76. Lexington: University Press of Kentucky.

Almond, Gabriel. 1950. *The American People and Foreign Policy.* New York: Harcourt Brace.

Alter, Jonathan. 2020. *His Very Best: Jimmy Carter, A Life.* New York: Simon & Schuster.

Althaus, Scott L., and Devon M. Largio. 2004. "When Osama Became Saddam: Origins and Consequences of the Change in America's Public Enemy #1." *PS: Political Science and Politics* 37 (4): 795–99. doi:10.1017/s1049096504045172.

Ambrose, Stephen. 1989. *Nixon: The Triumph of a Politician.* New York: Simon & Schuster.

Anand, Sowmya, and Jon A. Krosnick. 2003. "The Impact of Attitudes toward Foreign Policy Goals on Public Preferences among Presidential Candidates: A Study of Issues Publics and the Attentive Public in the 2000 U.S. Presidential Election." *Presidential Studies Quarterly* 33 (1): 31–71. doi:10.1177/0360491802250541.

Asselin, Pierre. 2002. *A Bitter Peace: Washington, Hanoi, and the Making of the Paris Agreement.* Chapel Hill: University of North Carolina Press.

Bacevich, Andrew J. 2020. *Age of Illusions: How America Squandered Its Cold War Victory.* New York: Metropolitan Books.

Baker, Peter. 2014. *Days of Fire: Bush and Cheney in the White House.* New York: Anchor Books.

Barabas, Jason, and Jennifer Jerit. 2010. "Are Survey Experiments Externally Valid?" *American Political Science Review* 104 (2): 226–42. doi:10.1017/s0003055410000092.

Bartels, Larry M. 1991. "Constituency Opinion and Congressional Policy Making: The Reagan Defense Buildup." *American Political Science Review* 85 (2): 457–74.

Berinsky, Adam J. 2009. *In Time of War: Understanding American Public Opinion from World War II to Iraq.* Chicago: University of Chicago Press.

Berman, Larry. 2001. *No Peace, No Honor: Nixon, Kissinger, and Betrayal in Vietnam.* New York: Free Press.

Berman, William C. 1988. *William Fulbright and the Vietnam War: The Dissent of a Political Realist.* Kent, OH: Kent State University Press.

Betts, Richard K. 2000. "Is Strategy an Illusion?" *International Security* 25 (2): 5–50.

Biden, Joe. 2008. *Promises to Keep: On Life and Politics.* New York: Random House.

Bishop, George. 1989. "Manipulation and Control of People's Responses to Public Opinion Polls." In *The Orwellian Moment: Hindsight and Foresight in the Post-1984 World*, edited by Robert L. Savage, James Combs, and Dan Nimmo, 119–29. Fayetteville: University of Arkansas Press.

Blanken, Leo J., Hy S. Rothstein, and Jason J. Lepore. 2015. *Assessing War: The Challenge of Measuring Success and Failure.* Washington, DC: Georgetown University Press.

Bond, Charles F., Jr., and Bella M. DePaulo. 2006. "Accuracy of Deception Judgments: Appendix B." *Personality and Social Psychology Review* 10 (3): 214–34. doi:10.1207/s15327957pspr1003_2b.

"Bosnian War Sparks Conflict at Home." 1996. *1995 Congressional Quarterly Almanac* 51. http://library.cqpress.com/cqalmanac/cqal95-1099599.

Boys, James D. 2015. *Clinton's Grand Strategy: U.S. Foreign Policy in a Post-Cold War World.* London: Bloomsbury.

Boys, James D. 2021. "Grand Strategy, Grand Rhetoric, and the Forgotten Covenant of Campaign 1992." *Politics* 41 (1): 80–94. doi:10.1177/0263395720935782.

Branch, Taylor. 2009. *The Clinton Tapes: Wrestling History with the President.* New York: Simon & Schuster.

Brands, Hal. 2018. *American Grand Strategy in the Age of Trump.* Washington, DC: Brookings Institution Press.

Brands, Hal, and Peter Feaver. 2017. "Was the Rise of ISIS Inevitable?" *Survival* 59 (3): 7–54.

Brigham, Robert K. 2018. *Reckless: Henry Kissinger and the Tragedy of Vietnam.* New York: PublicAffairs.

Caddell, Patrick H. 1981. "The Democratic Strategy and Its Electoral Consequences." In *Party Coalitions in the 1980s*, edited by Seymour Martin Lipset, 267–306. San Francisco: Institute for Contemporary Studies.

Campbell, Angus, Philip E. Converse, Warren E. Miller, and Donald E. Stokes. 1960. *The American Voter.* New York: J. Wiley & Sons.

Campbell, James E. 2005. "Why Bush Won the Presidential Election of 2004: Incumbency, Ideology, Terrorism, and Turnout." *Political Science Quarterly* 120 (2): 219–41. doi:10.1002/j.1538-165x.2005.tb00545.x.

Carnegie, Allison, and Austin Carson. 2019. "Reckless Rhetoric? Compliance Pessimism and International Order in the Age of Trump." *The Journal of Politics* 81 (2): 739–46. doi:10.1086/702232.

Carroll, Susan J. 2009. "Reflections on Gender and Hillary Clinton's Presidential Campaign: The Good, the Bad, and the Misogynic." *Politics and Gender* 5 (1): 1–20. doi:10.1017/s1743923x09000014.

Carson, Austin. 2018. *Secret Wars: Covert Conflict in International Politics.* Princeton, NJ: Princeton University Press.

Cassata, Donna. 1995. "Congress Bucks White House, Devises Its Own Bosnia Plan." *Congressional Quarterly* 53 (23): 1653–54.

Chester, Lewis, Godfrey Hodgson, and Bruce Page. 1969. *An American Melodrama: The Presidential Campaign of 1968.* New York: Viking.

Chivvis, Christopher S. 2014. *Toppling Qaddafi: Libya and the Limits of International Intervention.* New York: Cambridge University Press.

Chollet, Derek H. 2005. *The Road to the Dayton Accords: A Study of American State-craft.* New York: Palgrave Macmillan.

Chollet, Derek H. 2016. *The Long Game: How Obama Defied Washington and Redefined America's Role in the World.* New York: PublicAffairs.

Chollet, Derek H., and James M. Goldgeier. 2008. *America Between the Wars, 11/9 to 9/11: The Misunderstood Decade Between the End of the Cold War and the Start of the War on Terror.* New York: PublicAffairs.

Clinton, Hillary Rodham. 2015. *Hard Choices.* New York: Simon & Schuster.

Clodfelter, Mark. 1989. *The Limits of Airpower: The American Bombing of North Vietnam.* New York: Free Press.

Cohen, Jeffrey E. 2015. *Presidential Leadership in Public Opinion: Causes and Consequences.* New York: Cambridge University Press.

Colgan, Jeff D., and Robert O. Keohane. 2017. "The Liberal Order Is Rigged." *Foreign Affairs* 96 (3): 36–44. http://www.jstor.org/stable/44823729.

Craig, Campbell, and Fredrik Logevall. 2009. *America's Cold War: The Politics of Insecurity.* Cambridge, MA: The Belknap Press of Harvard University Press.

Cramer, Jane Kellett. 2007. "Militarized Patriotism: Why the U.S. Marketplace of Ideas Failed Before the Iraq War." *Security Studies* 16 (3): 489–524. doi:10.1080/09636410701547949.

Crane, Phillip M. 1978. *Surrender in Panama: The Case Against the Treaty.* New York: Dale Books.

Daalder, Ivo H. 2000. *Getting to Dayton: The Making of America's Bosnia Policy.* Washington, DC: Brookings Institution.

Daddis, Gregory. 2015. "Choosing Progress: Evaluating the Salesmanship of the Vietnam War in 1967." In *Assessing War: The Challenge of Measuring Success and Failure,* edited by Leo J. Blanken, Hy Rothstein, and Jason J. Lepore, 173–96. Washington, DC: Georgetown University Press.

Dana, Jason, Robyn Dawes, and Nathanial Peterson. 2013. "Belief in the Unstructured Interview: The Persistence of an Illusion." *Judgment and Decision Making* 8 (5): 512–20. https://journal.sjdm.org/12/121130a/jdm121130a.pdf.

Delli Carpini, Michael X., and Scott Keeter. 1996. *What Americans Know About Politics and Why It Matters.* New Haven, CT: Yale University Press.

Downs, Anthony. 1957. *An Economic Theory of Democracy.* New York: Harper and Row.

Drew, Elizabeth. 1981. *Portrait of an Election: The 1980 Presidential Campaign.* New York: Simon & Schuster.

Drew, Elizabeth. 1994. *On the Edge: The Clinton Presidency.* New York: Simon & Schuster.

Druckman, James N., Lawrence R. Jacobs, and Eric Ostermeier. 2004. "Candidate Strategies to Prime Issues and Image." *The Journal of Politics* 66 (4): 1180–1202. doi:10.1111/j.0022-3816.2004.00295.

Dumbrell, John. 2009. *Clinton's Foreign Policy: Between the Bushes, 1992–2000.* New York: Routledge.

Dumbrell, John. 2017. "Internationalism Challenged: Foreign Policy Issues in the 1992 Presidential Election" In *U.S. Presidential Elections and Foreign Policy,* edited by Andrew Johnstone and Andrew Priest, 317–35. Lexington: University Press of Kentucky.

Egan, Patrick J. 2013. *Partisan Priorities: How Issue Ownership Drives and Distorts American Politics*. New York: Cambridge University Press.

Ehrlichman, John. 1982. *Witness to Power: The Nixon Years*. New York: Simon & Schuster.

Eichenberg, Richard C. 2005. "Victory Has Many Friends: U.S. Public Opinion and the Use of Military Force, 1981–2005." *International Security* 30 (1): 140–77. doi:10.1162/0162288054894616.

Eichenberg, Richard C., and Richard J. Stoll. 2017. "The Acceptability of War and Support for Defense Spending." *Journal of Conflict Resolution* 61 (4): 788–813. doi:10.1177/0022002715600760.

Ellis, Sylvia. 2017. "Leadership Experience in the Cold War." In *US Presidential Elections in Foreign Policy*, edited by Andrew Johnstone and Andrew Priest, 128–53. Lexington: University Press of Kentucky.

Fearon, James D. 1995. "Rationalist Explanations for War." *International Organization* 49 (3): 379–414. doi:10.1017/s0020818300033324.

Fenno, Richard Francis. 1978. *Home Style: House Members in Their Districts*. Boston: Little, Brown.

Fiorina, Morris P. 1981. *Retrospective Voting in American National Elections*. New Haven, CT: Yale University Press.

Fridkin, Kim L., and Patrick J. Kenney. 2011. "The Role of Candidate Traits in Campaigns." *Journal of Politics* 73 (1): 61–73. doi:10.1017/s0022381610000861.

Friedberg, Aaron L. 2000. *In the Shadow of the Garrison State: America's Anti-Statism and Its Cold War Grand Strategy*. Princeton, NJ: Princeton University Press.

Friedman, Jeffrey A. 2022. "Is U.S. Grand Strategy Dead? The Political Foundations of Deep Engagement after Donald Trump." *International Affairs* 98 (4): 1289–305. doi:10.1093/ia/iiac112.

Friedman, Jeffrey A. 2023. "Issue-Image Tradeoffs and the Politics of Foreign Policy: How Leaders Use Foreign Policy Positions to Shape Their Personal Images." *World Politics* 75 (2): in press.

Funk, Carolyn L. 1999. "Bringing the Candidate into Models of Candidate Evaluation." *Journal of Politics* 61 (3): 700–20. doi:10.2307/2647824.

Gadarian, Shana K. 2010. "Foreign Policy at the Ballot Box." *Journal of Politics* 72 (4): 1046–62. doi:10.1017/S0022381610000526.

Gates, Robert. 2014. *Duty: Memoirs of a Secretary at War*. New York: Knopf.

Gaubatz, Kurt Taylor. 1999. *Elections and War: The Electoral Incentive in the Democratic Politics of War and Peace*. Stanford, CA: Stanford University Press.

Gelpi, Christopher, and Joseph M. Grieco. 2015. "Competency Costs in Foreign Affairs: Presidential Performance in International Conflicts and Domestic Legislative Success." *American Journal of Political Science* 59 (2): 440–56. doi:10.1111/ajps.12169.

Gelpi, Christopher, Jason Reifler, and Peter Feaver. 2007. "Iraq the Vote: Retrospective and Prospective Foreign Policy Judgments on Candidate Choice and Casualty Tolerance." *Political Behavior* 29 (2): 151–74. doi:10.1007/s11109-007-9029-6.

Gershkoff, Amy, and Shana Kushner. 2005. "Shaping Public Opinion: the 9/11-Iraq Connection in the Bush Administration's Rhetoric." *Perspectives on Politics* 3 (3): 525–37. doi:10.1017/s1537592705050334.

Gewen, Barry. 2020. *The Inevitability of Tragedy: Henry Kissinger and His World*. New York: W. W. Norton & Company, Inc.

Gholz, Eugene, Daryl G. Press, and Harvey M. Sapolsky. 1997. "Come Home, America: The Strategy of Restraint in the Face of Temptation." *International Security* 21 (4): 5–48. doi:10.1162/isec.21.4.5.

Glaser, Charles L. 2010. *Rational Theory of International Politics: The Logic of Competition and Cooperation*. Princeton, NJ: Princeton University Press.

Goldman, Peter, and Tony Fuller. 1985. *The Quest for the Presidency 1984*. New York: Bantam Books.

Gooch, Andrew, Alan S. Gerber, and Gregory A. Huber. 2021. "Evaluations of Candidates' Non-Policy Characteristics from Issue Positions: Evidence of Valence Spillover." *Electoral Studies* 69: 1–10. doi:10.1016/j.electstud.2020.102246.

Gordon, Philip H. 2020. *Losing the Long Game: The False Promise of Regime Change in the Middle East*. New York: St. Martin's Press.

Gries, Peter Hays. 2014. *The Politics of American Foreign Policy: How Ideology Divides Liberals and Conservatives over Foreign Affairs*. Stanford, CA: Stanford University Press.

Groseclose, Tim. 2001. "A Model of Candidate Location When One Candidate Has a Valence Advantage." *American Journal of Political Science* 45 (4): 862–86. doi:10.2307/2669329.

Haass, Richard N. 2020. "Present at the Disruption: How Trump Unmade U.S. Foreign Policy." *Foreign Affairs* 99 (5): 24–34. doi:10.1007/978-3-030-45050-2_6.

Halberstam, David. 2001. *War in a Time of Peace: Bush, Clinton, and the Generals*. New York: Scribner.

Halpin, John, Brian Katalis, Peter Juul, Karl Agne, Jim Gerstein, and Nisha Jain. 2019. "America Adrift." Center for American Progress, May 5. https://www.americanprogress.org/article/america-adrift/.

Hames, Tim. 1993. "Foreign Policy and the American Elections of 1992." *International Relations* 11 (4): 315–30. doi:10.1177/004711789301100402.

Hanhimäki, Jussi. 2003. "Selling the 'Decent Interval': Kissinger, Triangular Diplomacy, and the End of the Vietnam War, 1971–73." *Diplomacy and Statecraft* 14 (1): 159–94. doi:10.1080/09592290412331308771.

Harris, John F. 2005. *The Survivor: Bill Clinton in the White House*. New York: Random House.

Hartley, Thomas, and Bruce Russett. 1992. "Public Opinion and the Common Defense: Who Governs Military Spending in the United States?" *American Political Science Review* 86 (4): 905–15. doi:10.2307/1964343.

Harvey, Frank P. 2011. *Explaining the Iraq War: Counterfactual Theory, Logic and Evidence*. New York: Cambridge University Press.

Hastings, Michael. 2012. *The Operators: The Wild and Terrifying Inside Story of America's War in Afghanistan*. New York: Plume.

Healy, Andrew, and Neil Malhotra. 2013. "Retrospective Voting Reconsidered." *Annual Review of Political Science* 16 (1): 285–306. doi:10.1146/annurev-polisci-032211-212920.

Heffington, Colton. 2018. "Do Hawks and Doves Deliver? the Words and Deeds of Foreign Policy in Democracies." *Foreign Policy Analysis* 14 (1): 64–85. doi:10.1093/fpa/orw011.

Heffington, Colton, Brandon Beomseob Park, and Laron K. Williams. 2019. "The 'Most Important Problem' Dataset (MIPD): A New Dataset on American Issue Importance." *Conflict Management and Peace Science* 36 (3): 312–35. https://doi.org/10.1177/0738894217691463.

Hermann, Margaret G., Thomas Preston, Baghat Korany, and Timothy M. Shaw. 2001. "Who Leads Matters: The Effects of Powerful Individuals." *International Studies Review* 3 (2): 83–131. doi:10.1111/1521-9488.00235.

Hess, Gary R. 2006. "Presidents and the Congressional War Resolutions of 1991 and 2002." *Political Science Quarterly* 121 (1): 93–118. doi:10.1002/j.1538-165x.2006.tb00566.x.

Hillygus, D. Sunshine, and Todd G. Shields. 2005. "Moral Issues and Voter Decision Making in the 2004 Presidential Election." *PS: Political Science and Politics* 38 (2): 201–9. doi:10.1017/s1049096505056301.

Holbrooke, Richard C. 1998. *To End a War.* New York: Random House.

Holsti, Ole R. 2011. *American Public Opinion on the Iraq War.* Ann Arbor: University of Michigan Press.

Hsee, Chrisopher K., George F. Loewenstein, Sally Blount, and Max H. Bazerman. 1999. "Preference Reversals between Joint and Separate Evaluations of Options: A Review and Theoretical Analysis." *Psychological Bulletin* 125 (5): 576–90. doi:10.1037/0033-2909.125.5.576.

Hsee, Christopher K., and Jiao Zhang. 2010. "General Evaluability Theory." *Perspectives on Psychological Science* 5 (4): 343–55. doi:10.1177/1745691610374586.

Hughes, Ken. 2015. *Fatal Politics: The Nixon Tapes, the Vietnam War, and the Casualties of Reelection.* Charlottesville: University of Virginia Press.

Hung, Nguyen Tien, and Jerrold L. Schecter. 1986. *The Palace File.* New York: Harper & Row.

Ikenberry, G. John. 2020. *A World Safe for Democracy: Liberal Internationalism and the Crises of Global Order.* New Haven, CT: Yale University Press.

Imai, Kosuke, Luke Keele, Dustin Tingley, and Teppei Yamamoto. 2010. "Unpacking the Black Box of Causality: Learning about Causal Mechanisms from Experimental and Observational Studies." *American Political Science Review* 105 (4): 765–89. doi:10.1017/s0003055411000414.

Isaacson, Walter. 1992. *Kissinger: A Biography.* New York: Simon & Schuster.

Isikoff, Michael, and David Corn. 2006. *Hubris: The Inside Story of Spin, Scandal, and the Selling of the Iraq War.* New York: Crown.

Jacobs, Lawrence R., and Benjamin I. Page. 2005. "Who Influences U.S. Foreign Policy?" *American Political Science Review* 99 (1): 107–23. doi:10.1017/s000305540505152x.

Jacobs, Lawrence R., and Robert Y. Shapiro. 1994. "Issues, Candidate Image, and Priming: The Use of Private Polls in Kennedy's 1960 Presidential Campaign." *American Political Science Review* 88 (3): 527–40. doi:10.2307/2944793.

Jacobs, Lawrence R., and Robert Y. Shapiro. 2000. *Politicians Don't Pander: Political Manipulation and the Loss of Democratic Responsiveness.* Chicago: University of Chicago Press.

Jamieson, Kathleen Hall. 1992. *Dirty Politics: Deception, Distraction, and Democracy.* New York: Oxford University Press.

Jamieson, Kathleen Hall. 1996. *Packaging the Presidency: A History and Criticism of Presidential Campaign Advertising.* New York: Oxford University Press.

Jamieson, Kathleen Hall. 2006. *Electing the President, 2004: The Insiders' View.* Philadelphia: University of Pennsylvania Press.

Jervis, Robert. 1978. "Cooperation Under the Security Dilemma." *World Politics* 30 (2): 167–214. doi:10.2307/2009958.

Jervis, Robert. 1997. *System Effects: Complexity in Political and Social Life.* Princeton, NJ: Princeton University Press.

Jervis, Robert, Francis J. Gavin, Joshua Rovner, and Diane N. Labrosse. 2018. *Chaos in the Liberal Order: The Trump Presidency and International Politics in the Twenty-First Century.* New York: Columbia University Press.

John F. Kennedy School of Government. 2006. *Campaign for President: The Managers Look at 2004.* Lanham, MD: Rowman & Littlefield.

John F. Kennedy School of Government. 2017. *Campaign for President: The Managers Look at 2020.* Lanham, MD: Rowman & Littlefield.

Johns, Andrew L. 2020. *The Price of Loyalty: Hubert Humphrey's Vietnam Conflict.* Lanham, MD: Rowman & Littlefield.

Johns, Andrew L. 2010. *Vietnam's Second Front: Domestic Politics, the Republican Party, and the War.* Lexington: University Press of Kentucky.

Johnson, Dominic D. P. 2020. *Strategic Instincts.* Princeton, NJ: Princeton University Press.

Johnson, Robert David. 2009. *All the Way with LBJ: The 1964 Presidential Election.* New York: Cambridge University Press.

Johnstone, Andrew, and Andrew Priest. 2017. *US Presidential Elections and Foreign Policy: Candidates, Campaigns, and Global Politics from FDR to Bill Clinton.* Lexington: University Press of Kentucky.

Kahneman, Daniel, and Jonathan Renshon. 2007. "Why Hawks Win." *Foreign Policy* 158: 34–38. http://www.jstor.org/stable/25462124.

Kaplan, Fred M. 2013. *The Insurgents: David Petraeus and the Plot to Change the American Way of War.* New York: Simon & Schuster.

Karol, David, and Edward Miguel. 2007. "The Electoral Cost of War: Iraq Casualties and the 2004 U.S. Presidential Election." *The Journal of Politics* 69 (3): 633–48. doi:10.1111/j.1468-2508.2007.00564.x.

Kelley, Stanley. 1983. *Interpreting Elections.* Princeton, NJ: Princeton University Press.

Kennan, George F. 1951. *American Diplomacy.* Chicago: University of Chicago Press.

Kennedy, John F. 1960. *The Strategy of Peace.* New York: Harper.

Kerry, John. 2018. *Every Day Is Extra.* New York: Simon & Schuster.

Kertzer, Joshua D. 2016. *Resolve in International Politics.* Princeton, NJ: Princeton University Press.

Kertzer, Joshua D., Deborah Jordan Brooks, and Stephen G. Brooks. 2021. "Do Partisan Types Stop at the Water's Edge?" *Journal of Politics* 83 (4): 1764–82. doi:10.1086/711408.

Kertzer, Joshua D., Marcus Holmes, Brad L. LeVeck, and Carly Wayne. 2022. "Hawkish Biases and Group Decision Making." *International Organization* 76 (3): 513–48. doi:10.1017/s0020818322000017.

Key, V. O. 1966. *The Responsible Electorate: Rationality in Presidential Voting, 1936–1960.* Cambridge, MA: Harvard University Press.

Kimball, Jeffrey P. 1999. *Nixon's Vietnam War*. Lawrence: University Press of Kansas.

Kimball, Jeffrey. 2003. "Decent Interval or Not? The Paris Agreement and the End of the Vietnam War." *Passport: The Newsletter of the Society for Historians of American Foreign Relations* 34 (3): 26–31.

Kinder, Donald R. 1986. "Presidential Character Revisited." In *Political Cognition*, edited by Richard Lau and David Sears. Hillsdale, NJ: Lawrence Erlbaum.

Kinder, Donald R., Mark D. Peters, Robert P. Abelson, and Susan T. Fiske. 1980. "Presidential Prototypes." *Political Behavior* 2 (4): 315–37. doi:10.1007/bf00990172.

Kissinger, Henry. 1979. *White House Years*. Boston: Little, Brown.

Kissinger, Henry. 2022. *Leadership: Six Studies in World Strategy*. New York: Penguin Press.

Klarevas, Louis. 2002. "The 'Essential Domino' of Military Operations: American Public Opinion and the Use of Force." *International Studies Perspectives* 3 (4): 417–37. doi:10.1111/1528-3577.t01-1-00107.

Kleinberg, Jon, Himabindu Lakkaraju, Jure Leskovec, Jens Ludwig, and Sendhil Mullainathan. 2018. "Human Decisions and Machine Predictions." *Quarterly Journal of Economics* 133 (1): 237–93. doi:10.3386/w23180.

Kleinberg, Katja B., and Benjamin O. Fordham. 2018. "Don't Know Much about Foreign Policy: Assessing the Impact of 'Don't Know' and 'No Opinion' Responses on Inferences about Foreign Policy Attitudes." *Foreign Policy Analysis* 14 (3): 429–48. doi:10.1093/fpa/orw060.

Klinkner, Philip A. 2006. "Mr. Bush's War: Foreign Policy in the 2004 Election." *Presidential Studies Quarterly* 36 (2): 281–96. doi:10.1111/j.1741-5705.2006.00303.x.

Klofstad, Casey A., Rindy C. Anderson, and Susan Peters. 2012. "Sounds Like a Winner: Voice Pitch Influences Perceptions of Leadership Capacity in Both Men and Women." *Proceedings of the Royal Society B: Biological Sciences* 279 (1738): 2698–704. doi:10.1098/rspb.2012.0311.

Knock, Thomas J. 2016. *The Rise of a Prairie Statesman: The Life and Times of George McGovern*. Princeton, NJ: Princeton University Press.

Krebs, Ronald R., and Jennifer K. Lobasz. 2007. "Fixing the Meaning of 9/11: Hegemony, Coercion, and the Road to War in Iraq." *Security Studies* 16 (3): 409–51. doi:10.1080/09636410701547881.

Kreps, Sarah E. 2011. *Coalitions of Convenience: United States Military Interventions After the Cold War*. New York: Oxford University Press.

Kreps, Sarah E., Elizabeth N. Saunders, and Kenneth A. Schultz. 2018. "The Ratification Premium: Harks, Doves, and Arms Control." *World Politics* 70 (4): 479–514. doi:10.1017/s0043887118000102.

Krogstad, Jens Manuel. 2020. "Americans Broadly Support Legal Status for Immigrants Brought to the U.S. Illegally as Children." *Pew Research Center*, June 17. https://www.pewresearch.org/fact-tank/2020/06/17/americans-broadly-support-legal-status-for-immigrants-brought-to-the-u-s-illegally-as-children/.

Kull, Steven, and Clay Ramsay. 2017. "Americans on U.S. Role in the World." *Program for Public Consultation*, January. https://publicconsultation.org/wp-content/uploads/2017/01/PPC_Role_in_World_Report.pdf.

Kupchan, Charles A. 2020. *Isolationism: A History of America's Efforts to Shield Itself from the World*. New York: Oxford University Press.

Kuperman, Alan J. 2013. "A Model Humanitarian Intervention? Reassessing NATO's Libya Campaign." *International Security* 38 (1): 105–36. doi:10.1162/isec_a_00126.

Lacatus, Corina. 2021. "Populism and President Trump's Approach to Foreign Policy." *Politics* 41 (1): 31–47. doi:10.1177/0263395720935380.

LaFeber, Walter. 2005. *The Deadly Bet: LBJ, Vietnam, and the 1968 Election.* Lanham, MD: Rowman & Littlefield.

Lake, Anthony. 2008. *6 Nightmares: Real Threats in a Dangerous World and How America Can Meet Them.* Boston: Little, Brown.

Lau, Richard R., and David O. Sears. 1986. *Political Cognition.* Hillsdale, NJ: Lawrence Erlbaum.

Lawson, Chappell, Gabriel S. Lenz, Andy Baker, and Michael Myers. 2010. "Looking Like a Winner: Candidate Appearance and Electoral Success in New Democracies." *World Politics* 62 (4): 561–93. doi:10.1017/s0043887110000195.

Ledbetter, James. 2011. *Unwarranted Influence: Dwight D. Eisenhower and the Military-Industrial Complex.* New Haven, CT: Yale University Press.

Levendusky, Matthew S., and Michael C. Horowitz. 2012. "When Backing Down Is the Right Decision: Partisanship, New Information, and Audience Costs." *Journal of Politics* 74 (2): 323–38. doi:10.1017/s002238161100154x.

Lewis-Beck, Michael S., Helmut Norpoth, William G. Jacoby, and Herbert F. Weisberg. 2008. *The American Voter Revisited.* Ann Arbor: University of Michigan Press.

Lipset, Seymour Martin. 1981. *Party Coalitions in the 1980s.* San Francisco: Institute for Contemporary Studies.

Lodge, Milton, and Charles S. Taber. 2013. *The Rationalizing Voter.* New York: Cambridge University Press.

Mann, Jim. 2012. *The Obamians: The Struggle Inside the White House to Redefine American Power.* New York: Viking.

Mann, Robert. 2011. *Daisy Petals and Mushroom Clouds: LBJ, Barry Goldwater, and the Ad That Changed American Politics.* Baton Rouge: Louisiana State University Press.

Manza, Jeff, Fay Lomax Cook, and Benjamin I. Page. 2002. *Navigating Public Opinion: Polls, Policy, and the Future of American Democracy.* New York: Oxford University Press.

Marsh, Kevin. 2014. "Obama's Surge: A Bureaucratic Politics Analysis of the Decision to Order a Troop Surge in Afghanistan." *Foreign Policy Analysis* 10 (3): 265–88. doi:10.1111/fpa.12000.

Mattes, Michaela, and Jessica L. Weeks. 2019. "Hawks, Doves, and Peace: An Experimental Approach." *American Journal of Political Science* 63 (1): 53–66. doi:10.1111/ajps.12392.

McChrystal, Stanley A. 2013. *My Share of the Task: A Memoir.* New York: Portfolio.

McDermott, Rose. 2008. *Presidential Leadership, Illness, and Decision Making.* New York: Cambridge University Press.

McGovern, George. 1974. *An American Journey: The Presidential Campaign Speeches of George McGovern.* New York: Random House.

McHugh, Kelly. 2015. "A Tale of Two Surges: Comparing the Politics of the 2007 Iraq Surge and the 2009 Afghanistan Surge." *SAGE Open* 5 (4): 215824401562195. doi:10.1177/2158244015621957.

Mearsheimer, John J. 2018. *The Great Delusion: Liberal Dreams and International Realities.* Cambridge, MA: The Belknap Press of Harvard University Press.

Mercieca, Jennifer R. 2020. *Demagogue for President: The Rhetorical Genius of Donald Trump*. College Station: Texas A&M University Press.

Merolla, Jennifer Lee, and Elizabeth J. Zechmeister. 2009. *Democracy at Risk: How Terrorist Threats Affect the Public*. Chicago: University of Chicago Press.

Miller, Warren Edward, and J. Merrill Shanks. 1996. *The New American Voter*. Cambridge, MA: Harvard University Press.

Milner, Helen V., and Dustin H. Tingley. 2015. *Sailing the Water's Edge: The Domestic Politics of American Foreign Policy*. Princeton, NJ: Princeton University Press.

Miroff, Bruce. 2007. *The Liberals' Moment: The McGovern Insurgency and the Identity Crisis of the Democratic Party*. Lawrence: University Press of Kansas.

Moïse, Edwin E. 1996. *Tonkin Gulf and the Escalation of the Vietnam War*. Chapel Hill: University of North Carolina Press.

Mondak, Jeffery J. 1995. "Competence, Integrity, and the Electoral Success of Congressional Incumbents." *The Journal of Politics* 57 (4): 1043–69. doi:10.2307/2960401.

Moore, Jonathan. 1986. *Campaign for President: The Managers Look at '84*. Dover, MA: Auburn House Publishing Company.

Morris, Dick. 1998. *Behind the Oval Office: Getting Reelected Against All Odds*. New York: Renaissance Books.

Mueller, John E. 2006. *Overblown: How Politicians and the Terrorism Industry Inflate National Security Threats, and Why We Believe Them*. New York: Free Press.

Nelson, Michael. 2014. *Resilient America: Electing Nixon in 1968, Channeling Dissent, and Dividing Government*. Lawrence: University Press of Kansas.

Nelson, Michael. 2018. "Lost Confidence: The Democratic Party, the Vietnam War, and the 1968 Election." *Presidential Studies Quarterly* 48 (3): 570–85. doi:10.1111/psq.12449.

Nguyen, Lien-Hang T. 2012. *Hanoi's War: An International History of the War for Peace in Vietnam*. Chapel Hill: University of North Carolina Press.

Nomikos, William G, and Nicholas Sambanis. 2019. "What Is the Mechanism Underlying Audience Costs? Incompetence, Belligerence, and Inconsistency." *Journal of Peace Research* 56 (4): 575–88. doi:10.1177/0022343319839456.

Norpoth, Helmut, and Andrew H. Sidman. 2007. "Mission Accomplished: The Wartime Election of 2004." *Political Behavior* 29 (2): 175–95. doi:10.1007/s11109-007-9036-7.

Obama, Barack. 2020. *A Promised Land*. New York: Crown.

Offner, Arnold. 2018. *Hubert Humphrey: The Conscience of the Country*. New Haven, CT: Yale University Press.

O'Hanlon, Michael E. 2022. "Qassem Soleimani and Beyond." Brookings, March 9. https://www.brookings.edu/blog/order-from-chaos/2020/01/03/qassem-soleimani-and-beyond/.

Ornstein, Norman J., and Mark Schmitt. 1989. "The 1988 Election." *Foreign Affairs* 68 (1): 39–52. doi:10.2307/20043883.

Page, Benjamin I. 1978. *Choices and Echoes in Presidential Elections*. Chicago: University of Chicago Press.

Page, Benjamin I. 1994. "Democratic Responsiveness? Untangling the Links Between Public Opinion and Policy." *PS: Political Science & Politics* 27 (1): 25–29. doi:10.1017/s1049096500039834.

Page, Benjamin I., and Marshall M. Bouton. 2006. *The Foreign Policy Disconnect: What Americans Want from Our Leaders but Don't Get*. Chicago: University of Chicago Press.

Page, Benjamin I., and Richard A. Brody. 1972. "Policy Voting and the Electoral Process: The Vietnam War Issue." *American Political Science Review* 66 (3): 979–95. doi:10.2307/1957489.

Panetta, Leon, and Jim Newton. 2014. *Worthy Fights: A Memoir of Leadership in War and Peace.* New York: Penguin Publishing Group.

Payne, Andrew. 2021. "Bringing the Boys Back Home: Campaign Promises and US Decision-Making in Iraq and Vietnam." *Politics* 41 (1): 95–110. doi:10.1177/0263395720937205.

Payne, Andrew. 2023. *War on the Ballot: How the Electoral Cycle Shapes Presidential Decision-Making in War.* New York: Columbia University Press.

Payne, Lee W. 2013. "'If Elected, I [Still] Promise'; American Party Platforms, 1980–2008." *Journal of Political Science* 41 (1). https://digitalcommons.coastal.edu/jops/vol41/iss1/2/.

Perlstein, Rick. 2020. *Reaganland: America's Right Turn 1976–1980.* New York: Simon & Schuster.

Peter G. Peterson Foundation. 2022. "U.S. Defense Spending Compared to Other Countries," May 11. https://www.pgpf.org/chart-archive/0053_defense-comparison.

Petrocik, John R. 1996. "Issue Ownership in Presidential Elections, with a 1980 Case Study." *American Journal of Political Science* 40 (3): 825–50. doi:10.2307/2111797.

Phelan, Julie E., and Laurie A. Rudman. 2010. "Prejudice Toward Female Leaders: Backlash Effects and Women's Impression Management Dilemma." *Social and Personality Psychology Compass* 4 (10): 807–20. doi:10.1111/j.1751-9004.2010.00306.x.

Popkin, Samuel L. 1994. *The Reasoning Voter: Communication and Persuasion in Presidential Campaigns.* Chicago: University of Chicago Press.

Porter, Patrick. 2018. "Why America's Grand Strategy Has Not Changed: Power, Habit, and the U.S. Foreign Policy Establishment." *International Security* 42 (4): 9–46. doi:10.1162/isec_a_00311.

Posen, Barry. 2014. *Restraint: A New Foundation for US Grand Strategy.* Ithaca, NY: Cornell University Press.

Posen, Barry R., and Andrew L. Ross. 1996. "Competing Visions for U.S. Grand Strategy." *International Security* 21 (3): 5–53. doi:10.2307/2539272.

Powell, Robert. 1999. *In the Shadow of Power: States and Strategies in International Politics.* Princeton, NJ: Princeton University Press.

Power, Samantha. 2019. *The Education of an Idealist: A Memoir.* New York: Dey Street Books.

Preble, Christopher A. 2003. "'Who Ever Believed in the 'Missile Gap'?': John F. Kennedy and the Politics of National Security." *Presidential Studies Quarterly* 33 (4): 801–26. doi:10.1046/j.0360-4918.2003.00085.x.

Preble, Christopher A. 2004. *John F. Kennedy and the Missile Gap.* DeKalb: Northern Illinois University Press.

Rathbun, Brian C. 2019. *Reasoning of State: Realists, Romantics and Rationality in International Relations.* New York: Cambridge University Press.

Renshon, Stanley Allen, and Deborah Welch Larson. 2003. *Good Judgment in Foreign Policy: Theory and Application.* Lanham, MD: Rowman & Littlefield.

Rhodes, Ben. 2018. *The World as It Is: A Memoir of the Obama White House.* New York: Knopf.

Rice, Condoleezza. 2000. "Promoting the National Interest." *Foreign Affairs* 79 (1): 45–62. doi:10.2307/20049613.

Rice, Susan. 2019. *Tough Love: My Story of the Things Worth Fighting For.* New York: Simon & Schuster.

Richards, Diana, Clifton T. Morgan, Rick K. Wilson, Valerie L. Schwebach, and Garry D. Young. 1993. "Good Times, Bad Times, and the Diversionary Use of Force." *Journal of Conflict Resolution* 37 (3): 504–35. doi:10.1177/0022002793037003005.

Romer, Daniel, Kate Kenski, Kenneth Winneg, Christopher Adasiewicz, and Kathleen Hall Jamieson. 2006. *Capturing Campaign Dynamics, 2000 and 2004: The National Annenberg Election Survey.* Philadelphia: University of Pennsylvania Press.

Rorabaugh, W. J. 2009. *The Real Making of the President: Kennedy, Nixon, and the 1960 Election.* Lawrence: University Press of Kansas.

Rove, Karl. 2010. *Courage and Consequence: My Life as a Conservative in the Fight.* New York: Threshold.

Rudman, Laurie A. 1998. "Self-Promotion as a Risk Factor for Women: The Costs and Benefits of Counterstereotypical Impression Management." *Journal of Personality and Social Psychology* 74 (3): 629–45. doi:10.1037/0022-3514.74.3.629.

Ryan, David. 2017. "1984, Regional Crises, and Morning in America." In *US Presidential Elections and Foreign Policy*, edited by Andrew Johnstone and Andrew Priest, 271–92. Lexington: University Press of Kentucky.

Saunders, Elizabeth N. 2011. *Leaders at War: How Presidents Shape Military Interventions.* Ithaca, NY: Cornell University Press.

Saunders, Elizabeth N. 2023. *War and the Inner Circle.* Princeton, NJ: Princeton University Press.

Savage, Robert L., James E. Combs, and Dan D. Nimmo. 1989. *The Orwellian Moment: Hindsight and Foresight in the Post-1984 World.* Fayetteville: University of Arkansas Press.

Scanlon, Sandra. 2017. "Vietnam, American National Identity, and the 1968 Presidential Election" Essay. In *U.S. Presidential Elections and Foreign Policy*, edited by Andrew Johnstone and Andrew Priest, 177–202. Lexington: University Press of Kentucky.

Schelling, Thomas C. 1960. *The Strategy of Conflict.* Cambridge, MA: Harvard University Press.

Schuessler, John M. 2015. *Deceit on the Road to War: Presidents, Politics, and American Democracy.* Ithaca, NY: Cornell University Press.

Schwartz, Joshua A., and Christopher W. Blair. 2020. "Do Women Make More Credible Threats? Gender Stereotypes, Audience Costs, and Crisis Bargaining." *International Organization* 74 (4): 872–95. doi:10.1017/s0020818320000223.

Schwartz, Thomas Alan. 2020. *Henry Kissinger and American Power: A Political Biography.* New York: Hill and Wang.

Shapiro, Robert Y. 2001. *Marshall Plan: Fifty Years After.* New York: Palgrave Macmillan.

Shepsle, Kenneth A. 1972. "The Strategy of Ambiguity: Uncertainty and Electoral Competition." *American Political Science Review* 66 (2): 555–68. doi:10.2307/1957799.

Shrum, Robert. 2007. *No Excuses: Confessions of a Serial Campaigner.* New York: Simon & Schuster.

Smith, Alastair. 1996. "Diversionary Foreign Policy in Democratic Systems." *International Studies Quarterly* 40 (1): 133–53. doi:10.2307/2600934.

Smith, Alastair. 1998. "International Crises and Domestic Politics." *American Political Science Review* 92 (3): 623–38. doi:10.2307/2585485.

Snead, David L. 1999. *The Gaither Committee, Eisenhower, and the Cold War*. Columbus: Ohio State University Press.

Sobel, Richard. 2000. "To Intervene or Not to Intervene in Bosnia: That Was the Question for the United States and Europe." In *Decisionmaking in a Glass House: Mass Media, Public Opinion, and American and European Foreign Policy in the 21st Century*, edited by Brigitte L. Nacos, Robert Y. Shapiro, and Pierangelo Isernia, 111–31. Lanham, MD: Rowman & Littlefield.

Soderberg, Nancy E. 2005. *The Superpower Myth: The Use and Misuse of American Might*. New York: Wiley.

Solberg, Carl. 1984. *Hubert Humphrey: A Biography*. New York: W.W. Norton.

Sorensen, Theodore C. 1965. *Kennedy*. New York: Harper & Row.

Soroka, Stuart Neil, and Christopher Wlezien. 2010. *Degrees of Democracy: Politics, Public Opinion, and Policy*. New York: Cambridge University Press.

Spielvogel, Christian. 2005. "'You Know Where I Stand': Moral Framing of the War on Terrorism and the Iraq War in the 2004 Presidential Campaign." *Rhetoric and Public Affairs* 8 (4): 549–69. doi:10.1353/rap.2006.0015.

Stephanopoulos, George. 1999. *All Too Human: A Political Education*. Boston: Little, Brown.

Stimson, James A. 2004. *Tides of Consent: How Public Opinion Shapes American Politics*. New York: Cambridge University Press.

Stokes, Donald E. 1963. "Spatial Models of Party Competition." *American Political Science Review* 57 (2): 368–77. doi:10.2307/1952828.

Stone, Walter J., and Elizabeth N. Simas. 2010. "Candidate Valence and Ideological Positions in U.S. House Elections." *American Journal of Political Science* 54 (2): 371–88. doi:10.1111/j.1540-5907.2010.00436.x.

Thomson, Robert, Terry Royed, Elin Naurin, Joaquín Artés, Rory Costello, Laurenz Ennser-Jedenastik, Mark Ferguson, Petia Kostadinova, Catherine Moury, François Pétry, and Katrin Prapotnik. 2017. "The Fulfillment of Parties' Election Pledges: A Comparative Study on the Impact of Power Sharing." *American Journal of Political Science* 61 (3): 527–42. doi:10.1111/ajps.12313.

Thorpe, Rebecca U. 2014. *The American Warfare State: The Domestic Politics of Military Spending*. Chicago: University of Chicago Press.

Todorov, Alexander, Anesu N. Mandisodza, Amir Goren, and Crystal C. Hall. 2005. "Inferences of Competence from Faces Predict Election Outcomes." *Science* 308 (5728): 1623–26. doi:10.1126/science.1110589.

Tomz, Michael, Jessica L. P. Weeks, and Keren Yarhi-Milo. 2020. "Public Opinion and Decisions about Military Force in Democracies." *International Organization* 74 (1): 119–43. doi:10.1017/s0020818319000341.

Walt, Stephen M. 2018. *The Hell of Good Intentions: America's Foreign Policy Elite and the Decline of U.S. Primacy*. New York: Farrar, Straus, and Giroux.

Warren, Elizabeth. 2019. "A Foreign Policy for All." *Foreign Affairs* 98 (1): 50. https://heinonline.org/HOL/P?h=hein.journals/fora98&i=52.

Wattenberg, Martin P. 1991. *The Rise of Candidate-Centered Politics*. Cambridge, MA: Harvard University Press.

Webb, Daryl. 1998. "Crusade: George McGovern's Opposition to the Vietnam War." *South Dakota History* 28 (3): 161–90. https://www.sdhspress.com/journal/south -dakota-history-28–3/crusade-george-mcgoverns-opposition-to-the-vietnam -war/vol-28-no-3-crusade.pdf.

Weisberg, Herbert F., and Dino P. Christenson. 2007. "Changing Horses in War-time? The 2004 Presidential Election." *Political Behavior* 29 (2): 279–304. doi:10.1007/s11109-007-9026-9.

Wertheim, Stephen. 2020a. "The Price of Primacy." *Foreign Affairs* 99 (2): 19–29. https://heinonline.org/HOL/P?h=hein.journals/fora99&i=229.

Wertheim, Stephen. 2020b. *Tomorrow, the World: The Birth of U.S. Global Supremacy.* Cambridge, MA: The Belknap Press of Harvard University Press.

Western, Jon. 2005. "The War Over Iraq: Selling War to the American Public." *Security Studies* 14 (1): 106–39. doi:10.1080/09636410591002518.

Whalen, Richard J. 1972. *Catch the Falling Flag: A Republican's Challenge to His Party.* Boston: Houghton Mifflin.

White, Theodore H. 2009. *The Making of the President 1960.* New York: Harper/ Perennial.

Wildavsky, Aaron B. 1991. *The Beleaguered Presidency.* New Brunswick, NJ: Transaction Publishers.

Wirthlin, Richard B., Vincent Breglio, and Richard Beal. 1981. "Campaign Chronicle." *Public Opinion* 4: 43–49.

Wirthlin, Richard B., and Wynton C. Hall. 2004. *The Greatest Communicator: What Ronald Reagan Taught Me About Politics, Leadership, and Life.* Hoboken, NJ: Wiley.

Witcover, Jules. 1977. *Marathon: The Pursuit of the Presidency, 1972–1976.* New York: Viking Press.

Wittkopf, Eugene R. 1990. *Faces of Internationalism: Public Opinion and American Foreign Policy.* Durham, NC: Duke University Press.

Woods, Randall Bennett. 1995. *Fulbright: A Biography.* New York: Cambridge University Press.

Woodward, Bob. 1996. *The Choice.* New York: Simon & Schuster.

Woodward, Bob. 2004. *Plan of Attack.* New York: Simon & Schuster.

Yarhi-Milo, Keren. 2018. *Who Fights for Reputation: The Psychology of Leaders in International Conflict.* Princeton, NJ: Princeton University Press.

Zaller, John R. 1992. *The Nature and Origins of Mass Public Opinion.* New York: Cambridge University Press.

Zaretsky, Natasha. 2011. "Restraint or Retreat? The Debate over the Panama Canal Treaties and U.S. Nationalism After Vietnam." *Diplomatic History* 35 (3): 535–62. doi:10.1111/j.1467-7709.2011.00962.x.

Index

closed-ended survey data, 31, 43–44, 125
Cold War, 46, 64, 70, 79
communism/anti-communism: and
    defense spending, 64, 67–68, 79; in
    image-making, 15–16; in issue-image
    tradeoffs, 1–2, 101; toughness/softness
    on, 1–2, 15–16, 64, 66, 79, 89, 91, 105, 107–8;
    in Vietnam War politics, 89, 91, 97–98,
    101–2, 103, 105, 107–8. *See also* Soviet
    Union/US-Soviet relations
compromise, 3, 13–14, 15, 143–44, 147
concealment, 24–25, 89–90
concessions, diplomatic, 16, 18, 96–98,
    100–101, 103–5
Congress: Iraq War authorization by,
    113–14, 133–38, 194n56; issue-image
    trade-offs in behavior of, 7–8, 133–34;
    in military intervention in Bosnia, 132;
    policy positions, in image of, 180n21;
    responsiveness of, to public opinion on
    defense spending, 85–86; Vietnam War
    authorization by, 91–92, 107–8
Connell, William, 96–97
cooperation/cooperative internationalism:
    in foreign policy politics, 4; and the
    hawk's advantage, 53; in image-making,
    15, 16; and invasion of Iraq, 134; in
    issue-image trade-offs, 149; in surveys
    and experiments, 27–28, 35–37
counterterrorism, 139, 192n45. *See also*
    terrorism
Cramer, Jane Kellett, 135
credibility: and defense spending, 69,
    81; of experts in military intervention,
    139–40; in image-making, 16; issue-
    image trade-offs in, 153; on Vietnam, in
    the 1968 election, 95
crises, international, 12–13, 18, 81–82

"Daisy Ad," 90–91
Darman, Richard, 80
Dayton Accords, 1992, 132
Deaver, Michael, 80
"decent interval" in Vietnam, 100–103
decisiveness: on Iraq in the 2004 election,
    114, 125–26; and military intervention,
    131–32, 133, 140–41; in public discourse
    on the commander-in-chief test, 157A; in
    Reagan's defense buildup, 72–74, 81; in
    Vietnam War politics, 91–92, 95–96, 98,
    107–8
defense spending: democratic responsive-
    ness on, 83–86; documentation of data on,
    168–70A; and the hawk's advantage,
    47–53; in issue voting, 28–30; in Ken-
    nedy's 1960 election, 63–72; partisanship
    in preferences on, 28–30; popular opinion

in politics of, 62–63, 71–72; raising of, in
    projecting strength, 1; in Reagan's "Peace
    through Strength" program, 72–83
deferral, 24–25, 102, 105–7, 130, 137–38
Democrats: in Congressional politics of the
    Iraq War, 135–38; dovish image of, 21–22;
    and the hawk's advantage, 47–48
Devenish, Nicolle, 111–12
Devine, Tad, 115
discipline, rhetoric of, 150–51
discretion, 154–55
distortions of foreign policy, 4–5, 11, 15–17,
    107, 154–56
Dole, Bob, 132
domestic policy/programs, 41–42, 102, 127,
    129, 153–54
dovishness/dovish foreign policies: in
    avoiding issue-image trade-offs, 150;
    defined, 174n17, 180–81n24; as good
    judgment, 15, 19, 46, 57, 79–80; in image-
    making, 15, 16, 19, 20–21, 24; and Rea-
    gan's defense buildup, 79, 81–82; in
    shaping personal images, 46, 47–48, 57;
    in Vietnam War politics, 99–100, 105–6.
    See also hawkishness/hawk's advantage
Dowd, Matthew, 111
Drew, Elizabeth, 130
Dukakis, Michael, 83–84
Dulles, Allen, 69

economic issues/approval, 7, 119, 129, 148,
    170–71A
Ehrlichman, John, 102
Eisenhower, Dwight D., and administra-
    tion, 67–68, 69–70, 71, 174n8 (intro.)
election, presidential of 2004: advisers on
    strategies in, 110–17; and Iraq, in the
    NAES survey, 117–23; issue-image
    trade-offs on the Iraq War in, 109–10;
    level importance in, 119–23, 170–72A;
    reinterpreting the politics of Iraq in,
    123–26
elections, presidential: of 1952 and 1956,
    174n8 (intro.); of 1960, 62, 63–72; of 1964,
    87–93; of 1968, 94–100; of 1972, 100–107; of
    1976, 61, 154; of 1980, 62, 73–75; of 1984,
    62, 78–83; of 1988, 83–85; of 1992, 128,
    129–30; of 1996, 131–33; of 2000, 29–30,
    150; of 2004, 109–26, 170–72A; of 2008,
    138, 144; of 2012, 144, 157; of 2016, 1–2, 16,
    147–48, 152–53, 157A; of 2020, 18–19, 27;
    image-making in, 22; as short-term focus
    of public opinion, 6
elites, foreign policy and national security:
    on the commander-in-chief test, 158A; in
    defense spending, 85–86; and issue-
    image trade-offs, 150, 152; in military